Gays, Lesbians, and Consumer Behavior: Theory, Practice, and Research Issues in Marketing

Daniel L. Wardlow, PhD
Editor

Gays, Lesbians,
and Consumer Behavior

...gnition of customer groups based ...demographic, psychographic and ...variables is a hallmark of mar-...since scholars and managers ...ly ignored the lesbian and gay ...wledge about gay and lesbian ...is based more on inaccurate ...on the voice and experi-...nsumers. This long overdue ...me does a superb job of ...by exploring a variety of ...ssues ranging from the size ...the lesbian and gay market ...esbian consumer behaviors ...marketplace discrimination, ...esearch and market to gay ...stomers.

...niel Wardlow and all the ...ve recognition and thanks ...excellent and courageous ...This very important vol-...e as an invaluable resource, ...be required reading for ...ket researchers and market-

...I. Bristor, PhD
...t *Professor of Marketing*
...ity of Houston

This book provides a very broad-sweeping look at gay and lesbian consumers. Prof. Wardlow has brought together an interesting and diverse group of authors to provide a refreshing analysis of these important, yet under-studied, groups of American consumers. The chapter authors represent a wide range of academic disciplines, including Psychology, Marketing Communications, Advertising, Consumer Sciences, Social Work, and Counseling. The result of bringing together such a diverse group is a refreshing tone of openness and acceptance, as reflected in the range of methods and intellectual perspectives that are brought to bear in the present volume.

Examinations of homosexual consumer groups range from thought-provoking, theoretical treatments to more concrete, socio-political analyses. Many marketing strategies attempt to satisfy the needs of different sub-cultural groups, while other approaches begin with empirically based market segments. One of the important conceptual issues that is dealt with in the present volume is the question of how to distinguish empirically derived market segments from sub-culture groups. This distinction has important ramifications for the development of effective marketing strategies and for advancing our understanding of the motivations and perceptions of different consumer groups. The analyses of this distinction, how to define it and its various consequences for marketers and consumers alike, represent but one of the important focal points of the book.

The book is remarkable for its balance between critical analysis of marketing practices and their consequence, on the one hand, and consideration of how better to market products and services to gay and lesbian consumers, on the other. Another distinctive feature of the present collection of chapters is their dual emphasis on the perceptions and practices of consumers and marketers. Readers will find themselves reconsidering their preconceptions of gay and lesbian consumers. The volume should stimulate academic debate on this topic and contribute to marketing practice as well.

Basil G. Englis, PhD
Assistant Professor of Marketing,
Rutgers University

Gays, Lesbians, and Consumer Behavior: Theory, Practice, and Research Issues in Marketing

Daniel L. Wardlow, PhD
Editor

Gays, Lesbians, and Consumer Behavior: Theory, Practice, and Research Issues in Marketing, edited by Daniel L. Wardlow, was simultaneously issued by The Haworth Press, Inc., under the same title, as a special issue of *Journal of Homosexuality*, Volume 31, Numbers 1/2, 1996, John P. De Cecco, Editor.

Harrington Park Press
An Imprint of
The Haworth Press, Inc.
New York • London

ISBN 1-56023-0770

Published by

Harrington Park Press, 10 Alice Street, Binghamton, NY 13904-1580 USA

Harrington Park Press is an Imprint of the Haworth Press, Inc., 10 Alice Street, Binghamton, NY 13904-1580 USA.

Gays, Lesbians, and Consumer Behavior: Theory, Practice, and Research Issues in Marketing has also been published as *Journal of Homosexuality*, Volume 31, Numbers 1/2, 1996.

The development, preparation, and publication of this work has been undertaken with great care. However, the publisher, employees, editors, and agents of The Haworth Press and all imprints of The Haworth Press, Inc., including The Haworth Medical Press and Pharmaceutical Products Press, are not responsible for any errors contained herein or for consequences that may ensue from use of materials or information contained in this work. Opinions expressed by the author(s) are not necessarily those of The Haworth Press, Inc.

Library of Congress Cataloging-in-Publication Data

Gays, lesbians, and consumer behavior : theory, practice, and research issues in marketing / Daniel L. Wardlow, editor.
     p. cm.
    Includes bibliographical references and index.
    ISBN 1-56024-761-4 (Haworth Press). – ISBN 1-56023-077-0 (Harrington Park Press)
    1. Gay consumers–United States. 2. Lesbian consumers–United States. 3. Marketing research–United States. 4. Advertising–United States. I. Wardlow, Daniel L.
HF5415.33.U6G38 1996
658.8'348–dc20
                                96-4209
                                 CIP

INDEXING & ABSTRACTING

Contributions to this publication are selectively indexed or abstracted in print, electronic, online, or CD-ROM version(s) of the reference tools and information services listed below. This list is current as of the copyright date of this publication. See the end of this section for additional notes.

- *Abstracts in Anthropology*, Baywood Publishing Company, 26 Austin Avenue, P.O. Box 337, Amityville, NY 11701

- *Abstracts of Research in Pastoral Care & Counseling*, Loyola College, 7135 Minstrel Way, Suite 101, Columbia, MD 21045

- *Academic Abstracts/CD-ROM*, EBSCO Publishing, P.O. Box 2250, Peabody, MA 01960

- *Academic Search: database of 2,000 selected academic serials, updated monthly,* EBSCO Publishing, 83 Pine Street, Peabody, MA 19060

- *Applied Social Sciences Index & Abstracts (ASSIA) (Online: ASSI via Data-Star) (CD-Rom: ASSIA Plus)*, Bowker- Saur Limited, Maypole House, Maypole Road, East Grinstead, West Sussex RH19 1HH England

- *Book Review Index,* Gale Research, Inc., P.O. Box 2867, Detroit, MI 48231

- *Cambridge Scientific Abstracts*, *Risk Abstracts*, Environmental Routenet (accessed via INTERNET) 7200 Wisconsin Avenue, #601, Bethesda, MD 20814

- *CNPIEC Reference Guide: Chinese National Directory of Foreign Periodicals,* P.O. Box 88, Beijing, People's Republic of China

- *Criminal Justice Abstracts*, Willow Tree Press, 15 Washington Street, 4th Floor, Newark NJ 07102

- *Criminology, Penology and Police Science Abstracts*, Kugler Publications, P.O. Box 11188, 1001 GD-Amsterdam, The Netherlands

(continued)

- *Current Contents* . . . . . see: Institute for Scientific Information

- *Digest of Neurology and Psychiatry*, The Institute of Living, 400 Washington Street, Hartford, CT 06106

- *Excerpta Medica/Secondary Publishing Division*, Elsevier Science, Inc./Secondary Publishing Division, 655 Avenue of the Americas, New York, NY 10010

- *Expanded Academic Index*, Information Access Company, 362 Lakeside Drive, Forest City, CA 94404

- *Family Life Educator "Abstracts Section,"* ETR Associates, P.O. Box 1830, Santa Cruz, CA 95061-1830

- *Family Violence & Sexual Assault Bulletin*, Family Violence & Sexual Assault Institute, 1310 Clinic Drive, Tyler, TX 75701

- *HOMODOK/"Relevant" Bibliographic database, Documentation Centre for Gay & Lesbian Studies, University of Amsterdam (selective printed abstracts in "Homologie" and bibliographic computer databases covering cultural, historical, social and political aspects of gay & lesbian topics),* ILGA Archive, O.Z. Achterburgwal 185, NL-1012 DK Amsterdam, The Netherlands

- *Index Medicus/MEDLINE*, National Library of Medicine, 8600 Rockville Pike, Bethesda, MD 20894

- *Index to Periodical Articles Related to Law*, University of Texas, 727 East 26th Street, Austin, TX 78705

- *INFO-SOUTH Abstracts: contemporary, social, political, and economic information on Latin America; available on-line,* North-South Center Consortium, University of Miami, Miami, FL 33124

- *Institute for Scientific Information, 3501 Market Street, Philadelphia, Pennsylvania 19104. Coverage in:*
  a) Social Science Citation Index (SSCI): print, online, CD-ROM
  b) Research Alerts (current awareness service)
  c) Social SciSearch (magnetic tape)
  d) Current Contents/Social & Behavioral Sciences (weekly current awareness service)

(continued)

- *INTERNET ACCESS (& additional networks) Bulletin Board for Libraries ("BUBL"), coverage of information resources on INTERNET, JANET, and other networks.*
  - JANET X.29: UK.AC.BATH.BUBL or 00006012101300
  - TELNET: BUBL.BATH.AC.UK or 138.38.32.45 login 'bubl'
  - Gopher: BUBL.BATH.AC.UK (138.32.32.45). Port 7070
  - World Wide Web: http: / / www.bubl.bath.ac.uk./BUBL/ home.html
  - NISSWAIS: telnetniss.ac.uk (for the NISS gateway)
  The Andersonian Library, Curran Building, 101 St. James Road, Glasgow G4 ONS, Scotland

- *Inventory of Marriage and Family Literature (online and CD/ROM),* Peters Technology Transfer, 306 East Baltimore Pike, 2nd Floor, Media, PA 19063

- *Leeds Medical Information,* University of Leeds, Leeds LS2 9JT, United Kingdom

- *MasterFILE: updated database from EBSCO Publishing,* 83 Pine Street, Peabody, MA 01960

- *Mental Health Abstracts (online through DIALOG)*, IFI/Plenum Data Company, 3202 Kirkwood Highway, Wilmington, DE 19808

- *MLA International Bibliography,* Modern Language Association of America, 10 Astor Place, New York, NY 10003

- *PASCAL International Bibliography T205: Sciences de l'information Documentation*, INIST/CNRS-Service Gestion des Documents Primaires, 2, allée du Parc de Brabois, F-54514 Vandoeuvre-les-Nancy, Cedex, France

- *Periodical Abstracts, Research I (general and basic reference indexing and abstracting data-base from University Microfilms International (UMI), 300 North Zeeb Road, P.O. Box 1346, Ann Arbor, MI 48106-1346)*, UMI Data Courier, P.O. Box 32770, Louisville, KY 40232-2770

(continued)

- *Periodical Abstracts, Research II (broad coverage indexing and abstracting data-base from University Microfilms International (UMI), 300 North Zeeb Road, P.O. Box 1346, Ann Arbor, MI 48106-1346)*, UMI Data Courier, P.O. Box 32770, Louisville, KY 40232-2770

- *PsychNet*, PsychNet Inc., P.O. Box 470250, Aurora, CO 80047-0250

- *Public Affairs Information Bulletin (PAIS)*, Public Affairs Information Service, Inc., 521 West 43rd Street, New York, NY 10036-4396

- *Religion Index One: Periodicals*, American Theological Library Association, 820 Church Street, 3rd Floor, Evanston, IL 60201

- *Sage Family Studies Abstracts (SFSA)*, Sage Publications, Inc., 2455 Teller Road, Newbury Park, CA 91320

- *Social Planning/Policy & Development Abstracts (SOPODA)*, Sociological Abstracts, Inc., P.O. Box 22206, San Diego, CA 92192-0206

- *Social Sciences Index (from Volume 1 & continuing)*, The H.W. Wilson Company, 950 University Avenue, Bronx, NY 10452

- *Social Science Source: coverage of 400 jounals in the social sciences area; updated monthly,* EBSCO Publishing, 83 Pine Street, Peabody, MA 01960

- *Social Work Abstracts*, National Association of Social Workers, 750 First Street NW, 8th Floor, Washington, DC 20002

- *Sociological Abstracts (SA)*, Sociological Abstracts, Inc., P.O. Box 22206, San Diego, CA 92192-0206

- *Studies on Women Abstracts*, Carfax Publishing Company, P.O. Box 25, Abingdon, Oxfordshire OXI4 3UE, United Kingdom

- *Violence and Abuse Abstracts: A Review of Current Literature on Interpersonal Violence (VAA),* Sage Publications, Inc., 2455 Teller Road, Newbury Park, CA 91320

Book reviews are selectively excerpted by the Guide to Professional Literature of the Journal of Academic Librarianship.

CONTENTS

ALL HARRINGTON PARK PRESS BOOKS
ARE PRINTED ON CERTIFIED
ACID-FREE PAPER

ABOUT THE EDITOR

Daniel L. Wardlow, PhD, is Associate Professor of Marketing at the College of Business, San Francisco State University in California. His main research interests are in logistics organization and strategy, public policy and advertising, advertising effects, and philosophy of social science. He has authored, co-authored, or edited numerous books and journals. Dr. Wardlow is certified as a Diplomate by the International Advertising Association.

Preface

The genesis for this special volume came in a casual suggestion from the *Journal of Homosexuality* editor, John DeCecco, over lunch in the faculty club at San Francisco State University in late 1992. We had been discussing the growing interest of marketers in a supposed "dream segment": gay and lesbian consumers. Our discussion revolved around speculated and imagined consumption differences between homosexuals and heterosexuals. As we progressed, we realized that in many respects gays and lesbians may indeed be different as consumers responding in the marketplace, and that marketers' response to gays and lesbians should be driven by knowledge about their consumption behavior. At that point, John suggested we issue a call for papers for research in that general area in order to put together a special edition.

We issued the call in May 1993, allowing a year to promote and develop research in homosexuality and consumer behavior. In summer 1993, I travelled to the Gender Conference of the Association for Consumer Research held in Salt Lake City to gather suggestions and ideas for the special edition, and to promote the call for papers. I met a number of researchers there from a variety of academic disciplines, all conducting research on gender and consumption, and through those contacts encouraged submissions to the special edition. Many of the authors represented here contacted me early in the research process, and their continued input helped to guide the final shape of this volume.

The research presented here draws from a diverse collection of

[Haworth co-indexing entry note]: "Preface." Wardlow, Daniel L. Co-published simultaneously in *Journal of Homosexuality* (The Haworth Press, Inc.) Vol. 31, No. 1/2, 1996, pp. xix-xxi; and: *Gays, Lesbians, and Consumer Behavior: Theory, Practice, and Research Issues in Marketing* (ed: Daniel L. Wardlow) The Haworth Press, Inc., 1996, pp. xv-xvii; and: *Gays, Lesbians, and Consumer Behavior: Theory, Practice, and Research Issues in Marketing* (ed: Daniel L. Wardlow) Harrington Park Press, an imprint of The Haworth Press, Inc., 1996, pp. xiii-xv. Single or multiple copies of this article are available from The Haworth Document Delivery Service [1-800-342-9678, 9:00 a.m. - 5:00 p.m. (EST)].

xiii

academic disciplines and fields of inquiry to present a glimpse at the consumption behavior of gay men, lesbians, and bisexuals, and at the marketing response to these different populations. We believe this volume is the first academic research compilation to explore the topic. While I believe the papers presented here make substantial contributions to knowledge, I do not represent this volume as comprehensive in scope. Rather, our first attempts at academic research in the area point out broad swaths of uncharted territory. Each of the papers takes its first steps, acknowledges the unknown, and points the way for future research in a fascinating field.

ACKNOWLEDGMENTS

A special edition, especially one that so readily crosses disciplinary boundaries, is no easy task to assemble. I am grateful for the initial interest, encouragement, and suggestions of Janeen Arnold Costa of the University of Utah and Barbara B. Stern at Rutgers University. Janeen Arnold Costa wrote the Foreword for this volume. She is the editor of an excellent research compilation titled "Gender Issues and Consumer Behavior" (Sage, 1994). John DeCecco provided editorial guidance and direction for this project; I thank him for this opportunity and for his advice.

Each of the contributors to this volume was also asked to be a reviewer, and I am grateful to them for their "double duty" service. In addition, a number of additional reviewers volunteered their efforts in evaluating manuscripts: Kenneth Danko (Department of Accounting, San Francisco State University), Patricia J. Daugherty (Department of Marketing and Distribution, University of Georgia), Diane Halstead (Department of Marketing, University of Kentucky), Mary Joyce (Department of Communication Studies, Emerson College), Steven W. Kopp (Department of Marketing, University of Arkansas), and Jay Siskin (Department of Romance Languages, Brandeis University). I am grateful to these reviewers for their prompt and insightful comments and for the improvements they brought to each article.

I wish to thank Kyle James of the Development Department at Project Open Hand, San Francisco, for his informed and critical reading of the final manuscript submissions, and for his disciplined copyediting and final manuscript preparation. Last and certainly not least, my thanks to my partner Blue Moor for tea and sympathy throughout.

Daniel L. Wardlow, PhD
Associate Professor of Marketing
San Francisco State University
Editor

Foreword

Janeen Arnold Costa, PhD
University of Utah

Social systems are reflections, sometimes instruments, of power. Typically, they justify, enact, and engage differential access to power. So, in all but the extremely rare "egalitarian" societies, the social structure is pervaded by inequity, dominance and subordination, and political, social, and economic maneuvering. The power itself is expressed in different ways. Not only is power found through control of and access to resources of all kinds; power is manifest as group and individual expressions of identity. It is often the case that the latter are a response to the former, as the members of subordinated or marginalized social groups seek identity, control, and recognition in the context of a society dominated economically, politically, and in other ways by specific groups.

Thus we come to American society, dominated by a white, male, heterosexual, Christian culture. The dominant group expresses its power in and through the control of critical aspects of business, government, home life, education, etc. In addition, the accompanying ideological system often serves to legitimate and support that

Janeen Arnold Costa is Assistant Professor of Marketing, David Eccles School of Business, and Adjunct Assistant Professor of Anthropology, University of Utah. Correspondence should be addressed to: Department of Marketing, 107 KDGB, University of Utah, Salt Lake City, UT 84112. E-mail: *mktjac@business. utah.edu*

[Haworth co-indexing entry note]: "Foreword." Costa, Janeen Arnold. Co-published simultaneously in *Journal of Homosexuality* (The Haworth Press, Inc.) Vol. 31, No. 1/2, 1996, pp. xxiii-xxvi; and: *Gays, Lesbians, and Consumer Behavior: Theory, Practice, and Research Issues in Marketing* (ed: Daniel L. Wardlow) The Haworth Press, Inc., 1996, pp. xix-xxii; and: *Gays, Lesbians, and Consumer Behavior: Theory, Practice, and Research Issues in Marketing* (ed: Daniel L. Wardlow) Harrington Park Press, an imprint of The Haworth Press, Inc., 1996 pp. xvii-xx. Single or multiple copies of this article are available from The Haworth Document Delivery Service [1-800-342-9678, 9:00 a.m. - 5:00 p.m. (EST)].

xvii

control. The material and the ideological work in concert with one another, reinforcing the societal hierarchy and making it seem "natural," "right," both to those in the position of dominance and to many of those who are themselves dominated. The ideology is reinforced, the "correctness" of the inequity re-created, over and over again, through the machinations of culture.

One gender, one sexual orientation, one religious affiliation, and one color of skin are seen as mainstream, while all others fall outside this social category. What is more, the ideology is designed and manipulated to emphasize the "otherness" of the non-dominant groups and individuals. The outcome can be a social system in which "other" is not only distinctive and subordinated, but is feared and systematically isolated. The fear and the isolation result in, and from, discrimination, and so it continues. Those who are part of the white mainstream populace fear the potential power of the non-mainstream; they fear what they are not, or they find it offensive. Furthermore, those who are *not* in the mainstream may fear the consequences of identifying themselves as "other," because of the vast ideological, social and material forces that can then be brought into play against them.

One domain of the cultural machinations of inequity in American society is in marketing and consumption. Here, the ideology of white, Christian, male heterosexuality is again framed as superior to non-white, non-Christian, female heterosexual, and male or female of homosexual orientation. The selection and production of goods and services, the promotional appeals, the interactions of the sales force, and the spread of consumer culture to "developing" societies are all examples of marketing practices which may maintain and further the societal status quo. When the advertisement for a car or for a brand of beer is based upon a portrayal of a scantily-clad female, when "sexual joking" is a critical part of the interaction between salesperson and customer, when consumer culture "penetrates" developing societies in the "battle" for markets, the rhetoric of white male heterosexual dominance is invoked.

On the other hand, marketing holds within it the seeds of recognition and empowerment through diversity. The "marketing concept" recognizes the need to understand the consumer, to address and meet his/her concerns, wants, and requirements with respect to the marketer's product. The strategy of segmentation is a further manifestation of marketing's recognition of diversity. Consumers, businesses, channels of distribution, and media forms are all segmented, addressing a diversity of attitudes and behaviors, and reaching consumers through targeted marketing. Yet, despite this apparent willingness to acknowledge diversity and to serve consumers whose interests are dissimilar to those of the mainstream, the overall culture of marketing and of business remains dominated itself by male heterosexuality.

Thus, while American society is multi-cultural and multi-dimensional, it is, nevertheless, a society dominated by male heterosexuals. It is against this social mosaic, with its hierarchical implications, that American homosexuality is most productively analyzed. Like other dimensions on which multiculturalism is predicated, homosexuality is not a characteristic which is unidimensional or which forms, in and of itself, a single cohesive social group. While it is based on sexual preference, this apparent basis does not define or describe homosexuality in a full sense. Rather, again as with other subcultures such as ethnic groups, homosexuality often entails a fully elaborated lifestyle, many details of which revolve around, and reflect differences from, mainstream society. Variation also exists *within* the group and among individuals who identify themselves as homosexual.

In addition, as with all processes of identity and social organization in a complex society, both *individuals* and *groups* are involved and deserve separate consideration. Group formation, individual and group identity, strategies of assimilation to, and separation from, the dominant society and from the subcultural category/group are all issues in homosexuality, as they are with other subcultures in American society.

Do these similarities in processes of identity on the individual and group level mean that homosexuality is merely another basis for social differentiation in the varied tapestry that is American life today? Such a representation of homosexuality would be both simplistic and naïve. On the contrary, it is clear that homosexuality in American society is also somewhat different from the other bases for subcultural identity and group formation. Of all the variations of "other," homosexuality invokes the most phobic reaction, making it the most stigmatized basis for identity in a society full of "otherness." Because sexuality itself is so closely monitored, is treated conservatively, even repressively, in American culture, sexual representations, acts, and preferences are a source of societal apprehension, even trepidation. The "otherness" of homosexuality invokes greater anxiety than do differences in religion, skin color, ethnic affiliation, or perceived changes in gender roles. As a result, we would expect manifest differences in the lifestyles, expressions and experiences of identity, and of group formation among homosexuals, when compared to other subcultural or individual bases for social variations in American society.

This foreword was originally requested to be a positioning piece, relating the studies of homosexuality in marketing to extant studies on gender and marketing, specifically gender and consumer behavior. It is clear that the similarity between the two fields of study and of experience lies within the context of American power structures. Many American women struggle for power, recognition, and identity in a social system dominated politically, economically, socially, and ideologically by male heterosexuality. The circumstances of their experience are framed definitively by male expressions of authority and superordination. In the context of consumer behavior, the literature has focused on both errors and truisms in the stereotypes of women in American society. The result has been a push toward greater understanding of women as consumers. Another outcome has been a deeper recognition of the power structure of American male heterosexuality.

This volume is composed of articles which attempt to present and represent homosexuality in the context of marketing and consumption in American society. I would suggest that both the similarities and differences between the experience of homosexuality and of female heterosexuality in American society are critical aspects of these studies. Some of the articles also address analogous behaviors and contexts in comparing homosexuality with ethnicity or other social bases for forming identities separate from mainstream American society. All of these comparisons are apt and informative within the framework of white, Christian, male heterosexuality.

The studies presented herein are useful; the authors, editor, and publisher should be commended for pushing forward the understanding of homosexuality as it relates to marketing and consumer behavior. It is an area of research which has been relatively under-explored; this collection of essays is an important beginning.

Introduction

Daniel L. Wardlow, PhD

San Francisco State University

Since the organization of consumer behavior as an integrated field of studies during the 1970s, marketing scholars have pursued lines of inquiry into differences in consumption behaviors across cultural and sub-cultural boundaries. The melding of diverse bodies of theory from psychology, social psychology, sociology, social and cultural anthropology, and economics has resulted in a convergent literature which helps us to understand the complexities of consumption in a wide variety of contexts and individual situations.

In consumer behavior research, as in all social sciences, practice generally leads the theoreticians. Such has been the case in recent years, as marketers of all kinds have suddenly "discovered" the gay and lesbian marketplace. Concurrent with an explosion of media targeted to gay and lesbian consumers, we have seen a great deal of privately conducted descriptive consumer research reported in the popular press. Gays and lesbians have variously been described as a "dream market" segment and as one which is too small and unreachable to be practical for the mass marketplace. As a "dream segment," gays and lesbians are reported to have significantly higher-than-average disposable incomes and a near-rabid desire for consumption. Gays and lesbians may also be a small and

---

Daniel L. Wardlow is Associate Professor of Marketing at San Francisco State University. Correspondence should be addressed to: Department of Marketing, San Francisco State University, 1600 Holloway Avenue, San Francisco, CA 94132. E-mail: *dwardlow@sfsu.edu*

[Haworth co-indexing entry note]: "Introduction." Wardlow, Daniel L. Co-published simultaneously in *Journal of Homosexuality* (The Haworth Press, Inc.) Vol. 31, No. 1/2, 1996, pp. 1-8; and: *Gays, Lesbians, and Consumer Behavior: Theory, Practice, and Research Issues in Marketing* (ed: Daniel L. Wardlow) The Haworth Press, Inc., 1996, pp. 1-8; and: *Gays, Lesbians, and Consumer Behavior: Theory, Practice, and Research Issues in Marketing* (ed: Daniel L. Wardlow) Harrington Park Press, an imprint of The Haworth Press, Inc., 1996, pp. 1-8. Single or multiple copies of this article are available from The Haworth Document Delivery Service [1-800-342-9678, 9:00 a.m. - 5:00 p.m. (EST)].

unreachable segment, although this critical description is often tied to the highly varied and controversial population estimates. With no surprise, the "dream segment" promoters have tended to come from the ranks of gay-owned consumer research organizations and from the gay-targeted media. The opposing position is spoken aloud a little less publicly by marketers, and often seems to come with a cautionary note attached and aimed at the mass market, for whom the concept of gays and lesbians as consumers is threatening in its ordinary worldliness.

This volume represents the first scholarly attempt that we know of to examine the nuance and subtlety of the world between those two perspectives. Some twenty-five authors have contributed to this effort through three essays, eleven empirical or descriptive papers, and a comment. The book that you hold is the product of almost two years of work, from the initial call for research through final publication. The authors were given maximum leeway in carving out their topics. No research areas or methodologies were specified in order to encourage broad-based, multi-method research for this first effort at academic inquiry into gays, lesbians, and consumption.

Four themes have emerged from this assembled research to guide the order of presentation in this volume:

1. Consumption Rituals
2. Presentation Through Consumption
3. Discrimination and Tolerance
4. Application and Accommodation.

As the reader will notice in reading this work, there is a circularity to the ordering of these themes. Consumption rituals, for example, may aid in understanding questions of presentation through consumption. Presentation is a social phenomenon, as are issues of discrimination and tolerance in the marketplace. Application and accommodation necessarily affect change in consumption rituals.

CONSUMPTION RITUALS

Given the thematic circularity, a bridging work was chosen to lead. In her paper titled "We're Here, We're Queer, and We're Going Shopping! A Critical Perspective on the Accommodation of Gays and Lesbians in the U.S. Marketplace," author Lisa Peñaloza conceptualizes lesbians and gays as "a part of a consumer subculture that encompasses distinct dimensions of identity, social practices, and community formations." Peñaloza offers us the additional insight of a social movement as a market segment, thus politicizing consumption by attaching a social significance to its rituals among a defined group. She writes:

> As members of a social movement, gays and lesbians have developed a consciousness of themselves as a people as the result of a history of common interests and experiences, particularly their exclusion, mobilization, and struggle in response to how they have been treated by others. . . . (I)t is also necessary to expand measures of consumption patterns to account for differences in the meanings of uses accorded various products, services, and other marketing stimuli among various consumer subcultures even when there is no apparent difference in the consumption patterns themselves.

Thus, the symbolic nature of the consumption behavior both helps to define the consumer as well as reflects the aggregate social, political, and cultural experience of the individual. Peñaloza also points out that social validation and legitimization are experienced by gays and lesbians as a result of market accommodation. In this sense, marketing is seen as an institution which may further (or inhibit) social change. The social context, then, of both performance ritual and meaning in consumption carries significance.

Margaret Rucker, Anthony Freitas, and Oscar Huidor, in a paper titled "Gift-Giving Among Gay Men: The Reification of Social Relations," examine a significant consumption ritual among gay men: gift-giving. They examine dimensions of "social support, sensitivity to behavioral and product codes, equality and meanings of intimacy, and uses of humor to manage personal conditions and social relations." Using depth interviews with a small sample and interpretation with illustration from the interview text, the authors come to several important conclusions. Relationship building and maintenance figure prominently in the selection of gifts, implying that the symbolic value of the gift carries a high degree of significance for both giver and recipient. In the area of egalitarianism and perceptions of equity, the authors found a sensitivity to a balance between sentiment and cost, again pointing to the social implications of the exchange. Thus a consumption ritual exchange affirms the abstractions of the relationship.

In a paper titled "Mainstream Legitimization of Homosexual Men Through Valentine's Day Gift-Giving and Consumption Rituals," authors Peter J. Newman, Jr., and Michelle R. Nelson find significant similarities and differences between heterosexual and homosexual men in a particular gift-giving ritual. An additional dimension of inclusion is present in the ritual for gay men, in that they "may use the holiday as an opportunity to engage in self-affirmation against an 'oppressive society' and express their gay pride." Furthermore, gay men were found to draw a larger circle of inclusion for this holiday's celebration rather than focusing on a single romantic partner. Both of these findings serve to support and illustrate Peñaloza's contentions on social validation and legitimization through market behavior. Rucker, Freitas, and Huidor also found higher levels of enjoyment of gift-giving among gay men than among heterosexual men.

In an essay titled "Desire and Deviate Nymphos: Performing Inversion(s) as a Lesbian Consumer," author sidney matrix engages the reader in an infinite hall-of-mirrors excursion into the dynamic reflexivity of a lesbian consuming lesbophobic imagery in the form of a postcard. The subtle nuances of meaning are explored, highlighting the importance of understanding the sub-cultural context of lesbian identity, social practice, and consumption in a lesbian community, as well as the contradictions inherent with a reconciliation of a consumption symbol to any other sense of self, dyadic relationship, or community.

PRESENTATION THROUGH CONSUMPTION

The role of the consumption of goods in defining and delineating gays and lesbians, and their roles in the creation and utilization of such definitions and boundaries are explored by two works in this volume. Anthony Freitas, Susan Kaiser, and Tania Hammidi, in their paper titled "Communities, Commodities, Cultural Space, and Style," draw important relationships between the existence of a community, its symbols of identity in the form of style, and the functionality of style as market commodity. Through depth interviews, they discern a "conceptual space" which connects commodity and symbolic values of style. They explore the duality of target market and subculture through the lens of individual members' perceptions and conclude that members of this community engage in a conscious reflexivity that embraces both a consumerist viewpoint and an "ongoing search for a link between playfulness and seriousness in everyday life (expressed) through style."

In her paper titled "Appearance and Self-Presentation Research in Gay Consumer Culture: Issues and Impact," Nancy A. Rudd reports on two empirical studies involving gay men. In the first, Rudd explores the semiotic codes resident in attire and self-presentation and their effects on gay men's perceptions of desirability of social interaction. The results indicate the existence of an aesthetic appearance code which carries substantial meaning through self-presentation. To begin to establish parameters for this code, Rudd next explored the differences in aesthetic responses to appearance between heterosexual and homosexual men. Significant differences in perception and understanding between the two groups were found, leading Rudd to confirm the popular image of a subset of gay men as preferring novel, trendy, or other creative ways of self-presentation.

In addition to the findings of the two studies, Rudd explores a list of problems and concerns related to conducting research on the gay consumer culture including managing confidentiality and risk, sample selection and settings, and measurement of sexual orientation or gay identity. Her research concludes with a number of recommendations to marketing managers concerning the unique positioning characteristics necessary to reach various gay subcultural groups.

DISCRIMINATION AND TOLERANCE

The extent to which gay and lesbian consumers face discrimination in the marketplace is explored in two articles in this volume. A third paper deals with how a viewer's level of tolerance of homosexuality affects their attitudes toward advertising which features images suggesting homosexuality.

In a very creative "real-world" empirical study, Andrew S. Walters and Maria-Cristina Curran show significant differences in the ways in which presumed heterosexual and homosexual customers are treated by retail sales staff. In their paper titled "'Excuse Me, Sir? May I Help You and Your Boyfriend?': Salespersons' Differential Treatment of Homosexual and Straight Customers," Walters and Curran place confederates in a natural setting–a shopping mall–and observe salespersons' responses to the confederates' portrayals of gay male, lesbian, and straight couples while shopping. They found significant differences in service levels between heterosexual and homosexual shopping couples involving response time, friendliness, and a general reluctance to serve and an avoidance of perceived gay and lesbian couples. Their research featured a follow-up with store managers, which itself reveals substantial gaps in management knowledge of employee behavior and attitudes. The anecdotal reporting of employee comments indicates the complex nature of the reasons behind the differences in service and point to the need for additional research beyond this pioneering effort.

David A. Jones's article, titled "Discrimination Against Same-Sex Couples in Hotel Reservation Policies," also explores issues of discrimination and tolerance. In a simple experimental design using actual hotels and their reservations procedures, Jones found that hotels generally granted fewer reservation requests when couples could be identified as same sex. He found a greater level of discrimination in smaller hotels (bed and breakfasts), and a generally greater degree of discrimination against female-female couples than against male-male couples. Jones speculates on reasons behind these differences and suggests additional courses of research to identify sources of prejudice in business practice.

Subodh Bhat, Thomas W. Leigh, and Daniel L. Wardlow examine the effects that the use of homosexual imagery in advertising might have on viewers' attitudes toward the ad. Their research, reported here under the title "The Effect of Homosexual Imagery in Advertising on Attitude Toward the Ad," measured the relative level of condemnation or tolerance for homosexuality and compared this to the respondent's attitudes toward two different treatments (homosexual and heterosexual) in each of two simulated magazine advertisements. They found that among respondents who were relatively tolerant of homosexuality, attitudes toward homosexual imagery in advertising were more positive than among those who were less tolerant. Conversely, they found that those less tolerant held more positive attitudes toward the heterosexual version of the ad than the homosexual version. They conclude their article with a number of suggestions for marketing managers wishing to target gay and lesbian consumers, along with reporting several incidental findings which suggest the importance of considering the symbolic value of brands among gay and lesbian consumers.

APPLICATION AND ACCOMMODATION

Four articles in this volume deal with applications of marketing, and with issues of accommodation in the marketplace. The first of these is titled "The Social Marketing of Project ARIES: Overcoming Challenges in Recruiting Gay and Bisexual Males for HIV Prevention Counseling," and was submitted by the Innovative Programs Research Group of the School of Social Work at the University of Washington (authors Douglass S. Fisher, Rosemary Ryan, Anne W. Esacove, Steven Bishofsky, J. Marc Wallis, and Roger A. Roffman). This study reports on the development, implementation, and evaluation of a social marketing campaign. The objective of the campaign was to recruit high-risk gay and bisexual men for HIV-prevention counseling. Project ARIES used a classic differentially targeted, integrated marketing communications approach, and found that different marketing communications vehicles were better at reaching different target markets. For example, the researchers found that public relations coverage in the mainstream press was highly effective in reaching closeted men, men less active in the gay community, and men who did not self-identify as gay.

Their study is significant as it points out the importance and challenges of pinpoint targeting to smaller segments within the homosexual and bisexual population. Substantial detail is provided for each step in the marketing plan, making this paper a model for the design of similar social marketing campaigns. One reviewer of this paper noted enthusiastically "This is a paper which NEEDS to be published. . . . This is the kind of relevant research that can actually help to save lives."

The second of the four papers in this section, "Marketing to the Homosexual (Gay) Market: A Profile and Strategy Implications" by M. Wayne DeLozier and Jason Rodrigue, provides a description of a prototypical gay marketplace. The authors provide insight into some of the traditional segmentation criteria (demographics, psychographics, personality) as applied in a particular segment. They conclude with a composite profile, and offer a number of marketing strategy suggestions in the areas of niche marketing, packaging and brand names, and marketing communications.

Following on DeLozier and Rodrigue's descriptive article, Subodh Bhat offers an editor-invited comment. Bhat's perspectives on market segmentation differ radically from Delozier and Rodrigue. Bhat rejects the notion of a cohesive or uniform "homosexual" segment in the market. He argues that differential responsiveness to a marketing mix is the key to segmentation, and builds on Delozier and Rodrigue's static approach to descriptive segmentation to offer a dynamic strategy for segmenting the gay and lesbian market.

Both the DeLozier and Rodrigue article and the comment by Bhat help to illuminate the application of segmentation strategy described in the Fisher et al. report on Project ARIES. The reader will note that the differential responsiveness to marketing communications vehicles reported in the Fisher et al. study is related to sub-segments in the market for HIV-prevention counseling. These sub-segments likely are distinctive, measurable, and accessible; thus are amenable to the development of different marketing mixes to satisfy different sub-segment needs.

The final article in the volume, by John E. Bowes, is titled "Out of the Closet and into the Marketplace: Meeting Basic Needs in the Gay Community." Bowes offers a complex picture of the gay community, and traces much of the complexity to the community's history of exclusion and discrimination. Using data gathered from gays and lesbians in the Seattle area, Bowes argues that the marketplace is not seen as uniformly accessible by the gay community. He notes a disconnection between the goals of marketers in serving gay and lesbian consumers and the needs of the consumers themselves. Bowes points to a general blindness of marketing efforts to the psychosocial complexities of suspicion, concealment, and alienation which exist among these consumers. The article includes discussions of the fulfillment of basic needs in the community and the roles the different media play in the marketing dialogue. The Bowes article also lends additional insight into the communications challenges faced by the Project ARIES team as reported by Fisher et al.

At this point, the reader is redirected to the opening article in this volume. A re-read of Lisa Peñaloza's article from a perspective of accommodation and tolerance will help to solidify the importance of the last four articles, as well as assist in generalizing the collective findings of the entire volume.

WHERE DO WE GO FROM HERE?

As is the case in any pioneering research effort, more questions are raised than answered. Each of the articles presented here simply scratches the surface of complex phenomena, revealing to both researcher and reader our dearth of knowledge, raising questions, and provoking our desire to uncover and learn. While many of the articles offer explicit advice to managers, all implicitly lend a greater understanding of lesbians', gays', and bisexuals' consumer behavior. As marketing practice continues to forge ahead with this community, we sincerely hope we have made a contribution with this volume and that the work presented here is a spur to further inquiry.

We're Here, We're Queer, and We're Going Shopping! A Critical Perspective on the Accommodation of Gays and Lesbians in the U.S. Marketplace

Lisa Peñaloza, PhD

University of Colorado

SUMMARY. This paper draws from studies of social movements, consumer culture, and postmodern cultural theory to argue that gays and lesbians constitute a viable market segment in the U.S. Marketing practices targeting gays and lesbians are then critically analyzed, with attention to their impact on the U.S. market, on individual gays and lesbians, and on gay/lesbian communities. While marketing incorporation of gays and lesbians offers a strong sense of legitimation in capitalist society, these marketing representations tend to provide a

Lisa Peñaloza is Assistant Professor of Marketing at the University of Colorado. The author would like to thank the reviewers, Nan Alamilla Boyd, Zhenya Gallon, and Sylvia Allegretto for their constructive comments on earlier drafts of this manuscript. Correspondence should be addressed to: College of Business, University of Colorado, CB 419, Boulder, CO, 80309-0419. E-mail: *Penaloza @ spot. colorado.edu*

[Haworth co-indexing entry note]: "We're Here, We're Queer, and We're Going Shopping! A Critical Perspective on the Accommodation of Gays and Lesbians in the U.S. Marketplace." Peñaloza, Lisa. Co-published simultaneously in *Journal of Homosexuality* (The Haworth Press, Inc.) Vol. 31, No. 1/2, 1996, pp. 9-41; and: *Gays, Lesbians, and Consumer Behavior: Theory, Practice, and Research Issues in Marketing* (ed: Daniel L. Wardlow) The Haworth Press, Inc., 1996, pp. 9-41; and: *Gays, Lesbians, and Consumer Behavior: Theory, Practice, and Research Issues in Marketing* (ed: Daniel L. Wardlow) Harrington Park Press, an imprint of The Haworth Press, Inc., 1996, pp. 9-41. Single or multiple copies of this article are available from The Haworth Document Delivery Service [1-800-342-9678, 9:00 a.m. - 5:00 p.m. (EST)].

9

somewhat distorted perspective of gay and lesbian life and culture, and for this reason merit serious critical attention. *[Article copies available from The Haworth Document Delivery Service: 1-800-342-9678.]*

INTRODUCTION

It is altogether fitting that the call for papers for this volume coincides with the 25th anniversary of the Stonewall Rebellion. Businesses catering to a gay/lesbian clientele, such as the Stonewall Inn and other nightclubs, cafés, bookstores, and coffeehouses, have been at the center of gay/lesbian communities historically (Wilson 1991; Trumbach 1991; Myrick 1972), and continue to be an important hub of contemporary social activism.

In recent years, marketing and media attention has begun to be directed to gays and lesbians as a distinct consumer group. This market segment has been dubbed the "Dream Market," with estimates of the numbers of gays and lesbians reaching 18.5 million, and estimates of spending power topping $514 billion (Johnson 1993a). Businesses targeting gays and lesbians have expanded beyond clubs and bookstores to comprise virtually a full service market that includes media, merchandise catalogues (see Photo 1, Shocking Gray), vacation companies (see Photo 2, Olivia, and Photo 3, RSVP), and legal, medical, financial and communications services, to name a few.[1] Together, these businesses create an environment in which gay and lesbian consumer culture thrives.[2]

With this increased attention by marketing practitioners, marketing and consumer behavior scholars have begun to think about lesbians and gays as a market. In one of the first academic studies on this topic, Fugate (1993) concluded that gays and lesbians did not qualify as a market segment because this group did not satisfy the traditional criteria of being identifiable, accessible, and of sufficient size. This paper provides an alternative view of gays and lesbians as a market segment and draws from studies of the new social movements, consumer culture, and postmodern cultural theory. My argument is that the segmentation criteria rely on outdated assumptions regarding the nature of consumers, marketing activities, and media, and require modifications for the contemporary marketplace. Specifically, this research recognizes the important intersection of market segments and social movements and addresses the marketing implications of increasing consumer subjectivity and agency, and of market and media heterogeneity.[3]

The objectives of this research are twofold. First, I reevaluate the question of whether gays and lesbians constitute a viable market segment. Second, I critically evaluate implications of gay and lesbian marketing with respect to the structure of the U.S. marketplace, to individual gays and lesbians, and to gay/lesbian communities.

PHOTO 1. Reprinted with permission of Shocking Gray.

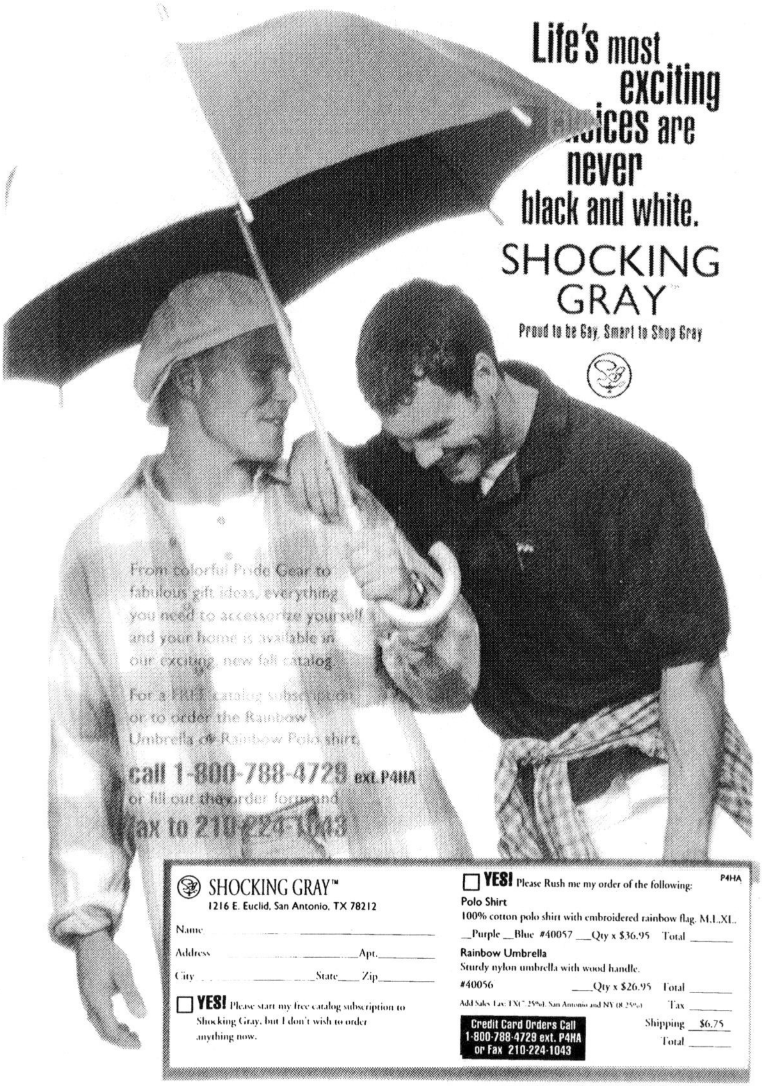

PHOTO 2. Reprinted with permission of Olivia Records and Travel.

PHOTO 3. Reprinted with permission of RSVP Travel Productions, Inc.

In addressing the first objective, I begin by briefly overviewing the literature on social movements before turning to gay/lesbian social movements. The dual status of gays and lesbians as both a social movement and a market segment raises a number of important theoretical questions for marketers and academics. Issues such as identity, subjectivity, and agency, which are central to studies of social movements, are also critical in understanding the place gays and lesbians occupy in the contemporary market economy. Social movements have historically played a significant role in enfranchising socially subordinated groups. Towards this end, members of social movements tend to have a heavily sensitized concern for the impact of marketing communications on group interests (e.g., critiques of the Frito Bandito and Aunt Jemima among Latinos and blacks, respectively). Equally important, relationships among social groups and conflicts of interests must be taken into account. Gays and lesbians historically have been stigmatized in U.S. society, particularly by those religious groups that see homosexuality as immoral. Their political mobilization against gay and lesbian interests continues to affect both marketers' decisions to target members of these groups and gays' and lesbians' attempts to achieve full political enfranchisement.

My second step in moving toward an evaluation of the gay/lesbian market is to compare its development with that of the Latino market. Significantly, there are similarities between what is currently said about the gay market and what was said about the Latino market in its early stages. Both of these groups of people, while seemingly recent market "discoveries," have long, rich histories of social movement activism and their study generates important insights into the contemporary marketplace. In particular, both groups share positioning outside mainstream U.S. culture, yet receive important social legitimation in market targeting.

Having reviewed the social movement literature and compared developments of the Latino market with that of gays/lesbians, I then turn to the evaluation of gays and lesbians as a viable market segment. I proceed through each of the segmentation criteria, with attention to its assumptions and its propriety for gays and lesbians in the contemporary marketplace. Further, I question the use of the term "lifestyle" to describe gays and lesbians, particularly when gay/lesbian life and culture is reduced to sexuality.

The second part of the paper consists of a critical examination of writings on the gay/lesbian market in the marketing literature. Statistics on the market as a whole, as well as characteristics and profiles of gay/lesbian consumers are reviewed, with attention to the role and interests of advertising, market research, and media agents and institutions. Key concerns are the strategies employed in promoting this group as a market and the representativeness of the data provided with regard to the larger population of gays and lesbians.

Finally, I evaluate the implications of marketing to gays and lesbians. Regarding the implications of marketing to gays and lesbians on the structure of the U.S. marketplace, increased fragmentation and specialization are both the result of and chief factors spurring segmentation strategies targeting market subgroups, such as gays and lesbians, as well as blacks, the elderly, men, Latinos, etc. These market segmentation strategies may be seen to operate as democratizing mechanisms, in the sense that they include people who are not typically included in more narrow conceptualizations of the U.S. market. Indeed, there is a profound sense of social validation and legitimation that is experienced by individual gays and lesbians and gay/lesbian communities as the result of increased accommodation as a market in capitalist society. Further, the gay/lesbian market brings a number of job opportunities as it grows. Less positive effects include distorted representations of gays and lesbians both within and outside these communities, such as an inflated socioeconomic status attributed to gays and lesbians that not only misrepresents the conditions and experiences of a number of gays and lesbians, but has also been used by radical right religious organizations in their efforts to repeal gay/lesbian protection legislation.

MARKETING AND SOCIAL DIFFERENCE: THE INTERSECTION OF SOCIAL MOVEMENTS AND MARKET SEGMENTS

The world regards sexuality as the secret of cultural life, it is rather a process of our having to create a new cultural life underneath the ground of our sexual choices. Not only do we have to defend ourselves, we have to affirm ourselves, not only as an identity, but as a creative force.

–Michel Foucault

Since the mid-1960s there has been a documented shift in marketing practice from targeting the mainstream or mass market to including more specialized niche markets (Smith 1965; Engel, Fiorillo and Cayley 1971). This shift in marketing strategy is the result of a number of factors, including increasing levels of competition for the mass market, shifts in demographic growth rates and geographic patterns of residence for the U.S. population, and the increasing availability of specialized media products.

Together, these factors have contributed to the recent visibility of the gay/lesbian market. Research and media companies specializing in the gay market have dubbed it the "Dream Market," promising U.S. firms direct access to millions of gay and lesbian consumers with billions of dollars in annual income (Miller 1990; 1992).

Partly in response to this increasing marketing and media attention, marketing scholars have questioned whether gays and lesbians comprised a market segment. In this section, I draw from the literature on social movements because this work offers new insight into the market accommodation of minority populations. Significantly, it is the gains of the gay/lesbian social movement, together with the development of a marketing infrastructure, that render gays and lesbians a viable market segment.[4]

The Social Movement Literature

It is more than a coincidence that marketing theorists began to exhort the benefits of tailoring products and/or services to particular groups of people on the basis of their unique characteristics in the 1960s (Engel, Fiorillo, and Cayley 1971). At this time there was much social activism in the U.S., and the development of these segmentation strategies may be seen as both the result of and a contributing factor to the social changes these movements brought about. In fact, many civil rights gains were and continue to be manifest in the marketplace–at the lunch counters, in bus and retail service, in hotel accommodations, and in socially acceptable standards of dress. In this sense, the marketplace may be viewed as an important domain of social contestation whereby disenfranchised groups engage in ongoing struggles for social and political incorporation.

Social movement theory is particularly useful in this research because it attends to: (1) the ways in which particular groups of people in society come together in the development and pursuit of their interests and (2) the ways in which their strategic actions are incorporated and/or resisted by institutions within a society, particularly governmental and educational institutions. Classic studies in this literature have documented the differential trajectories and strategies of various social movements as people within them work to mobilize people and resources in the development and pursuit of their objectives (Piven and Cloward 1977; Petracca 1993). Also of interest have been "free riders," people who benefit from movement gains, but do not contribute directly to the effort and who may or may not identify themselves as group members. My interest lies in exploring the relationship between gay/lesbian activism and the accommodation of gay/lesbian consumers in the marketplace. It is suggested that as civil rights gains are made by gay/lesbian activists, the social climate becomes more favorable to individual gays and lesbians in claiming and expressing this part of themselves as well as to firms interested in targeting members of this group.

A second stream of this literature, labeled the "new social movements," emphasizes the development of identity, subjectivity, and agency both within and outside the movement, and goes beyond traditional notions of social movements based on socioeconomic status to include social movements formed around issues of race/ethnicity, gender, and sexuality. This literature examines how people within the movement are mobilized and politicized as a subculture, as well as how those outside the movement are mobilized and politicized both in support and in opposition to it (Morris and Mueller 1992). Issues of identity, subjectivity, and agency are integral to the analysis of contemporary gay marketing because these aspects of individual and collective behavior contribute to our understanding of how gays and lesbians constitute themselves and their relations towards others.

Finally, a third stream of this research is relevant to the present study. This work incorporates theoretical advances in poststructuralism to examine the ways in which the subject of social movements is constituted in social discourse (Butler and Scott 1992; Shapiro 1992). This work is particularly useful in examining representations of gay/lesbian consumers in the discourses of marketing and advertising. Marketing activities targeting gays and lesbians typically do so by including elements of gay identity and experience. Because these representations provide a mirroring function for gay/lesbian people, they potentially have an effect upon gay subjectivity and agency, i.e., how gays and lesbians think of themselves and how they view marketing practices and consumption behaviors in relation to group interests.

While offering a number of theoretical contributions to this research, the social movement literature has virtually neglected the role of marketing institutions in furthering or inhibiting social change. This view of business ignores some strategically useful aspects of business activity, namely the social legitimation that comes as the result of market targeting. This is not to suggest that marketing attention is always a positive thing for the people or the social movement in question, however. Because market targeting has both positive and negative implications, it merits serious critical analysis. Towards this end, I turn now to the gay/lesbian movement.

The Gay/Lesbian Social Movement

A complete recounting of the history of gay/lesbian social movements is beyond the scope of this paper; however, a few points are noteworthy.

Historians and social theorists have documented the trajectory of gay/lesbian movements, situating them within the larger field of the history of sexuality, and noting various shifts in the ontological status of same-sex love and sexual desire from a universal human capability to the deviant behavior of a stigmatized people, to a criminal activity, to a clinical disorder, to a positive social identity and subculture (D'Emilio and Freedman 1988; Foucault 1978; Weeks 1985; D'Emilio 1983; Kennedy and Davis 1994).

Particularly relevant are earlier manifestations of gay/lesbian/bisexual/transgender practices, communities, and social movements, together with their reception by business and other social institutions because this lays the historical groundwork for the contemporary marketplace response to gays and lesbians. In early examples, Trumbach (1991) wrote of historical and literary accounts of hermaphrodites (i.e., the vernacular sodomite or molly in the case of men and sapphist or tommy for women) in London as early as the eighteenth century, and Wilson (1991) located a thriving area of restaurants, cafes, and theater in Paris in the late nineteenth century. It is likely that these consumer subcultures had an influence on the early sexologists, such as Magnus Hirschfeld (1910) and Havelock Ellis (1925), whose work took seriously the study of sexual behavior. These consumer subcultures reached a peak in Europe in the 1930s and 1940s, before being run underground by the Nazis (Plant 1986).

In the U.S., gay and lesbian communities have been located as early as the late nineteenth and early twentieth centuries (Chauncey 1994). However, for the most part gay/lesbian social activism in the U.S. is traced to the late 1940s and 1950s (D'Emilio 1983; Bérubé 1990; Kennedy and Davis 1994; Boyd 1995). While it pales somewhat in contrast to the more radical activism that would follow thirty years later, its contributions were no less significant. At this time gay and lesbian organizations such as the Matachine Society and the Daughters of Bilitis were formed. These organizations were largely middle class in composition and featured a fairly conservative, assimilationist strategy in their attempt to gain civil rights and acceptance by the larger society.

The most recent wave of gay/lesbian social activism is marked by the Stonewall Rebellion in 1969 in New York. At that time, homosexuality was listed as a mental disorder by the American Psychological Association and police raids of bars, in which drag queens and crossdressing butches were hauled off and often beaten, were common (Nestle 1992; D'Emilio 1994; Thompson 1994). As in other social movements, a key event is seldom as important as what it comes to symbolize. The Stonewall Rebellion has gained notoriety because it is used by the contemporary gay/lesbian community to mark the beginning of gay/lesbian pride and to communicate the message that gays/lesbians will no longer tolerate subordinate status. Nevertheless, like the importance granted to Rosa Parks in the Black civil rights movement, the happenings that night at the Stonewall Inn were necessarily predated and accompanied by the work of countless unrecognized individuals and groups. Partly in response to gay and lesbian social activism, but also in response to the research of Evelyn Hooker (1956; 1957), homosexuality was removed from the list of disorders of the American Psychological Association in 1973. This institutional breakthrough served to further spur the movement.

Over the years, many gay/lesbian organizations have come and gone, and while some of the items on the agendas of these groups have changed, the struggle for basic rights continues. Organizations vary widely in their composition and aims. Examples such as the National Gay and Lesbian Task Force, GLAAD, Society of Janus, PFLAG, ACT UP, Queer Nation, and the Victory Fund have worked for and continue to work to address such issues as decriminalization of sexual practices, job discrimination, violence against gays and lesbians, teen suicide, freedom of sexual expression, family understanding, the AIDS crisis, and political enfranchisement.[5] It is also significant to note that gays and lesbians have come together despite differences over the years, partly in response to the AIDS epidemic, but also as a pragmatic strategy that has served to bolster the numbers collectively and render the group a more formidable force for positive social change. Currently, the most pressing issue facing the gay/lesbian movement is arguably the rash of state and local initiatives sponsored by the radical Christian right that seeks to repeal gay protection legislation. Marketing to gays/lesbians is best understood when situated within the sociohistorical context of these movements.

A Comparison of the Development of the Gay/Lesbian and Latino Markets

As suggested previously, there is a close temporal relationship between social movement gains and market targeting. In the 1970s, marketing studies flourished that prescribed strategies for targeting women and Blacks. Analogously, the Latino market was "discovered" in the 1980s, while the gay market is a 1990s phenomenon. Significantly, each of these market segments followed on the heels of social movement gains, but with different time lags.

The gay/lesbian market offers a number of differences and similarities when compared to that of Latinos.[6] Both groups are positioned outside the imagined community (Anderson 1983) of U.S. culture, but for different reasons and to different degrees. Both groups have different distributions of sociodemographic characteristics, such as income, education, and occupation. Gays and lesbians tend to be thought of as primarily middle class and white, although there are many working class and racial/ethnic minority gays and lesbians in this country; Latinos tend to be thought of as unskilled workers for the most part, although many professionals are found within their ranks.

In addition, issues of agency characterize both groups. Regarding gays and lesbians, there is much debate concerning whether homosexuality is chosen or genetic, yet for the most part public sentiment is in line with the former. It is the "choice" to love someone of the same sex that goes against U.S. heterosexual norms, even as many gays' and lesbians' whiteness and middle class status is consistent with the U.S. mainstream culture. Regarding Latinos, those born outside of the U.S. have moved to the U.S. to flee economic hardship, to improve their standard of living, and to better their education and that of their children. In these ways, their movement is consistent with the U.S. work ethic, even as their color goes against the U.S.'s self image of whiteness (Peñaloza 1994).

Most importantly for purposes of this paper, however, is the fact that both gays/lesbians and Latinos have a history of social activism and are considered examples of the new social movements (Morris and Mueller 1992). For both groups, the constitution of themselves as a subculture has had much to do with the revaluation of an identity that had been imbued with negative qualities by the larger culture. Further, marketing incorporation has helped facilitate the social legitimation of both groups, even as the marketplace remains contested terrain in their struggles.

Re-evaluating Gays and Lesbians as a Viable Market Segment

Partly the result of the stigma attached to homosexuality, but also due to the dearth of statistics on this "new" market, many firms remain doubtful about its potential, even as they are strongly financially motivated to seek out new profitable market segments. In his evaluation of the gay/lesbian market, Fugate (1993) positioned it as a lifestyle segment and concluded that gays/lesbians were not a viable market segment because they did not satisfy the segmentation criteria of being identifiable, accessible, and of sufficient size and stability to be feasible (Cravens, Hill and Woodruff 1987). Yet, while Fugate produced a rigorous, comprehensive piece of scholarship, there are some noteworthy limitations.

The first limitation of Fugate's (1993) work relates to his operationalization of the segmentation criteria. These criteria tend to be used in ways that treat marketers as active agents who must clearly identify more passive potential customers prior to being able to target them. Thus, these criteria posit rather traditional roles for marketers, media, and consumers even as these roles have been called into question (Bristor and Fischer 1993). Indeed, Fugate (1993) was quite concerned with the dissension regarding the numbers of gay/lesbian consumers, particularly in people's propensity to identify as gays/lesbians. This also continues to be an issue for the Latino market, as Latinos vary in self-identification by generation, nationality, and socioeconomic level (Peñaloza 1994). Although self-identification is a notoriously unreliable construct in the case of socially subordinated groups, it is at best a good place to start. Yet, the issue is as much whether distinct consumption patterns deal solely with the segment determinant (i.e., race, ethnicity, gender, or in this case, sexuality), as whether these groups claim a distinct identity and subculture that is expressed in identifiable ways.

Similarly, the accessible criterion continues with the assumption of active marketers who contact passive consumers. This criterion also requires modification to reflect dramatic changes in media and in the marketplace that have occurred over the past 20 years, particularly the use of specialty media by marketers in their efforts to access special interest segments. Increasingly important in accessing consumers is providing materials that they will self-select, and then using these customer-initiated contacts in the form of interactive computer networks and cable, as well as the more traditional mail and telephone merchandising techniques, to build a reliable consumer database (Meyer 1994). This is especially the case for members of a stigmatized group, such as gays and lesbians, but is also appropriate for other segments that are difficult to access, such as the wealthy. A plethora of specialty print and broadcast media have entered the scene since 1970, rendering niche markets increasingly accessible and a good buy, especially when they are expanded beyond U.S. national borders to encompass their global counterparts.

Closely related to issues of identifiability and accessibility is the requirement that a market segment be of sufficient size to justify those additional costs needed to reach it. This criterion often assumes separate campaigns are necessary to reach each segment. Yet, companies often place the same advertisement in a number of media, relying on its placement to communicate a specialized message to each audience. In these cases, firms realize only those additional costs of media placement that often result in an economically efficient contact.

The stability criterion assumes an idealized level of social stability that is arguably a characteristic of modern, and not postmodern, society, as people move into and out of several categories daily, as well as over the course of their lives (Featherstone 1991). This is the case not only for gay/lesbian consumers, but also for consumers categorized by marketers based on ethnicity and race, or even by stage in family life cycle, simply because people's identification and experience change over time as the result of life events, and as the result of changes in the significance of social categories. Nevertheless, it is increasingly clear that consumers inhabit more than one of these domains and that the domains are themselves anything but distinct. Any one of them may be seen to include a wide variation in its delineating characteristics and marketplace expressions.

Finally, there is some question regarding the use of the term "lifestyle" to categorize gays/lesbians. Fugate (1993) noted that homosexual males and lesbians constituted a definable market segment only so long as *specific activities, interests, and opinions dealt with their sexuality* (p. 47, italics added). This categorization reduces gay and lesbian culture to sexuality, even as it smooths over existing variation in activities, interests, and opinions among lesbians and gay men. The term "lifestyle" has been used in an attempt to capture the complexity and subtlety of cultural differences that go beyond demographics, but with mixed success when tied to consumption behaviors (Lastovicka et al. 1990; Lastovicka 1982). While activities, interests, and opinions capture some aspects of gay/lesbian life, and while gay and lesbian culture certainly includes elements of sexuality in all of its diverse forms, designating gays and lesbians as a lifestyle limited to sexuality potentially trivializes the complexities of gay/lesbian lives. This reduction is perhaps best demonstrated by extrapolating the term "lifestyle" to other subcultural groups, such as Latinos, blacks, or women, while thinking of these subcultures solely in terms of race, ethnicity, and gender, respectively.

A key theoretical problem with the segmentation criteria is their inability to distinguish among types of market segments. There are key differences between dinks and yuppies on one hand, and Latinos, women, and gays/lesbians on the other. While both types of groups are market segments, the former represents sociodemographic groupings and lifestyles, while the latter are best understood as social movements. As members of a social movement, gays and lesbians have developed a consciousness of themselves as a people as the result of a history of common interests and experiences, particularly their exclusion, mobilization, and struggle in response to how they have been treated by others. This consciousness is only part of the foundation for the gay/lesbian market segment, however, as people vary in the degree to which they identify as group members.

For these reasons, it is necessary to move beyond the question of identity to include social practices and community formations in conceptualizing consumer subcultures such as gays and lesbians. Even with the gains of gay/lesbian movements, it is likely that the number of gays/ lesbians claiming a gay/lesbian identity is less than the total number of gays and lesbians due to the social stigma attached to homosexuality. Further, it is likely that the number of gays and lesbians working under the rubric of the gay/lesbian movement is less than the total number of gays and lesbians, given the presence of free riders. Marketers should be concerned with these latter operationalizations.

Reconceptualizing lesbians and gays as part of a consumer subculture that encompasses the distinct dimensions of identity, social practices, and community formations facilitates the inclusion of variations in identification and in consumption patterns. Yet, it is also necessary to expand measures of consumption patterns to account for differences in the meanings and uses accorded various products, services, and other marketing stimuli among various consumer subcultures even when there is no apparent difference in the consumption patterns themselves. In my work with Latino consumers, it became clear that the meanings they associated with many of the products and services they used were different than those associated with the same products and services for mainstream consumers (Peñaloza 1994). Thus, the segmentation view that requires people to have differences in consumption patterns can be misleading, especially when the differences stem from identity and group membership.

Including differences in the meanings attached to products, services, and marketing stimuli that tap into group identity and experience as measures of market segments yields a more sensitive measure of differences in subcultural consumption behaviors. As with other consumer subcultures, particular codes such as clothing styles, mannerisms, and language are used to communicate to other members of the group. With regard to gays and lesbians, it is likely that there are differences in meanings and uses for products and services as compared to heterosexual consumers. Further, these differences would not necessarily be limited to sexuality simply because this is only one dimension of gay/lesbian life experience, although an important one.

In sum, understanding the place of gays and lesbians in the contemporary market requires thoughtful reconsideration of the segmentation criteria. Based on my review of the literature on social movements and market segmentation, it appears that there is some theoretical basis for the constitution of gays and lesbians as a viable market segment. Perhaps the most compelling argument, however, is found in the acts of marketing practitioners targeting members of this group, a subject to which I now turn.

GAYS–A DREAM MARKET?!?

REACH THIS DREAM MARKET IN A STYLISH, REALITY BASED EDITORIAL ENVIRONMENT THAT SPEAKS DIRECTLY TO THEM

–A recent advertisement for the gay publication *Genre*

The above excerpt is but one of several advertisements and articles in marketing and advertising industry publications promoting the gay/lesbian market. This particular advertisement promised firms access to 200,000 potential customers per issue. In this section I examine the characteristics and potential of the gay/lesbian market, the role of gay/lesbian media, and the strategies used to target gays and lesbians.

The Making of the Gay/Lesbian Market

Accounting for the number of gays and lesbians in the U.S. has proven to be quite difficult and controversial. The numbers vary widely as the result of the use of various measures in various types of studies. Studies come from a number of disciplines, including sexuality, psychology, health care, and most recently, market research. Perhaps most famous is the 1948 Kinsey Institute study which found the ratio of heterosexuals to homosexuals to be 10:1. This study was replicated in 1993, with similar findings in *The Janus Report on Sexual Behavior* (Janus and Janus 1993). According to studies by the National Opinion Research Center at the University of Chicago, 2.8% of adult males and 2.3% of adult females identified themselves as homosexual (Rogers 1993). These lower figures may be attributable to the use of a more narrow definition of gay and lesbian that excluded bisexuals. At any rate, due to the controversial nature of homosexuality in U.S. society, measures typically consist of self-reports, which tend to be conservative in their estimates.

In addition, varying definitions and terms create a number of other data collection and tabulation problems. Definitions touch on the range of identities, sexual orientations, and behaviors encompassed by the general term "homosexual." Among scholars and activists alike, there is much disagreement regarding whether exclusive homosexual behaviors, identities, and orientations are requirements for members of this group. More liberal definitions include having engaged in homosexual behaviors or having claimed a gay/lesbian identity or orientation at any time during the life course.

Terminology used includes various combinations of homosexual, gay, lesbian, queer, dyke, bisexual, transgendered, transvestite, and transsexual, and each of these terms is further complicated by its generational and ideological connotations. It is significant to note that while queer theorists are adamant about including bisexuals and transgendered persons within the gay/lesbian movement in an attempt to move beyond the dualistic essentialisms of gender and to embrace the complexity, indeterminacy, and performance that homosexuality entails, marketing firms are intent on specifying the category.

Marketing and advertising studies of the gay market tend to focus on the numbers and on buying power. Overlooked Opinions, a market research firm in Chicago that specializes in the gay market, estimates it to consist of 18.5 million people with total annual income of $514 billion dollars (Johnson 1993a). More conservative figures have been provided by Nile Merton, publisher of *The Advocate*, who estimated the number of gay and lesbian consumers in the U.S. to be 5 million people (cited in Johnson 1993a), and Cyndee Miller (1990), who estimated gays' and lesbians' annual spending to be $382 billion.

Consumer Profile

For the most part, studies of gay/lesbian consumers have found their income to be higher than that of heterosexuals. According to a study done by Simmons Market Research Bureau of the readership of eight of the leading gay newspapers in the country, the figures for average individual income were $36,800 for gays/lesbians, as compared to census statistics of $32,287 for heterosexuals. Average household income figures were $55,430 for gays/lesbians, as compared to census figures of $32,114 for heterosexual households (cited in Miller 1990; Curiel 1991). This study has been criticized for providing a distorted characterization of gays and lesbians as the result of its reliance on the readership of gay newspapers.

More recently, the Yankelovich Monitor Survey has called into question the widespread belief that the income of gays and lesbians was greater than that of heterosexuals. According to their report, income for gays was $37,400, as compared to $39,300 for heterosexual men; and $34,800 for lesbians, as compared to $34,400 for heterosexual women. This study is significant in that it employed a nationally representative sample of self-selected gays and lesbians. In addition, the study compared the responses of heterosexual and homosexual men and women. Regarding education, 14% of gay/lesbian/bisexual respondents had attended graduate school, compared to 7% of heterosexuals; while 49% of gay/lesbian/bisexual respondents had attended some college, as compared to 37% of heterosexuals (Yankelovich 1994). Regarding occupation, 56% of gays/lesbians had professional and managerial jobs, compared to 16% of heterosexuals (cited in Curiel 1991).

Turning to consumption patterns, it has been widely reported that gays and lesbians are more willing to spend money than non-gays (Johnson 1993a; Fugate 1993). Gays/lesbians have been listed as spending dispro-portionate amounts on luxury and premium products, such as travel (But-ton 1993), vacations (Davis 1993), phone services, and books (Warren 1990; Summer 1992), recorded music, alcoholic beverages, theater (Elliot 1993b), clothing catalogues (Miller 1992; Elliot 1993c), and greeting cards (Button 1993). In addition, gay/lesbian consumers were found to be younger, more brand and fashion conscious, and more brand loyal than their heterosexual counterparts (Miller 1990).

While these statements appear to contradict the reservation discussed earlier that gays and lesbians were not identifiable in terms of distinct buyer behaviors from non-gays, it is important to keep in mind that most of these statements were not based on representative studies of the larger population of gays and lesbians. Only the Yankelovich Monitor survey was based on a nationally representative sample. Significantly, others like the Simmons survey were based on samples of gay/lesbian media audi-ences. In general, media audience studies tend to overestimate such con-sumer characteristics as income and purchase intentions for the general population because they draw from a distinct subgroup that tends to be better off financially. Most critically, these figures are used by marketing and media agencies to sell clients on the potential profits to be made from targeting that particular audience. As in other marketing appeals, what appears is part salesmanship and part truth, as illustrated in the quote at the beginning of this section. While the gay media are beginning to use audits to attain more independent audience figures (Johnson 1993a), even these results should be understood as *representative of their audiences, and not of the general population*, in this case, gays and lesbians in the U.S.

Finally, it is important to note that market studies tend to focus on gay men, even as lesbians are used to bolster their numbers. This is partly the result of the persistent difference in earnings for men as compared to women; on average women still earn two thirds of the amount men earn (Johnson 1993b). Of particular interest to marketers are gay male dinks (i.e., double income, no kids) because of their attractive levels of dispos-able income. Nevertheless, some differences in consumption patterns for lesbians as compared to gay men have been noted, and these differences, together with lower earnings may also help explain lesbians' lower per capita spending. Miller (1990) noted that lesbians tended to frequent bars less often and entertain at home more often than did gay men. Lesbians' relative invisibility in lesbian/gay consumer profiles may also reflect the legacy of anti-market sentiment among some lesbian-feminists, i.e., their equation of capitalism with patriarchy and resulting reluctance and/or resistance to market participation.

Access

Firms interested in tapping into the gay/lesbian market can do so with the help of a growing range of media. There are a number of local and regional gay/lesbian newspapers, together with national magazines, cable and public broadcasting service television programs, and radio shows. The newspapers typically have both paid and free distribution, and are sponsored largely by local gay/lesbian owned and operated firms that cater to gay/lesbian clientele.

A number of gay/lesbian magazines have come on the scene in recent years, joining the ranks of the more established. *Deneuve, Genre, Out, 10 Percent, QW,* and *50/50* (See Photo 4, 50/50) are some of the recent arrivals; while *The Advocate, On Our Backs* and *Outweek* have a longer history of service to the gay/lesbian community. A key debate that has followed in the wake of the new media is their future impact on the gay/lesbian community, as they are glossier and more image and fashion oriented than their more politically inclined predecessors. With the increased number of new magazines comes more competition in this burgeoning field and their positioning relative to the gay/lesbian community is an important factor affecting their chances of survival.

In addition to these gay/lesbian media, a number of advertising and marketing research companies now offer consulting services for firms interested in targeting gay and lesbian consumers. Examples include Overlooked Opinions, Direct Male, Mulryan/Nash, and Rivendell Marketing Company, Inc. These companies help firms develop marketing campaigns and place advertisements in gay/lesbian media, at gay/lesbian events such as the Gay Games and Gay/Lesbian Pride parades, and at gay/lesbian resorts.

As previously mentioned, access was cited as one of the disadvantages of the gay/lesbian market (Fugate 1993), yet problems of access seem unlikely given the increasing array of media and marketing research firms. Mainstream firms are beginning to advertise in gay/lesbian media, having been told that gays and lesbians value those firms they perceive to be supportive to them (See Photo 5, Miller Lite). In doing so, these firms join the ranks of those that have supported gay/lesbian media and events over the years. These firms should not expect gays and lesbians to be loyal customers simply because they have been targeted, however. For firms,

PHOTO 4. Reprinted with permission of *50/50* magazine.

PHOTO 5. Reprinted with permission of Miller Brewing Company.

the impact of gay/lesbian market targeting efforts are dependent upon both the quality and creativity of their campaigns, together with the relative number of advertisements consumers are exposed to. Presently, there are so few advertisements for the products and services of major corporations, that the advertisements of those companies targeting gays and lesbians enjoy a marked visibility. Over time, however, and with increases in the number of firms targeting gay/lesbian consumers, how gays and lesbians are portrayed in these advertisements will become an issue, just as portrayals of other minorities in advertisements have become issues for other minority communities following their initial market "discovery" period.

Strategies/Approaches Used to Target Gays and Lesbians

A number of strategies have been used to target gay/lesbian consumers. These vary from the simple extrapolation of a marketing campaign developed for other market(s) to the gay/lesbian market, to modifications of ongoing campaigns to tailor them to the gay/lesbian market, to the development of campaigns tailored uniquely for gay/lesbian consumers.

Redirecting a marketing campaign used to target heterosexuals to gay/lesbian media can be a cost-effective strategy, as firms can rely on the placement of their advertisements to communicate their desire to do business with gays and lesbians. Recent examples include Evian, Calvert Equity Fund, Calvin Klein, Levi's, and Gaultier jeans. This is not just a message of intention to do business, however, but also marks some solidarity with gay/lesbian communities, so long as religious groups threaten such firms with boycotts (Levin 1993).

In addition, while marketing campaigns that feature solely men or women invite gay/lesbian identification, campaigns that feature heterosexual references to the exclusion of any gay/lesbian iconography may preclude such identification. This is especially the case when these advertisements appear in proximity to advertisements with more direct appeals, and when gay/lesbian organizations disseminate critiques of these campaigns that feature their sponsor as merely targeting gays and lesbians as an afterthought, or in a tokenistic fashion.

A second marketing strategy, located on the other end of the continuum, entails the development of a separate campaign for gays/lesbians with readily identifiable appeals to members of these consumer subcultures. The most obvious examples include the use of same sex couples (see Photo 2, Olivia, and Photo 3, RSVP). Other examples would include the use of gay/lesbian iconography such as the rainbow or pink/black triangles. These advertisements present the greatest potential in terms of identification by gay/lesbian audiences and often minimize the risk of offending heterosexuals by their placement in gay/lesbian media, as marketers capitalize on self-selected gay/lesbian audiences. Examples include American Express's advertisements for joint travelers' checks featuring two male and two female signatures, and AT&T's use of the rainbow in advertisements placed in gay/lesbian media. A twist of this second strategy is to tie marketing campaigns to gay/lesbian community events, such as the 1994 Unity Games, as well as fundraisers and charities (see Photo 5, Miller Lite). In another example, Community Spirit, a telephone interconnect company, gave their service a gay reference by allocating 2% to the gay, lesbian, or AIDS charity of the consumer's choice (Button 1993).

Perhaps the most practical strategy is to combine the use of gay iconography with the reading strategies of gay/lesbian consumers. In ways not unlike "inside" jokes, these alternative reading strategies produce different messages for the same advertisement for gay/lesbian consumers as compared to heterosexual consumers as the result of shared subcultural understandings. For example, in Photo 5 the Miller Lite advertisement features the copy, "Pour on the Pride." While pride is certainly not limited to gay/lesbian consumers, this caption carries a special meaning for them when placed during the Gay/Lesbian Pride festivals. This strategy is potentially effective in campaigns placed in both the mainstream and in gay/lesbian media, as it achieves a cross-over appeal to both gays/lesbians and heterosexuals. Other examples include marketing campaigns that feature subtle gay and lesbian references because they may be read as close friendships by heterosexual men and women, at the same time they are accorded more intimate connotations by gays and lesbians.

DISCUSSION AND IMPLICATIONS

This could be the first time in the history of great American capitalists that they've avoided making an easy buck.

Richard Rouilard, editor-in-chief, *The Advocate,* quoted in Miller 1992, p. 15

Increasing appeals to the gay/lesbian market among mainstream marketing firms, together with the increased number of media and marketing firms serving gays/lesbians, suggest that this is a viable segment for many products and services. Particularly responsive product and service categories include books, music, film and theater, vacations, beverages (alcoholic and non-alcoholic), and clothing. The recent "discovery" of the gay market raises a number of important theoretical and practical issues, however. With the advent of recognition of the gay market, sexuality comes to the fore as a market designator. This promises to be at least as controversial as gender and race/ethnicity. Yet, as I have argued, the basis for the gay/lesbian market segment is found in the nexus of sexuality and social movement. Because of this unique configuration, studies of this market bring consumer agency to the fore.

As scholars interested in marketing and in homosexual issues, it is important to situate the recent recognition of gays and lesbians as a market segment within the larger trends that have brought this about. I have argued that changes in the nature of the marketplace, in competition, among consumers, and in media, as well as changes brought about by the gay/lesbian movement have worked in tandem to bring about the present reality of this market. The first implication of marketing to gays/lesbians to be discussed is its effect on the structure of the U.S. marketplace. Gay/lesbian market segmentation, like other forms of market segmentation, both contributes to and is the result of the increasing fragmentation and specialization of the U.S. market. As firms increasingly engage in niche marketing, targeting people with unique campaigns based on their unique features and relying on specialty media, they not only draw from these social differences, but also reproduce them in the marketplace and in the larger social milieu. By addressing gays and lesbians as consumers, then, marketers and advertisers constitute them in important ways (i.e., render them identifiable and intelligible), particularly in a capitalistic society. A gay/lesbian aesthetic, or sensibility, becomes visible in the form of advertising codes and conventions, specific product and service appeals, and media treatments designed both in response to and in anticipation of gay/lesbian market expressions and desires. As such, marketing to lesbians and gays may be seen to impact relations between gays and lesbians and the larger society. In particular, as the accommodation of gay and lesbian consumers in the marketplace serves to validate and legitimate them, it mobilizes those who oppose the full incorporation of gays and lesbians in U.S. society.

In addition to its impact on the U.S. market as a whole, gay/lesbian marketing potentially affects both gays and lesbians as individuals and as members of highly diverse, geographically dispersed communities. There is much economic power in the gay/lesbian market and it is increasingly global. It is a valuable affirmation for gays and lesbians to be able to go to almost any major city in the world and locate gay/lesbian clubs, media, bookstores, and hotlines. It is no less significant for gays and lesbians to see themselves, their heroines and their heroes in film, music, and in advertisements. Marketing to gays and lesbians serves to legitimize them in the U.S. as individuals and as members of a subculture.

At the individual level, this validation is important because sexuality is a fundamental part of human experience. For individual gays and lesbians, sexuality is one of several dimensions of their lives, along with those such as family, ethnicity/race, occupation, gender and religion. Because gay/lesbian identity and group affiliation remain stigmatized by many of the other groups of which they are a part, this market incorporation provides a vital sense of affirmation. At issue, then, for gay and lesbian consumers are questions regarding how these various groups to which they belong coexist, i.e., which conflict with and which reinforce each other, as well as how these various affiliations are reconciled within their psyches and how they are expressed within the marketplace.

Marketing and media attention also affect gay/lesbian communities, and while it is somewhat separate from political activism, it can help render gays and lesbians a force to be reckoned with politically (Mickens 1994). Alliances are invaluable in any social movement, and the gay/lesbian movement is no exception. Both within and outside the gay/lesbian community it is important to nurture alliances with the "others," be they marketers, working class people, people of color, bisexuals, transgendered persons or heterosexuals.

Marketing campaigns, in particular, add the critically important data points of buyer and income earner for those taking an oppositional stance towards homosexuality and who are accustomed to thinking of gays/lesbians solely in terms of sexuality. Noted Kevin Ray, president of aka Communications, a media and public relations agency specializing in the gay market, "business is exploding, firms are no longer willing to avoid the market out of fear of a backlash from straight consumers, now they're worried about a backlash against firms that appear to be homophobic" (cited in Miller 1992, p. 15). While this may be somewhat of an overstatement, let us not lose sight of the fact that in a capitalist society, market incorporation is of the utmost importance because it summons a social legitimation approaching that of citizen.

Yet, there are some downsides to this market recognition and targeting. Gays and lesbians are right to hold advertisers and companies that target them accountable for the images they use, and there are places to articulate these concerns in both mainstream and gay media, in letters to the editors of both gay/lesbian and mainstream media, and in boycotts. Here I make reference to the title of this paper, which is an intentional play on the earlier and opposite rallying cry, "We're Here, We're Queer, and We're Not Going Shopping," echoed along Fifth Avenue in New York on the twentieth anniversary of the

Stonewall Rebellion. That cry demonstrated gays' and lesbians' growing awareness of and intention to use strategically their buying power in the form of boycotts and purchases to express their disapproval or approval of corporate policies regarding employment practices, marketing and advertising campaigns and charitable and political contributions.

The marketplace has a tendency to distort not only the representations of those being targeted, but also their interests. For gays/lesbians, being targeted by marketers can be very seductive, particularly the portrayals of gays/lesbians as gorgeous, well-built, professionally successful, loved and accepted, especially in contrast to the legacy of negative treatment. Some aspects of gay/lesbian culture are forwarded at the expense of others in marketing and advertising appeals. Particularly noteworthy are the pervasive images of white, upper-middle class, "straight looking" people at the expense of those more distanced from and threatening to the mainstream, such as the poor, ethnic/racial/sexual minorities, drag queens, and butch lesbians.

In addition, it remains to be seen whether critical political agendas will be able to coexist with marketing interests in gay/lesbian media. Noted Dave Mulryan, director of business development at Mulryan/Nash Communications, "take away the politics and it's good, sound marketing." Mr. Mulryan's statement was made in reference to the elimination of sex advertisements in *The Advocate*, and their subsequent inclusion in a separate plastic envelope. Hermetically sealing and physically distancing the more controversial aspects of gay/lesbian culture may make sound business sense, as Mulryan noted, but it may not be in the best political interests of gay/lesbian communities. Effective marketing campaigns operationalized in terms of messages that are directed to the largest common denominator of a subculture within specialized media that avoid content that might offend advertisers do not necessarily deal with the central concerns of an audience, nor do they necessarily bring about the most effective social change. While marketers are not directly interested in the latter, media managers must deal with the former to maintain the publication's strong following.

A number of obstacles to gay/lesbian marketing have been identified. Even as this market has proven quite lucrative for some firms, the gay market remains a quandary for others, both marketing practitioners and academics, with only some of this ambivalence attributable to the stigma attached to homosexuality. As previously mentioned, marketing academics have been reluctant to view gays and lesbians as a market due to traditional conceptions of marketing segmentation. So long as marketers continue to see gays and lesbians through the reductive lenses of sexuality as opposed to the more comprehensive conceptualizations that take into account the social movements and consumer subcultures that have developed around gay/lesbian identities, marketing myopia regarding the potential of this market segment will persist.

Finally, fear of the stigma attached to homosexuality being linked to their products is no small obstacle for marketing practitioners. Noted Harry Taylor, National Ad Director for *Out*, "what I have to sell is a comfort level to people . . . it's more difficult to overcome the prejudice than to sell the product" (cited in Levin 1993). Homophobia on the part of upper management has been cited as a factor that has made selling of advertising space in gay media very difficult, according to Joe Di Sabato, President of Rivendell Marketing (cited in Miller 1990).

Added to this fear is the charge of immorality. The religious right has engaged a virtual assault on the civil rights of gays, lesbians, and bisexuals in recent years, and a key part of their strategy has involved targeting firms actively marketing their products and services to gays/lesbians. Noted Michel Roux, president of Carillon Inc., distributor of Absolut vodka and the first major company to advertise in *The Advocate* in 1979, "We've had people writing to us saying we will not use your product because you're advertising in a homosexual magazine and promoting homosexuality" (cited in Levin 1993, p. 30). While Roux did not withdraw the ads, there are numerous examples of companies that have withdrawn theirs. Ron McDonald, manager of *Genre*, reported that members of religious groups called in accusing Phillip Morris of targeting gays with their ad for Special Kings, and in response the company withdrew its ads (Levin 1993). In another example, Visa was the recent target of the religious right for having contributed $10,000 in support of the Gay Games.

Perhaps the most insidious deployment of gay/lesbian marketing information to date has been the use of the income figures from the Simmons study mentioned earlier by religious groups to argue that gays/lesbians did not need "special rights" (i.e., their choice of words to describe gay/lesbian protection ordinances). In a newspaper circulated to tens of thousands of voters in the state of Colorado in support of Amendment Two, the Coalition for Family Values cited Simmons Market Research figures showing average household incomes of $54,300 to argue that gays and lesbians were not economically disadvantaged, and therefore did not need protection from discrimination.[7] On one hand it is possible that it is because gays/lesbians have had some success in making civil rights gains that the religious right is determined to dispel them. More to the point of this paper, it is because gays and lesbians are making some headway in the marketplace, and because this market incorporation helps bring about a sense of social legitimation, that political opponents are so intent on contesting this strategically important social terrain.

CONCLUSION

While the increase in marketing attention provides a welcome sense of validation and legitimation, gays and lesbians must look at this relatively recent development with a critical eye. The earlier era of gay culture and visibility in the 1930s and 1940s in Europe culminated in black and pink triangles in Germany. Let us not forget that this was a capitalist country at the time. In fact, the vibrant gay culture existing in bars, restaurants, cafés and theaters in evidence at that time may have even fueled gays' and lesbians' genocide under Hitler since it made them more visible.

Since then many things have changed, both in the U.S. and in many parts of the world. The work of social movement activists and social scientists, each in their own ways and in their respective domains, has helped counter the legacy of stigma and institutionalized oppression. Closely linked to these gains, the gay/lesbian market has become increasingly visible, promoted in articles in marketing and media publications, in advertisements for gay/lesbian media, and in the plethora of marketers' attempts to target gay and lesbian consumers.

Market incorporation provides an important sense of social legitimation for gays and lesbians at both the individual and community levels. Yet, such incorporation is not without its limitations. Market legitimation was not enough in Nazi Germany, and it is not enough now. The futures of the gay/lesbian market and of the gay/lesbian movement are intricately connected, but they are not reducible to each other. Gays and lesbians cannot expect advertisers to engage in community activism–although they can and will benefit at times from advertisements, and some members of the advertising and marketing professional communities can and will advance gay/lesbian causes from time to time.

It is important to note differences between gays and lesbians as a market segment and as a social movement, even as both can and do benefit from each other's efforts. The gay and lesbian movement needs multiple approaches along multiple fronts, including the marketplace, to make the gains deemed desirable and to enjoy the basic human rights taken for granted by so many (e.g., freedom from job and housing discrimination based on suspicion of gay status, the right to marriage, insurance, and medical benefits). Unfortunately, the movement has been plagued by internal variation in politics, sexual and otherwise, and has gotten caught up in arguments for the one best approach. The gay/lesbian community's response to Amendment Two in Colorado was a recent example, yet there are numerous other examples of controversies within the community regarding whether the tactics of ACT UP, Queer Nation, the Lesbian Avengers, or the more conservative reformist tactics of those who infiltrate churches, workplaces, and other community spaces are the most effective means to further community interests that are at least as diverse as the tactics used to address them.

For the gay/lesbian community, gay target marketing is much more productively viewed as a critically important field of social struggle than as something to be avoided or prevented. Advertisements and other marketing artifacts such as products and services and popular cultural products such as film, books, recorded music, videos, etc. that incorporate aspects of gay/lesbian iconography potentially validate individual gays and lesbians and their communities, and can be used towards these communities' ends.

At the same time, gays and lesbians must be wary of distortions and appropriations in marketing appeals. While the advertisements may be quite flattering, it is important to remember that gays and lesbians do not enjoy the same standing in the marketplace in terms of income, status, and treatment by others. There are extreme subject positions within the communities that make mainstream advertisers nervous, and the ultimate test of gay and lesbian rights occurs at the extremes, not for those who can pass as heterosexual.

Lesbians and gays have come a long way, as the saying goes, but the struggle is far from over. In fact, it appears that the struggle is heating up, with the stakes getting much higher. The accommodation of gays and lesbians in the marketplace is a highly complex phenomenon that is at once as potentially validating as it is potentially alienating.

The arrival of this new market brings with it many more questions than answers. Further work is called for that focuses on the nexus of sexuality, social movement, and market segmentation in order to enhance our understanding of the intricate dynamics of gays' and lesbians' market incorporation. Further research is also called for that investigates expressions of subcultural membership and identification for individual gay and lesbian consumers, gay/lesbian communities, and their relationships to other subcultures in the U.S. The shift from mass to specialty markets, in all their diversity, together with the loss of audience figures for the mass media have been cited as contributing to the decay of not only the mainstream market, but also of mainstream U.S. culture. Yet, there is another interpretation. Instead of a nostalgic lament for the false unity and superiority of white, middle-class, heterosexual male culture, this shift in marketing strategy may be a part of a new era of inclusion, as both marketers and consumers realize increased tolerance for social difference.

NOTES

1. Glancing in one of the gay/lesbian phone directories available in most major cities attests to the wide range of businesses targeting gays and lesbians.

2. Age, gender, race/ethnicity, class, and sexual orientation are but a few designators of consumer cultures. The term "consumer culture" was first used in the critical tradition of the Frankfurt School to lament the impending social changes of western capitalism. More recently, in marketing and in cultural studies the term is used in reference to the marketplace expressions of a group of people (i.e., their shared aesthetics, attitudes, values and beliefs), necessarily including the marketing strategies employed to target them (Schudson 1984; Featherstone 1991). Thus, consumer cultures are hybrids of existing subcultures (e.g., blacks, Latinos, gays and lesbians, yuppies, the elderly) and their respective marketing artifacts (e.g., products and services, advertisements, and other marketing communications).

3. By subjectivity, I mean a person's sense of themselves and their place in the world, as well as their relationships towards others. I use the term agency to refer to one's ability to act in pursuit of their interests and desires.

4. This is not to suggest that all market segments are social movements or that all social movements are market segments.

5. This is not a comprehensive list, but rather serves to illustrate the wide array of lesbian and gay organizations and interests.

6. My purpose here is not to rank oppressions, but rather to analyze characterizations of these respective groups for insight as to their position and treatment in society. In this sense, this work represents an extension of my previous work on the incorporation of another type of social difference in the marketplace, namely that of ethnicity and nationality. I examined the role of marketing strategies in facilitating and inhibiting the incorporation of Mexican immigrants into U.S. society. My findings were that subcultural boundaries between Latinos and other consumer groups in the U.S. were raised by firms targeting Latinos with specially tailored products and services, even as these marketing strategies offered Latinos an important sense of social legitimation by institutionalizing aspects of Latino culture in this country (Peñaloza 1994).

7. Amendment Two stated, "Shall there be an amendment to article II of the Colorado Constitution to prohibit the state of Colorado and any of its political subdivisions from adopting or enforcing any law or policy which provides that homosexual, lesbian, or bisexual orientation, conduct, or relationships constitutes or entitles a person to claim any minority or protected status, quota preferences, or discrimination." The amendment passed by a slim margin, and a preliminary injunction ruling it unconstitutional was later upheld by the Colorado Supreme Court. On October 11, 1994 Amendment Two was ruled unconstitutional by the Court. It is currently under appeal to the U.S. Supreme Court. Estimates of losses in convention and tourist revenue in response to the passage of Amendment Two totaled 40 million dollars (Johnson 1994).

REFERENCES

Anderson, B. (1983). *Imagined Communities*. London: Verso.

Bérubé, A. (1990). *Coming Out Under Fire: The History of Gay Men and Women in World War II*. New York: Free Press.

Boyd, N. A. (1995). San Francisco was a Wide Open Town: Charting the Emergence of Lesbian and Gay Communities through the mid Twentieth Century. Unpublished doctoral dissertation, Department of American Civilization, Brown University.

Bristor, J. & Fisher, E. (1993). Feminist Thought: Implications for Consumer Research. *Journal of Consumer Research*, 19 (4) (March), 518-536.

Butler, J. & Scott, J. W. (Eds.) (1992). *Feminists Theorize the Political*. London: Routledge.

Button, K. (1990). The gay consumer. *Financial Times* (November 9), p. 10.

Chauncey, G. A. (1994). *Gay New York: Urban Culture and the Making of a Gay Male World, 1890-1940*. Ph.D. thesis, Yale University.

Cravens, D., Hills, G., & Woodruff, R. (1987). *Marketing Management*. Homewood, IL: Irwin.

Curiel, J. (1991). Gay Newspapers. *Editor and Publisher Fourth Estate*. 124 (3) (August), 14-19.

Davis, R. A. (1993). Sky's the limit for tour operators. *Advertising Age* (January 18), p. 36.

D'Emilio, J. (1983). *Sexual Politics, Sexual Communities: The Making of a Homosexual Minority in the U.S., 1940-1970*. Chicago: University of Chicago Press.

_____. (1994). *Making Trouble: Essays on Gay History, Politics and the University*. New York: Routledge.

D'Emilio, J. & Freedman, E. B. (1988). *Intimate Matters: A History of Sexuality in America*. New York: Harper and Row.

Duberman, M. (1993). *Stonewall*. New York: Dutton.

Elliott, S. (1993a). *Good Housekeeping* is drawing fire from homosexuals over ads dealing with family values. *New York Times* (May 7), p. C-15.

_____. (1993b). When a play has a gay theme, campaigns often tell it as it is. *New York Times* (June 15), p. C-15.

_____. (1993c). As the gay and lesbian market grows, a boom in catalogues that are out, loud and proud. *New York Times* (September 10), p. C-17.

Ellis, H. (1925). *Sexual Inversion*. Philadelphia: F.A. Davis.

Engel, J. F., Fiorillo, H., & Cayley, M. A. (1971). *Marketing Segmentation: Concepts and Applications*. New York: Holt, Rinehart and Winston.

Faderman, L. (1981). *Surpassing the Love of Men*. New York: William Morrow and Company.

Featherstone, M. (1991). *Consumer Culture and Postmodernism*. Newbury Park, CA: Sage.

Foucault, M. (1978). *The History of Sexuality*. New York: Pantheon Books.

Fugate, D. L. (1993). Evaluating the U.S. Male Homosexual and Lesbian Population as a Viable Target Market Segment: A Review with Implications. *Journal of Consumer Marketing*, 10 (4), 46-57.

Hirschfeld, M. (1910). *Transvestites: The Erotic Drive to Cross Dress.* Translated by M. A. Lombardi-Nash (1991). New York: Prometheus Books.

Hooker, E. (1956). A Preliminary Analysis of Group Behavior of Homosexuals. *Journal of Psychology*, 42, 219-225.

_____. (1957). The Adjustment of the Male Overt Homosexual. *Journal of Projective Techniques*, 21, 18-31.

Janus, S. & Janus, C. (1993). *The Janus Report on Sexual Behavior.* New York: John Wiley and Sons.

Johnson, B. (1993a). The gay quandary: Advertising's most elusive, yet lucrative target market proves difficult to measure. *Advertising Age*, 64 (18) (January 18) p. 29.

_____. (1993b). Economics holds back lesbian ad market. *Advertising Age*, 64 (18) (January 18), p. 34.

Johnson, D. (1994). Colorado Court Nullifies a Ban on Gay Rights. *New York Times*, (October 12), p. 1.

Kennedy, E. L. & Davis, M. D. (1994). *Boots of Leather, Slippers of Gold: The History of the Lesbian Community.* New York: Penguin Books.

Lastovicka, J. (1982). On the validation of lifestyle traits: A review and illustration. *Journal of Marketing Research*, 19 (1) (February), 126-138.

Lastovicka, J., Murray, J., Jr., & Joachimsthaler, E. (1990). Evaluating the Measurement Validity of Lifestyle Typologies With Qualitative Measures and Multiplicative Factoring. *Journal of Marketing Research*, 27 (1) (February), 11-23.

Levin, G. (1993). Mainstream's domino effect: Liquor, fragrance, clothing advertisers ease into gay magazines. *Advertising Age* (January 18), p. 30.

Meyer, C. (1994). Consumers and the Emerging Interactive Communications Infrastructure. Presented to the Association for Consumer Research Annual Conference, Boston, Massachusetts, October 20-23.

Miller, C. (1992). Mainstream marketers decide time is right to target gays. *Marketing News* (July 20), p. 8.

_____. (1990). Gays are affluent but often overlooked market. *Marketing News* (December 24), p. 2.

Mickens, E. (1994). Gay Money Gay Power. *The Advocate* (April 19), p. 41-45.

Morris, A. D. & Mueller, C. M. (Eds.) (1992). *Frontiers in Social Movement Theory.* New Haven, CT: Yale University Press.

Myrick, F.L. (1972). Structure and Function of Deviant Economic Institutions. Unpublished doctoral dissertation, University of Texas.

Nestle, J. (Ed.) (1992). *The Persistent Desire.* Boston: Alyson Publications.

New York Times (1990). The Media Business: Gay Press Looks to Madison Ave. *New York Times* (December 17), p. D-11.

Peñaloza (1994). Atravesando fronteras/border crossings: A critical ethnographic exploration of the consumer acculturation of Mexican immigrants. *Journal of Consumer Research*, 21 (1) (June), 32-54.

Peñaloza & Gilly, M. (1986). The Hispanic family: Consumer research issues. *Psychology and Marketing*, 3 (Winter), 291-303.

Petracca, M. (1993). *The Politics of Interests*. Boulder, CO: Westview Press.

Piven, F.F. & Cloward, R.A. (1977). *Poor People's Movements*. New York: Random House.

Plant, R. (1986). *The Pink Triangle and the Nazi War Against Homosexuals*. New York: Holt.

Rogers, P. (1993). Survey stirs debate on number of gay men in U.S. *New York Times*, 142, pp. A-10, A-20.

Schudson, M. (1984). *Advertising: The Uneasy Persuasion* New York, NY: Basic Books.

Schulman, S. (1994), *My American History: Lesbian and Gay Life During the Reagan/Bush Years*. New York: Routledge.

Shapiro, M.J. (1992). *Reading the Postmodern Polity: Political Theory as Textual Practice*. Minneapolis, MN: University of Minnesota Press.

Shilts, R. (1987). *And the Band Played On*. New York: St. Martin's Press.

Straub, K. (1991). The guilty pleasures of female theatrical cross-dressing and the autobiography of Charlotte Charke. In Straub, J. & Straub, K. (Eds.), *Body Guards*. London: Routledge.

Summer, B. (1992). A Niche Market Comes of Age. *Publishers Weekly* (June 29), p. 36-41.

Thompson, M. (1994). *Long Road to Freedom: The Advocate History of the Gay and Lesbian Movement*. New York: St. Martin's Press.

Warren, J. (1990). Vibrant subculture: Readers' buying power a key to a thriving gay press. *Chicago Tribune*, p. 2.

Weeks, J. (1985). *Sexuality and Its Discontents: Meanings, Myth and Modern Sexualities*. New York: Routledge.

Weinberg, G. (1972). *Society and the Healthy Homosexual*. New York: St. Martin's Press.

Wilson, M. (1991). "Sans les femmes, qu'est-ce qui nous resterait?": Gender and Transgression in Bohemian Montmartre. In Straub, J. & Straub, K. (Eds.), *Body Guards*. London: Routledge.

Wind, Y. (1978). Issues and Advances in Segmentation Research. *Journal of Marketing Research*, 15 (3) (August), 317-337.

Yankelovich (1994). Gay/Lesbian/Bisexual Monitor Survey. New York: Yankelovich and Associates, cited in *New York Times* (June 9), p. D-1.

Gift-Giving Among Gay Men:
The Reification of Social Relations

Margaret Rucker, PhD
Anthony Freitas, MS
Oscar Huidor, BS
University of California, Davis

SUMMARY. Previous work on gift-giving has shown the economic and social importance of this activity, ways in which it may reflect social relations, and characteristics of good and bad gift exchanges. This study examined gay gift-giving experiences to determine whether some of the propositions based almost exclusively on heterosexual data needed reinterpretation to be relevant to the homosexual community. It was found that, compared to previous research on gift-giving between heterosexual partners, gay males devoted more attention to selection or creation of gifts and they were also more concerned about the recipient's appreciation and utilization of the gift. On the other hand, they were less concerned with economic equity in the exchange process. These findings have implications for products offered as gifts as well as gift promotions that would be most suitable for this market. *[Article copies available from The Haworth Document Delivery Service: 1-800-342-9678.]*

Margaret Rucker is a professor in the Division of Textiles and Clothing at the University of California, Davis. Anthony Freitas is a doctoral student at the University of California, San Diego. Oscar Huidor is Junior Sales Manager at Lisa Jenks Jewelry in New York City. Correspondence should be addressed to Margaret Rucker, Division of Textiles and Clothing, University of California, Davis, CA 95616. E-mail: *mhrucker@ucdavis.edu*

[Haworth co-indexing entry note]: "Gift-Giving Among Gay Men: The Reification of Social Relations." Rucker, Margaret, Anthony Freitas, and Oscar Huidor. Co-published simultaneously in *Journal of Homosexuality* (The Haworth Press, Inc.) Vol. 31, No. 1/2, 1996, pp. 43-56; and: *Gays, Lesbians, and Consumer Behavior: Theory, Practice, and Research Issues in Marketing* (ed: Daniel L. Wardlow) The Haworth Press, Inc., 1996, pp. 43-56; and: *Gays, Lesbians, and Consumer Behavior: Theory, Practice, and Research Issues in Marketing* (ed: Daniel L. Wardlow) Harrington Park Press, an imprint of The Haworth Press, Inc., 1996, pp. 43-56. Single or multiple copies of this article are available from The Haworth Document Delivery Service [1-800-342-9678, 9:00 a.m. - 5:00 p.m. (EST)].

43

INTRODUCTION

As noted by Belk and Coon (1993) in their proposal of a new paradigm of gift-giving, economic exchange and social exchange models have been guiding work on gift-giving for over 50 years now. As a result, there is emerging a progressively clearer picture of both the economic and social effects of gifts and linkages between the two. As discussed below, while gift-giving is typically thought of in terms of positive effects, negative effects can occur as well.

Economic Effects of Gift-Giving

Economic analyses from a variety of sources suggest that gift-giving accounts for between 3% and 4% of consumers' yearly expenditures. For example, Davis (1972) estimated that gifts represented 4.3% of all consumer expenditures in the United Kingdom. Caplow (1982) used Christmas expenditures reported by consumers in a midwestern city to extrapolate a similar value for total spending on gifts among U.S. consumers. Based on national data from the 1984-85 U.S. Bureau of Labor Statistics Consumer Expenditure Survey, Garner and Wagner (1991) calculated that households spent an average of 3.5% of total expenditures on gifts. When households not buying gifts for people outside the household were excluded from the sample, the percentage increased to 3.7. As reported by Waldfogel (1993), this translates into expenditures for holiday gifts alone of about $40 billion per year.

Although Waldfogel (1993) acknowledged that holiday spending has a healthy effect on the macro-economy, the main point of his research was that there is a substantial deadweight loss for individual consumers. Deadweight loss refers to the difference between what the giver spent on a gift and the value assigned by the recipient. Based on data collected from university undergraduates, Waldfogel estimated that this loss ranged from 10% to 33% of the value of the gifts.

SOCIAL EFFECTS OF GIFT-GIVING

Camerer (1988) also noted the economic inefficiency of gift-giving, which he explained in terms of the dual role of gifts as economic signals and social symbols. In his model, gifts reflected the giver's intentions for further investment in the relationship and inefficient gifts were better in terms of this social signaling. (If the gift-giving system were efficient, partners who had no interest in the social relationship might still engage in the exchange process simply to collect the gifts.)

The role of gifts in initiating relationships and signaling commitment has been discussed in other work on gift-giving. For example, Belk (1979) proposed that "establishing, defining, and maintaining interpersonal relationships" as well as "the ceremonial recognition of social linkages" are major social functions of gift-giving. Sherry (1983) presented similar thoughts in his discussion of the social dimensions of gift-giving; he noted the interpretation of gift-giving as "an invitation to partnership" and also as a reflection of social integration. Baxter and Simon (1993) found gift-giving to be an important relationship maintenance strategy. Research by Rucker, Huidor, and Prato (1991) indicated that an object was apt to be viewed as a "good gift" if it represented a commitment to the relationship. Expensive gifts were thought to reflect more of a commitment than inexpensive ones; for any given price, durable gifts such as compact disks and jewelry were taken to signal greater commitment than nondurables such as a restaurant meal or an evening at the theater.

Gifts (or lack of gifts) can also serve to sever relationships and mirror the separation. Sherry, McGrath, and Levy (1993) discussed this issue at some length in their article on "the dark side of the gift." Some of the research by Caplow (1984) also showed how rejection of a person's gift is associated with rejection of that person. He found that a negative reaction to a gift was taken as a clear sign of alienation by the partner whose gift was refused. In fact, of the five couples among whom there had been a gift rejection at Christmas, two were found to have separated several weeks later. In work that considered the preparation and serving of food to be a type of obligatory gift-giving, Ellis (1983) provided documentation of the association between failure of the wife to have a hot meal on the table whenever her husband came home and episodes of domestic violence.

Another way in which gift-giving serves as a social symbol is by reflecting the structure of social relations in the culture in which the system is embedded. For instance, Cheal (1987) and Fisher and Arnold (1990), among others, have related women's responsibilities for maintaining social ties to their responsibilities for gift-giving. In work on the dynamics of the deferential dialectic in marriages, Bell and Newby (1976) argue that gifts are a means of social control. Husbands typically buy more expensive gifts than their wives do because of greater economic ability to be generous. This generosity demonstrates socioeconomic superiority and at the same time demands feelings of faithfulness and gratitude. Similarly, Caplow (1982) remarked on the unbalanced gift-giving from parents to children which continued even after the children had grown up and left home. Moschetti (1979) broadened the dominant-dependent analysis to include service personnel and support staff as well as family members. Again asymmetric gift exchanges were depicted as reflections of power differences.

Socializing individuals by transmitting a set of values is yet another social function of gift-giving (Belk, 1979; Sherry, 1983). Sherry cites toys and engagement rings as two gifts that perform this function in a relatively efficient manner; toys communicate gender expectations and engagement rings transmit fidelity expectations.

PEOPLE-OBJECT RELATIONS AND GIFT-GIVING

Theories and models of the ways in which people relate to each other and objects in their material environment, including gift-giving formulations, have been based almost exclusively on heterosexual data and therefore may need to be modified to be relevant for the homosexual community. Examples to be considered in this paper include the gift evaluation models of Rucker, Huidor, and Prato (1991) and Belk (1994). In their work, Rucker et al. proposed that gifts tend to be evaluated positively if they represent a commitment to the relationship, are obviously expensive, or are a good match to the recipient's wants, needs, and interests. On the other hand, they are rated negatively to the extent that they are perceived to be tokens (low cost/low effort), generic (would suit anyone), jokes, what the giver always wanted, what the giver always wanted the recipient to be, additions to a collection, or practical items. These attributes are consistent with the characteristics of the perfect gift proposed by Belk (1994); he stated that the perfect gift is marked by sacrifice of money, time or effort, altruism, luxury, appropriateness, surprise and delight.

In addition, dominance-deference models of heterosexual gift-giving will be compared with the data on gift exchanges among gay men (Bell and Newby, 1976; Caplow, 1982; Moschetti, 1979). The economic/instrumental orientation of males versus social/relational orientation of females to gift exchanges (cf. Rucker, Leckliter, Kivel, Dinkel, Freitas, Wynes, and Prato, 1991) and possessions in general (cf. Wallendorf and Arnould, 1988) will also be considered.

GIFT-GIVING IN A HOMOSEXUAL CONTEXT

As pointed out by Berger (1990) and Meyer (1989), the study of male couple relationships is relatively recent and therefore information on factors associated with relationship formation, maintenance, and dissolution is scarce. However, enough is known to ascertain that heterosexual models of relationships do not adequately address homosexual relationships (Klinkenberg and Rose, 1994). By the same token, theories about consumerism and the relationship of people to objects are mainly based on heterosexuals and heterosexual norms and therefore may not apply to the homosexual community (Clark, 1993).

Several characteristics of gay relationships and life experiences in general suggest that perceptions of gifts and the effects of various gift-giving experiences on homosexual relationships merit independent study. These characteristics have to do with social support, sensitivity to behavioral and product codes, equality and meanings of intimacy, and uses of humor to manage personal conditions and social relations.

A number of authors have noted that in the homosexual experience, it is often difficult to procure satisfactory levels of social support (cf. Telljohann and Price, 1993; Remafedi, 1987; Berger, 1990; Hetrick and Martin, 1987; D'Emilio, 1993). Limited availability of social support is apt to be most keenly felt in adolescence when gay males face all of the difficult developmental tasks of that time of life as well as adjusting, often alone, to the role of being gay. Whereas other minorities may typically count on family support, gay males are apt to encounter family rejection as well as peer rejection. Therefore, when peer attachments are made, these relationships are apt to become especially close and central to one's well being. As D'Emilio stated:

> Already excluded from families as most of us are, we have had to create, for our survival, networks of support that do not depend on the bonds of blood or the license of the state, but that are freely chosen and nurtured. The building of an "affectional community" must be as much a part of our political movement as are campaigns for civil rights. (p. 475)

If relationships are especially important to gay males, one might expect symbols of those relationships and tools for their maintenance to receive close attention. Since gifts are such symbols, the gift-giving process, from efforts to select an appropriate gift to concern for the disposition of one's gift by its recipient, might be expected to elicit more concern among homosexual than heterosexual consumers. (Refer to Sherry's 1983 article for a detailed model of the gift exchange process.) Gifts may receive even more attention from gay partners because, as argued by Meyer (1989), there are not the formal rituals to mark stages in the relationship that heterosexual couples have. Therefore, material goods such as rings and earrings that are given to one another may become potent symbols of relationship identity (Baxter, 1987). In contrast, to the extent relations are perceived to be relatively impermanent, psychological and monetary investments in the gift-giving process may be relatively low.

Just as all-too-pervasive homophobia may create problems in establishing social networks, it also is apt to prompt a greater sensitivity to behavioral and commodity codes. As Gonsiorek (1988) pointed out, the gay adolescent learns to constantly monitor appearances and behavior so as not to experience the negative sanctions that may occur when the gay identity is revealed. This sensitivity is useful initially for fitting in and later for choosing to masquerade or resist. This sensitivity also is evident in responses to marketing efforts. Aaker and Dean (1993), in their work on the non-target market effect, reported that gays were more sensitive than heterosexual males to visual cues in advertising campaigns.

Studies of the structure of gay relationships (Blumstein and Schwartz, 1983; McWhirter and Mattison, 1984), suggest that gays are more apt to strive for and achieve egalitarian relationships than are heterosexual couples. As McWhirter and Mattison explain:

> There are no set "husband" and "wife" roles. Each man can usually perform all necessary tasks at some level of competence. Men together learn early that it is equally blessed to give and to receive, even when the temptation is to prove love by giving more. (p. 31)

Just as dominant-dependent relations have been reflected in heterosexual partners' gift-giving, we might expect to find this egalitarian attitude reflected in gay gift-giving. For example, there may be less variation in price paid by each partner in a gift exchange and/or less concern about price equity.

McWhirter and Mattison (1984) also found that gay couples had to find alternative ways to maintain intimacy and sustain relationships. For example, sexual exclusivity was not a key factor in maintaining an intimate relationship. On the other hand, other aspects of intimacy such as self-disclosures and emotional expressiveness may be important across various types of male-male and male-female relationships (Monsour, 1992).

Finally, the way in which humor is used for interpersonal emotion management (Francis, 1994) may have an effect on gay relationships and gift-giving practices. Meyer (1989) mentioned playfulness as one characteristic of a male couple that stood out in their sample as having a particularly successful relationship. What may be more characteristic of the gay sensibility, however, is camp and the humor that represents the strategy of camp. Babuscio (1993) refers to camp humor as

> a means of dealing with a hostile environment and, in the process, of defining a positive identity. This humor takes several forms. Chief of

these is bitter-wit, which expresses an underlying hostility and fear. (p. 27)

Newton (1993) makes similar comments about camp humor:

There is no requirement that the jokes be gentle or friendly. A lot of camping is extremely hostile; it is almost always sarcastic. But its intent is humorous as well. (p. 51)

In the gift evaluation models described earlier, especially the work of Rucker et al. (1991), the practical joke gift was frequently mentioned as the worst gift *received* and noted for an association with strained relationships. Interestingly enough, there was less acknowledgement of joke gifts as worst gifts *given*. In a community or culture with a different orientation toward humor, however, one might expect to find a somewhat different set of associations.

The present study was designed as an exploratory investigation of gift-giving attitudes and practices of gay males and their relational implications. The objectives were to expand our understanding of gift-giving phenomenology and to determine whether norms and guidelines based on heterosexual experiences might benefit from modification for the gay community.

METHOD

Thirty-two men were recruited for this study from a university-based gay social organization and related friendship networks. These respondents ranged in age from 18 to 30 with a median age of 23. Self-reported ethnic data indicated that there were 15 White men, 8 Asian men, 4 Hispanic men and 1 Black man in the sample. An additional 4 men either reported some combination of ethnicities or did not respond to this question. The majority of the sample, 25 of the respondents, were employed, with the others receiving support from a variety of personal sources. Discretionary income ranged from $30 to $1,000 per month.

The men were interviewed individually by one of two gay male interviewers and asked for details regarding best and worst gifts given as well as received during the past year. They were also asked whether they would be willing to provide additional information on an exchange with a partner and its effect on the relationship. Ten pairs of respondents participated in this second phase of the study. (An eleventh respondent completed his half of the partner interview but his partner could not be reached for his input.)

In all but one case, both members of the pair came from the original pool of 32 volunteers. (The one exception was a heterosexual female friend of one of the informants.)

Interviews were recorded and transcribed for later analysis. The transcripts were read for themes developed from the review of the literature and other themes that emerged from the data. This variation of "interpretive tacking" (Geertz, 1983; Hirschman and Holbrook, 1992; Sherry, McGrath, and Levy, in press) or moving back and forth between models developed in other contexts and the new data set was intended to highlight both similarities and differences in homosexual and heterosexual gift exchange systems.

RESULTS AND DISCUSSION

Sensitivity to Objects and Relations

Compared to previous models and empirical research on male gift-giving (cf. Rucker et al. 1991; Rucker, Freitas, and Dolstra, 1994), the present interviews indicated more attention to selecting or creating the gift. Even if the gift were "only" a t-shirt, there was thought put into choosing one with a meaningful message that reflected the recipient's preferences and personality. Only one instance of something approaching the definition of a generic gift (would suit anyone, not particularized for that recipient) was mentioned and that was a gift certificate to a local music store. Even the certificate was more thoughtful than some gifts reported in earlier work on male gift-giving. In the present case, the giver was aware that the recipient purchased compact disks on a regular basis; for his part, the recipient perceived the certificate as a good gift because he could get exactly what he wanted. In other cases, there were enthusiastic expressions of appreciation for gifts that indicated knowledge of the recipient's favorite artist, action figure, or other collectible. This finding was somewhat at odds with previous work on good and bad gifts (Rucker, Huidor, and Prato, 1991). In that work, additions to a collection were most often described as bad gifts. Among heterosexual partners, there was more of a negative focus on the giver's lack of understanding of the criteria used to expand the collection whereas in this study, there was more of a positive focus on thoughtfulness of the giver (exceptions were recipients who had tired of their collections but had not yet had the heart to inform their friends).

In five of the eleven partner interviews, at least one of the gifts had been modified or personalized in some way. These modifications included engraving something on the gift, adding a personal picture or decorating it in some other way, as well as preparing the gift from basic ingredients (a dinner, a collage, a tape of favorite songs made from other tapes).

The interviews also suggested a relatively high concern with what the recipient did with the gift. This level of concern had not appeared in previous interviews on gift-giving. For example, the respondent who had made a collage of personal pictures to go in a frame for his friend was distressed that the friend would remove the collage and substitute his own picture; this treatment of the gift was mentioned at some length on two separate occasions during the interview. Comments at the end of the interview capture the feelings:

> I see it as we gave each other something we like and something we will always be able to use and give us memories about high school and stuff–hopefully if he puts that collage back in!

In another interview, hurt was expressed that a piece of jewelry was not being worn:

> [s]he never wears it. I told her last week why don't you just give it back to me and I will give you something else because I would wear it. I am trying to convince her to give it back to me. It is not her style.

Another informant complained that, as far as he could tell, his gift package was not even opened, suggesting that the recipient intended to recycle the gift rather than use it himself.

While not a topic of major interest to McWhirter and Mattison (1984), they also provided a quotation which seems to typify the type of resentment expressed in the present study over a gift that was not responded to as the giver had hoped:

> I used to love getting him flowers every Friday after work, but then it sort of got to be a chore. The fun went out of it. I kept doing it, thinking that his response would be my reward. He just started taking it for granted, like I was bringing home a quart of milk. (p. 56)

Another way in which these data diverged from the results of previous studies was the number of best gifts that were self-gifts or presents from the respondents to themselves. This finding offers support for the proposal by Schwartz (1967) that self-gifts are beneficial in compensating for lack of support from others when the surrounding environment is impersonal or even hostile.

Evidence of Humor

The interviews contained examples of several humorous gifts, camp and otherwise. For example, a gift picture described in one of the partner interviews showed the giver dressed up as Cybil Shepard.

In the individual interviews, good gifts were frequently associated with funny stories or inside jokes. On the other hand, there was a relatively high level of recognition among givers that joke gifts were generally not good gifts. Examples of joke gifts included a potato, a bar of soap, a tummy cruncher, and a Chippendale calendar. In only one case out of the 32 individual interviews did someone complain about receiving a joke gift.

Egalitarianism and Perceptions of Equity

The data on perceived power or "taking charge" of the relationship support the reports by McWhirter and Mattison (1984) and others that gay couples are more egalitarian than heterosexual couples. In fact, most of the respondents seemed puzzled by the question of who dominates or is in charge of the relationship. When a choice was made between partners, it tended to refer to who initiated or took charge of arranging the gift exchange rather than who took charge or dominated in the relationship.

As McWhirter and Mattison (1984, p. 31) explain the equality attitude, it "includes the expectation that each partner will take care of himself *and* try his best to meet his partner's needs." Sharing involves taking turns in providing whatever is needed in the relationship, be it financial, emotional, or some other form of support. This type of balance was reflected in answers to the question about equity in the partners' gift exchange interviews.

As noted previously in the work of Rucker et al. (1991), males tended to focus on economic contributions and want to trade dollar for dollar, whereas the females tended to focus on happiness of the recipients. In the present study, most of the responses reflected sensitivity to a balance between cost and sentiment as the following quotes illustrate:

> Even though my gift cost more, his gift was very sentimental and I really felt special.

> If you want it [equity] in terms of money, I guess not, but if you want it in terms of appreciation, yes.

> [The exchange was] probably not [equitable] in a financial sense but on a symbolic level, yes, because it was a very symbolic thing.

Other partners preferred to disregard or ignore the whole issue, as illustrated below:

> I don't really think about it that way but if you were going to pin me down, I would say yes it was a fair trade.

> I don't think the question is relevant. Because I didn't get that cookbook for Jim because he had gotten me a shirt. I got it because it was there and I felt like it.

CONCLUSIONS

Although one must be cautious in generalizing the findings of this study since it was conducted with a small sample in one geographical location, results do suggest that heterosexual gift-giving models need some modification before being applied to exchanges among gay men. Marketing activities based on heterosexual data will need some modification as well.

The sensitivity to different aspects of the gift-giving process, including gift selection as well as reactions of the recipient, is one finding with implications for marketing efforts that are relevant to the gay community. For example, the types of products selected to offer as gift items are most apt to be appreciated if they are in keeping with concerns about relationship building and maintenance. Examples of such products would be items that were intended to be personalized in some way or representative of the relationship (e.g., photo albums). Also, advertising appeals for gift items are apt to be better received if they emphasize a probable positive response from the recipient as opposed to a convenience factor such as already gift wrapped or an economic factor such as priced right.

Findings with respect to humor suggest that companies might be able to use a wider variety of humorous appeals in advertising to the gay market. However, this strategy should be approached with caution. If the best jokes are inside jokes, then ads with mass appeal would be difficult to construct. Additional research on humorous appeals might provide some useful guidelines. Another potentially fruitful area for further study is how feelings about equality in relationships and equity in gift exchanges translate into money and effort expended by each partner. Finally, the authors suggest that there should be more research on self-gifts. In cases where the support of an "affectional community" is limited, self-support may be the best gift of all.

REFERENCES

Aaker, J. L. & Dean, J. (1993). The non-target market effect: Associated feelings of acceptance, alienation or apathy. Paper presented at the annual meeting of the Association for Consumer Research, Nashville, Tennessee.

Babuscio, J. (1993). "Camp and the gay sensibility." In B. Bergman (Ed.), *Camp Ground: Style and Homosexuality.* Amherst: University of Massachusetts Press.

Baxter, L. A. (1987). Symbols of relationship identity in relationship cultures. *Journal of Social and Personal Relationships*, 4, 261-280.

Baxter, L. A. & Simon, E. P. (1993). Relationship maintenance strategies and dialectical contradictions in personal relationships. *Journal of Social and Personal Relationships*, 10, 225-242.

Belk, R. W. (1994). Altruism and gift-giving. Paper presented at the Association for Consumer Research Asia Pacific Conference, Singapore.

Belk, R. W. (1979). gift-giving behavior. *Research in Marketing*, 2, 95-126.

Belk, R. W. & Coon, G. S. (1993). gift-giving as agapic love: An alternative to the exchange paradigm based on dating experiences. *Journal of Consumer Research*, 20, 393-417.

Bell, C. & Newby, H. (1976). "Husbands and wives: The dynamics of the deferential dialectic." In D. L. Barker and S. Allen (Eds.), *Dependence and Exploitation in Work and Marriage.* London: Longman.

Berger, R. M. (1990). Men together: Understanding the gay couple. *Journal of Homosexuality*, 19 (3), 31-49.

Blumstein, P. & Schwartz, P. (1983). *American Couples: Money, Work, Sex.* New York: Morrow.

Camerer, C. (1988). Gifts as economic signals and social symbols. *The American Journal of Sociology*, 94, 180-214.

Caplow, T. (1982). Christmas gifts and kin networks. *American Sociological Review*, 47, 383-392.

_____ . (1984). Rule enforcement without visible means: Christmas gift-giving in Middletown. *American Journal of Sociology*, 89, 1306-1323.

Cheal, D. (1987). "Showing them you love them": gift-giving and the dialectic of intimacy. *Sociological Review*, 35 (1), 150-169.

Clark, D. (1993). Commodity lesbianism. In Abelove, H., Barale, M.A., & Halperin, D. M. (Eds.), *The Lesbian and Gay Studies Reader.* London: Routledge.

D'Emilio, J. (1993). Capitalism and gay identity. In Abelove, H., Barale, M.A., & Halperin, D. M. (Eds.), *The Lesbian and Gay Studies Reader.* London: Routledge.

Davis, J. (1972). Gifts and the U.K. economy. *Man*, 7, 408-429.

Ellis, R. (1983). The way to a man's heart: Food in the violent home. In Murcott, A. (Ed.), *The Sociology of Food and Eating.* Aldershot: Gower.

Fisher, E. & Arnold, S. J. (1990). More than a labor of love: Gender roles and Christmas gift shopping. *Journal of Consumer Research*, 17, 333-345.

Francis, L. E. (1994). Laughter, the best mediation: Humor as emotion management in interaction. *Symbolic Interaction*, 17 (2), 147-163.

Garner, T. I. & Wagner, J. (1991). Economic dimensions of household gift-giving. *Journal of Consumer Research*, 18, 368-379.

Geertz, C. (1983). *Local Knowledge: Further Essays in Interpretive Anthropology.* New York: Basic Books.

Gonsiorek, J. (1988). Mental health issues of gay and lesbian adolescents. *Journal of Adolescent Health Care*, 9, 114-122.

Hetrick, E. & Martin, A. (1987). Developmental issues and their resolution for gay and lesbian adolescents. *Journal of Homosexuality*, 14 (1/2), 25-43.

Hirschman, E. C. & Holbrook, M. B. (1992). *Postmodern Consumer Research: The Study of Consumption as Text.* Newbury Park, CA: Sage.

Klinkenberg, D. & Rose, S. (1994). Dating scripts of gay men and lesbians. *Journal of Homosexuality*, 26 (4), 23-35.

McWhirter, D. P. & Mattison, A. M. (1984). *The Male Couple: How Relationships Develop.* Englewood Cliffs, NJ: Prentice-Hall.

Meyer, J. (1989). Guess who's coming to dinner this time? A study of gay intimate relationships and the support for those relationships. *Marriage and Family Review*, 14, 59-82.

Monsour, M. (1992). Meanings of intimacy in cross- and same-sex friendships. *Journal of Social and Personal Relationships*, 9, 277-295.

Moschetti, G. J. (1979). The Christmas potlatch: A refinement on the sociological interpretation of gift exchange. *Sociological Focus*, 12 (1), 1-7.

Newton, E. (1993). Role models. In Bergman, D. (Ed.), *Camp Grounds: Style and Homosexuality.* Amherst: University of Massachusetts Press.

Remafedi, G. (1987). Male homosexuality: The adolescent's perspective. *Pediatrics*, 79, 326-330.

Rucker, M., Freitas, A. & Dolstra, J. (1994). A toast for the host? The male perspective on gifts that say thank you. In Allen, C.T. & John, D.R. (Eds.), *Advances in Consumer Research*, 21, 165-168.

Rucker, M., Huidor, O. & Prato, H. (1991). The good, the bad and the ugly: Analysis of successful and failed gift-giving situations. Paper presented at the annual meeting of the Popular Culture Association, San Antonio, TX.

Rucker, M., Leckliter, L., Kivel, S., Dinkel, M., Freitas, A., Wynes, M., & Prato, H. (1991). When the thought counts: Friendship, love, gift exchanges and gift returns. *Advances in Consumer Research*, 18, 528-531.

Schwartz, B. (1967). The social psychology of the gift. *American Journal of Sociology*, 73, 1-11.

Sherry, J. F., Jr. (1983). gift-giving in anthropological perspective. *Journal of Consumer Research*, 10, 157-168.

Sherry, J. F., Jr., McGrath, M. A., & Levy, S. J. (1993). The dark side of the gift. *Journal of Business Research*, 28, 225-244.

_____ . (in press). Monadic giving: Anatomy of gifts given to the self. In Sherry, J. F., Jr. (Ed.), *Contemporary Marketing and Consumer Behavior: An Anthropological Source Book.* New York: Sage.

Telljohann, S. K. & Price, J. H. (1993). A qualitative examination of adolescent homosexuals' life experiences: Ramifications for secondary school personnel. *Journal of Homosexuality*, 26 (1), 41-56.

Waldfogel, J. (1993). The deadweight loss of Christmas. *American Economic Review*, 83 (5), 1328-1336.

Wallendorf, M. & Arnould, E. J. (1988). "My favorite things": A cross-cultural inquiry into object attachment, possessiveness, and social linkage. *Journal of Consumer Research*, 14, 531-547.

Mainstream Legitimization of Homosexual Men Through Valentine's Day Gift-Giving and Consumption Rituals

Peter J. Newman, Jr., MA
Michelle R. Nelson, PhD (cand.)

University of Illinois at Urbana-Champaign

SUMMARY. Recently, the gay community has received increased attention from marketers through specially-made television commercials, direct mail pieces, and other media messages. However, little research in consumer behavior has examined the potential attitudinal and behavioral differences and similarities between heterosexuals and homosexuals. Specifically, this paper provides an exploratory look at the meaning and practices surrounding the consumer ritual of Valentine's Day from the perspective of homosexual men. Using depth interviews within an interpretative framework, our research sug-

---

Peter J. Newman, Jr., and Michelle R. Nelson are graduate students in the Department of Advertising at the University of Illinois at Urbana-Champaign. The authors would like to thank Dr. Cele Otnes for her guidance and help with this project. Correspondence should be addressed to Peter J. Newman, Jr., Department of Advertising, University of Illinois at Urbana-Champaign, 119 Gregory Hall, 810 S. Wright Street, Urbana, IL 61801. E-mail: *pnewman@uiuc.edu*

[Haworth co-indexing entry note]: "Mainstream Legitimization of Homosexual Men Through Valentine's Day Gift-Giving and Consumption Rituals." Newman, Peter J., Jr., and Michelle R. Nelson. Co-published simultaneously in *Journal of Homosexuality* (The Haworth Press, Inc.) Vol. 31, No. 1/2, 1996, pp. 57-69; and: *Gays, Lesbians, and Consumer Behavior: Theory, Practice, and Research Issues in Marketing* (ed: Daniel L. Wardlow) The Haworth Press, Inc., 1996, pp. 57-69; and: *Gays, Lesbians, and Consumer Behavior: Theory, Practice, and Research Issues in Marketing* (ed: Daniel L. Wardlow) Harrington Park Press, an imprint of The Haworth Press, Inc., 1996, pp. 57-69. Single or multiple copies of this article are available from The Haworth Document Delivery Service [1-800-342-9678, 9:00 a.m. - 5:00 p.m. (EST)].

57

gests similarities exist for the celebration of Valentine's Day between homosexual and heterosexual singles, while differences may exist for the functions of Valentine's Day gift-giving between these groups. Some homosexual couples feel they cannot "legitimately participate" in the dominant rituals associated with the holiday due to oppression by a "heterosexual society." Marketing implications are discussed. *[Article copies available from The Haworth Document Delivery Service: 1-800-342-9678.]*

INTRODUCTION

"Homosexuality is a way of being, one that can completely influence a person's life and shape its meaning and direction" (Grahn 1984). Today, through the potential *spending* opportunities offered by the gay community, marketers are beginning to recognize homosexuality as a way of life. A spokesperson for AT&T's long-distance telephone company explains, "The particular market segment [homosexual] is a good one to target because it's composed of affluent, highly-educated, and very brand-loyal consumers" (Fitzgerald 1994a). With the rise of upscale gay magazines such as *Out, Genre,* and *The Advocate,* and the promise of an affluent market niche, marketers are showing increased attention to the tailoring of messages and media especially for gays.

While marketing practitioners have recently begun targeting efforts to reach the gay community through special direct-mail pieces (Fitzgerald 1994a), television commercials, and print advertising in gay publications (Elliott 1994; Mathews 1992), academic consumer researchers have virtually ignored this area. Therefore, very little research has been conducted to explore attitudinal or behavioral differences among homosexuals. In particular, little is known about how this special group participates in mainstream consumer rituals.

Consumer rituals and gift-giving have received increased attention in the consumer literature (Sherry 1983; Belk, Wallendorf, and Sherry 1989; Belk 1989; Hirschman and LaBarbera 1989; Sherry and McGrath 1989; Wallendorf and Arnould 1991; Otnes, Ruth, and Milbourne 1994). However, all of these studies have used either heterosexual women or men in their samples in order to generalize among the particular gender and sexual orientation of the population. Our research suggests that mainstream meanings and practices may not always be generalizable to the homosexual population.

Employing depth interviews and interpretive methodology, this paper examines homosexual males' participation in a particular consumer ritual–that of Valentine's Day. Valentine's Day was chosen specifically because it is a holiday that is traditionally associated with the heterosexual exchange of romantic love. The present work is exploratory due to its sample size; we are looking at a specific and small segment of the gay community.

As a point of comparison for the current study, Otnes, Ruth, and Milbourne (1994) report findings of a survey of 105 male undergraduates about Valentine's Day gift-giving. Although the men considered Valentine's Day as a time to communicate feelings of affection for significant others, the results indicated that men often feel obligated to participate due to pressure exerted by significant others and social institutions. In addition, the lack of a romantic partner was a major reason why men did not give cards or gifts. The authors suggest that certain holidays and practices, such as Valentine's Day, "can exclude individuals who do not meet the criteria for inclusion in the celebration. As such, legitimacy of participation may be a salient issue for respondents who perceive they are excluded from valid participation."

This paper will consider the issue of legitimation while examining meaning and participatory scripts involved in Valentine's Day for gay men. Specifically, we were interested in: (1) identifying how single male homosexuals celebrate Valentine's Day; (2) discerning how gay couples celebrate the holiday; (3) determining the perceived differences in celebration between homosexuals and heterosexuals; and (4) recognizing some of the functions of Valentine's Day gift-giving for the homosexual population.

METHOD

The primary text for this project was generated via depth interviews conducted in a medium-sized midwestern city between February 10-20, 1994. Informants were recruited from a local gay bar, a university, and through snowball sampling. They ranged in age from the early twenties to the late forties. Two couples were involved in the study, four singles, and two partners of different couples. Three informants were Ph.D. students, one was an older part-time college student, and the remaining six were professionals. All informants were interviewed individually.

In order to construct an effective questionnaire for the depth interviews, a preliminary focus group was conducted to identify potential question topics. This took place on January 14, 1994 with eight gay male informants. Three couples participated and two singles; informants ranged in age from 26 to 32. The focus group was videotaped and transcribed. It lasted approximately 60 minutes and generated 34 pages of text. Text from this focus group was used to identify potential question topics and refine existing focus-group questions for use in the depth interviews.

Depth interviews for the present study lasted approximately 30 to 40 minutes. Informants were allowed to choose the sites for interviews. Interviews were taped and transcribed, yielding 87 pages of text. Coffee or food was provided as an incentive for participation unless the interviewer was invited to the informant's home.

The data analysis procedure was qualitative. The authors sought to identify emerging themes within the text and used a process of negotiation to arrive at the resulting representations of the emerging cultural categories.

As a reliability check, three willing and available informants were given a final draft of this work to read. The purpose was to assess the external validity of this paper and ensure that the authors' understanding of the text was accurate. The informants completely agreed that the uncovered categories were indicative of their personal experiences and feelings surrounding the ritual of Valentine's Day gift-giving.

FINDINGS

Participation Legitimacy

To legitimately participate in mainstream holidays and celebrations, individuals must follow dominant cultural norms and values. In the case of Valentine's Day, these norms have been created by institutions such as the media, the family, and businesses like Hallmark (makers of greeting cards). In fact, past research has shown individuals feel obligated to participate due to societal demands (Otnes, Ruth, & Milbourne 1994). Not only do institutions encourage participation with their constant barrage of messages, they also dictate the appropriate way to celebrate the holiday.

Indeed, many of our informants' responses about the "correct" way to celebrate Valentine's Day mirrored those iterated by heterosexual males from a previous study (Otnes et al., 1994). This "shared depiction" revealed a man and woman enjoying a romantic dinner with flowers, a card, and perhaps a gift. One of our informants said, "Well, of course you know everything is geared towards the straight world's view of Valentine's Day." Therefore, if men are not involved romantically with a significant other, or they are not a part of the heterosexual community, how do they feel about the holiday? And, how do they celebrate?

Similarities Among Single Males

From earlier research on heterosexual men, we learned the emphasis upon romantic love and couples in America may reinforce feelings of inadequacy among those who are not romantically involved. For instance, one of the Otnes et al. (1994) heterosexual male respondents said he felt anxiety during Valentine's Day due to "the fact that media and society kept reminding [him] what day it was and [he] didn't have a girlfriend." Similarly, one informant in our group indicated "there is a kind of status thing associated with being in a relationship, a certain amount of validation of attractiveness." Without this validation, inadequacy and depression can set in.

Specifically, Otnes et al. (1994) found that the lack of a significant other with whom to celebrate was the least liked aspect of the holiday and one of the prevalent reasons why men did not give cards or gifts. Generally, these same feelings were found among our group. We found men who were uninvolved with a romantic partner during Valentine's Day expressed several emotions, ranging from apathy and anxiousness to depression and anger. Resulting behaviors from these emotions followed two general themes: (1) ignoring the holiday (just another day); or (2) re-inventing the dominant ritual scripts to "protest" the holiday.

Valentine's Day Is Just Another Day

A number of our informants displayed apathetic feelings and indicated that the significance of the holiday depended upon whether or not they were in a relationship. One informant said, "If you are not seeing anybody at that particular time [Valentine's Day], I think that it is just basically another day." Another said that he "conditioned" himself to "not pay too much attention to the holiday because there really was never anyone there."

By avoiding the significance of the day, singles may be trying to deny their feelings of depression as well. When asked about the holiday, homosexual singles mentioned feelings of depression, much like those expressed in earlier research by single heterosexual men. One informant said, "I've seen people that think it is kind of a depressing holiday if you don't have someone to celebrate it with and you believe in it . . . I think it can cause depression if you are really into the holiday."

Several informants mentioned the societal pressure to participate more when they were single. When asked how Valentine's Day might change if he were in a relationship, one informant replied, "I think it would change significantly because I would probably do something special . . . maybe outside pressure would suggest that you do something." And another informant realized, "I seem to feel more pressure when I'm single at Valentine's Day. . . . you hear all your friends' plans and that kind of stuff."

Protesting the Holiday

Instead of engaging in an intimate dinner with a significant other, several informants talked about ways they "re-invented" the conventional Valentine's Day script to protest the holiday. These were events shared with a group of single friends, and often signified independence from the mainstream. One informant mentioned that "now a lot of bars have the anti-Valentine's Day" which was created to [according to him] "celebrate singledom, for people who feel like loser heads because the holiday makes them feel that way." Another informant discussed how he and his friend had attended "a black heart party," which was a "party for people who don't have any girlfriend or boyfriend and are not prepared to look for one in the party. We bitch about those things [not having anyone] . . . and people have cards and presents and stuff like that." In this way, singles were creating their own common script, within which they could legitimately participate in their version of the holiday.

Homosexual Couples

As discussed earlier, the importance of being in a relationship on Valentine's Day was a recurring theme among informants. The level of importance was dependent on whether or not they were in a relationship. One informant simply said that "it is when you are with someone that the holiday really is something special and . . . if you don't have certain ties, it loses something." Another informant said that he had "never actually paid much attention to Valentine's Day" and that "this year (was) my best Valentine's Day (so far), because I'm dating somebody."

Having a significant other seemed to be a pre-condition for the celebration of Valentine's Day. Being part of a couple provided the motivation for engaging in a significant level of involvement on this holiday. Several informants suggested that there were deeper meanings associated with being a couple on Valentine's Day because of their sexuality. One said that, "There is a kind of status thing associated with being in a relationship . . . a validation of attractiveness, being out and being gay . . . when you've got somebody to share it with at Valentine's Day." Achieving "status" and receiving this "validation" may provide self-confidence and pride for a group that generally feels oppressed in society.

Homosexual couples used Valentine's Day as an opportunity to publicly show the heterosexual world that gay people are not so different from straight people and that they have similar emotions, needs, and desires. One informant appreciated a media message that deviated from the mainstream depiction of relationships. He reported seeing a message placed on

MTV by a lesbian viewer for her partner, that read "Looking forward to seeing two brides on our wedding cake." He added, "you have to squint to find us, but we're out there," implying that homosexuals are being accepted into some mainstream media channels. Acceptance into mainstream media channels may allow homosexuals to feel like they are achieving higher participation legitimacy status.

Perceived Differences in the Meanings of Celebration

There was some discrepancy among informants as to whether or not Valentine's Day was celebrated the same with heterosexual couples as it was with homosexual couples. Some informants felt that there were very few differences *on the surface* between the way homosexuals versus heterosexuals celebrated Valentine's Day. When asked how he had celebrated Valentine's Day with women, one informant (who had been engaged to a woman for a number of years and has since been married to a man for ten years) said, "Usually, you know, dinner, flowers, basically not much different than now, there isn't really a difference." He went on to say, "I don't care if you are straight or gay, it is just the way you feel about the holiday."

Several informants did not agree that the holiday was celebrated the same by homosexuals and heterosexuals. They elicited statements such as, "Well, of course, you know everything is geared towards the straight world's view of Valentine's Day." But added, "I feel that the gay community is taking it upon itself to respond and make its own interpretation of this holiday. . . . Gay couples together at holidays have a tendency to really indulge, more so than heterosexual couples."

Providing a more detailed explanation, one informant said that there were not any differences in the way homosexuals and heterosexuals celebrated Valentine's Day *on the surface* level, but that " . . . the intentions are different. . . . For us the intentions are affirming through the homophobic society. The heterosexual intention is 'Let's go buy a card and some flowers and then [have sex]!'" When one of the authors asked the informant, "But didn't you do the same thing?" he responded "[no] . . . there is always for us . . . a sense that there is more tenderness than with [heterosexuals]."

He explained why he felt that there was a different level of emotion for homosexuals and heterosexuals on Valentine's Day, by saying "it is because the heterosexual form of love is so accepted that they are not even aware of what loving means in the general context. . . . [it's] as if heterosexuals don't have every day as the day for them to prance about, displaying emotions." Obviously upset, this informant added that "[homosexu-

als] are constantly reminded of what it means to be loving each other."
This informant was upset that he and his partner were not free to openly
express their emotions at any given time like heterosexuals have the
luxury of doing. In order to alleviate their feelings of oppression, the
informant and his partner decided to turn Valentine's day into "a day that
we could affirm ourselves as a queer couple and f___ everyone else." The
informant said that his purpose was "not so much for me to show my love
for a single person, but . . . uniting against an institution which is oppressive, which is another way of [showing] love."

Another informant verbalized his feelings about being in a marginal
group when he said "being a homosexual [in this society] is wrong, it is not
natural in heterosexuals' eyes." The informant reported that this creates
"hatred, stereotypes, and non-acceptance, [and it] makes people not be
themselves when they are around heterosexuals." When asked how homosexuals compensate for this on Valentine's Day, the informant said that:

> it is just a day that revolves around love, they are focused on love
> and showing that love and receiving it, they are very attentive, they
> are very in tune with their partner and that is really what makes it so
> special because they are listening and they are communicating
> whether it be words or physical contact.

Spending quality time with one's partner may help homosexuals avoid
some of the pain of oppression and make up for not being able to openly
express their love around heterosexuals.

The majority of informants felt that everything in society, including
Valentine's Day, was geared towards heterosexuals, and several agreed
with the description of Valentine's Day as a "breeder" (i.e., heterosexual)
holiday. Two informants disagreed though; one felt that gay people who
label things as "so heterosexual" or "breeder" are making themselves
"into victims . . . of society." He added that this notion was "ridiculous"
and said that even though Valentine's Day is "traditionally thought of as
heterosexual . . . love is not heterosexual." He explained, "Yes, we are
discriminated against, but to continue thinking of ourselves as victims, we
are not going to get anywhere." Another informant said, "We say these
things, but I don't think we should ostracize ourselves by labeling this as a
heterosexual/homosexual holiday. And putting barriers up like this really
pisses me off."

Gift-Giving Among Homosexual Men

Seven homosexual men in our sample were deeply involved in gift-giving and seemed to enjoy giving simple or extravagant gifts more than

receiving them. One informant said, "I feel better giving [gifts] than receiving them." This finding is inconsistent with prior evidence that indicated there was a tendency for heterosexual men to enjoy gift receipt more than gift-giving (Otnes et al., 1994). The phenomenon of homosexual men truly enjoying gift-giving was one instance where this marginal group deviated from the typical socialization process, where men are socialized to be the passive recipients of gift-giving efforts (cf., Otnes et al., 1994). Four purposes of gift-giving were identified among the men in our sample: altruism, compensation, involvement, and affirmation.

Altruism and Compensation

Otnes et al. (1994) suggest that among heterosexuals, feelings of obligation provided the motivation for gift-giving more so than the desire to spontaneously give gifts. Interviews with our informants suggested the opposite; two primary motivations for gift-giving were altruism or compensation for the unsatisfied needs of a recipient.

Several informants had engaged in altruistic gift-giving roles during the Valentine's Day holiday:

> Because to me Valentine's day is something within my heart, it is something that I do for people, not what people do for me.

> Just today I bought a bunch of kid cards in a package and I'm going to hand them out to my employees at the restaurant that I manage, it should cheer them up. It is something that hasn't been done around here in a long time.

> And for me it is a day to promote friendship, you know, the love that you feel for all kinds of people, not just one particular person.

Thus, for some informants, Valentine's Day served as a time to unselfishly spread love in addition to showing their love for one individual in particular.

Several informants engaged in compensatory roles, making up for the absence, or shortcomings, of boyfriends of their heterosexual female friends on Valentine's Day by buying them gifts or taking them out. Other informants played the part of a compensator for friends, strangers, or loved ones on Valentine's Day, providing them gifts they would not otherwise receive:

> Every Valentine's Day since I can remember I send my mother a card which I probably wouldn't have done if she would have got a card from a boyfriend or someone else.

> But I would say, my favorite Valentine's Day is, one year when I was still in high school, I bought one flower for all these people who I knew would never receive flowers.

Engaging in either altruistic or compensatory gift-giving roles contradicts equity theory which states that "one should receive gifts in direct proportion to the number that one gives, or perhaps more importantly, in proportion to the amount of money, time, and effort one puts into each gift he gives" (Poe 1977).

Involvement

Past literature has explored the underlying purpose of gifts, including the notion that they may demonstrate the importance of the person or the strengths of one's feelings (Otnes et al., 1994; Sherry 1993; Poe 1977). Likewise, the homosexual males interviewed for the current study used gifts to communicate their feelings about the level of commitment and seriousness of involvement within a relationship:

> If it is at the beginning of a relationship, there is a certain amount of antsiness about, well what is this relationship about right now? And, you have to consider appropriateness, level of intimacy, the symbolism of the gifts and what not.

> There are the frightening gifts and the disappointing gifts. Where the frightening ones are you're expecting things are fairly light and then all of a sudden they're sending you bouquets of balloons at work and you got them a card. The disappointing ones are the reverse of that, they have sent you a card when you cooked dinner, kind of an imbalance. That tends to occur more at the beginning of the relationship, not when you are deeper into it.

Since the "frightening gifts" may symbolize a request for deeper involvement than the recipient wishes, they may cause psychological reactance. Reactance theory says that anytime a "gift is perceived by the recipient as a threat to personal freedom, either implied or explicit, psychological reactance may occur" (Poe 1977). The recipient of a "frightening gift" may feel obligated to plunge deeper into a new relationship which he or she is unsure about.

Affirmation

Several informants either received or intended to give their Valentine's Day gifts publicly. The practice of public gift exchange is consistent with a theme of homosexuals affirming themselves through a heterosexual society. One informant said, "I think in some ways (giving gifts publicly) affirms the relationship, I know that is the big part of the reason I had my lover's flowers delivered at school." Interestingly, the reaction by heterosexual co-workers in this instance was one of disbelief; one woman was shocked and jealous that this homosexual man had received flowers. Often times gift exchange was publicly displayed to let others know that gay couples are not different from straight couples.

DISCUSSION

Although we found emotions (e.g., anxiousness and depression) elicited by single gay men similar to those found previously in research conducted with heterosexual men (Otnes et al., 1994), some of our conclusions regarding gay couples implied that attitudinal and behavioral differences do exist between homosexuals and heterosexuals *and* within the homosexual population with respect to Valentine's Day celebrations. According to the majority of media messages, legitimate participation in this holiday involves heterosexual couples engaged in romantic activities. Because they cannot participate in the dominant heterosexual rituals associated with Valentine's Day, especially public displays of affection, homosexual couples feel marginalized. As a result, homosexual couples may use the holiday as an opportunity to engage in self-affirmation against an "oppressive society" and express their gay pride. Although single gay men indicated that everything is geared toward the heterosexual celebration of Valentine's Day, they did not seem to be as agitated regarding oppression of gay public displays of affection. This was probably because they were not romantically involved at the time. Single gay men were more likely to ignore Valentine's Day or protest the holiday due to their lack of a significant other, rather than using the holiday as a way of opposing an oppressive institution or as a means of showing gay pride. In addition, homosexuals seemed to celebrate the holiday with a wide range of people, including co-workers, friends, and families, rather than concentrating solely on a single romantic partner. Finally, while homosexuals purchased standard gifts for the holiday (e.g., cards and flowers), they seemed to enjoy gift-giving more than had been found previously with heterosexual men.

These findings suggest a potential for greater marketing opportunities among the gay male population because they appear to enjoy gift-giving more and give to a wider range of people than their heterosexual counterparts. Businesses such as florists, greeting card companies, and confectioners that derive a large part of their sales from gift purchases should be interested in advertising in gay publications and promoting to gay communities. For any company that is attempting to advertise to gays, especially around holidays associated with gift-giving, the use of altruistic and compensator motivations as well as themes of self-affirmation and pride in the advertising copy could be beneficial.

The similarity of negative Valentine's Day experiences among homosexual and heterosexual singles (e.g., depression at being unattached) should signify to marketers that the singles segments of both markets are not being adequately addressed in the context of Valentine's Day and potentially around other holidays. For both segments, emphasizing the function of gifts to send messages other than those directly related to sexual intimacy such as friendship, thanks, thoughtfulness, and recognition could be appropriate. In terms of marketing to all singles on Valentine's Day, the concept of legitimate participation can be turned to an advertiser's advantage by emphasizing that the holiday is for all people and that the giving of Valentine's Day gifts goes well beyond the realm of established romantic relationships.

The differences reported from this study should be recognized in the context of a small sample size and concentration on one community. Perhaps a broader sample would still uncover similar results, but there may also be a greater diversity of gift-giving motivations and meanings that male homosexuals utilize during Valentine's Day. Future research should examine lesbians and additional gay men using a greater range of age and economic groups and geographic locations, and look at other consumer rituals such as Christmas gift-giving, garage sales, and replacement of old or lost possessions. Some potential sampling strategies could be through solicitations in gay publications for phone interviews, participant observation in gay community groups, or the recruitment of informants to fill out questionnaires at gay cultural events.

As marketing efforts to the gay community increase, so will the recognition within society of this subculture. Indeed, some marketers have suggested that increased marketing efforts can help homosexuals realize their "dream of the day when gays and lesbians will bend the mainstream" (Mathews 1992). Mathews advised that "such a change in American sensibility is unlikely, however, unless the gay press becomes much bigger and more profitable." The gay press is growing and gay advertising dollars are increasing; this has even led to the development of Gay Entertainment Television. Soon, the whole of society will have the ability to tune in to the gay subculture without leaving their sofas.

Contrary to Mathews' statement, the gay press is increasing in size, but one retailer has bypassed specific gay media altogether. IKEA, a Swedish furniture retailer, ran the first mainstream TV spot on March 28, 1994 featuring a "homosexual couple's relationship–including how they met and how they're getting along" (Fitzgerald 1994b). By carefully targeting both the homosexual singles' and couples' markets around Valentine's Day, and everyday, marketers could provide scripts that would legitimize the participation of these groups in society and, at the same time, increase their own profits.

REFERENCES

Belk, R. (1989). Materialism and the modern U.S. Christmas. In Hirschman, E. C. (Ed.), *Interpretative Consumer Research*. Provo, UT: Association for Consumer Research.

Belk, R., Wallendorf, M., & Sherry, J. (1989). The sacred and profane in consumer behavior: Theodicy on the odyssey. *Journal of Consumer Research*, 16, (June), 1-38.

Elliott, S. (1994). "Big marketers are divided on issue of homosexuality," *New York Times*, February 23, p. 1.

Fitzgerald, K. (1994a). AT&T addresses gay market. *Advertising Age*, May 16, p. 8.
_____. (1994b). Ikea dares to reveal gays buy tables, too. *Advertising Age*, March 28, pp. 3,41.

Grahn, J. (1984). *Another Mother Tongue*. Boston: Beacon Press.

Hirschman, E. & LaBarbera, P. (1989). The meaning of Christmas. In Hirschman, E. C. (Ed.), *Interpretative Consumer Research*. Provo, UT: Association for Consumer Research.

Mathews, J. (1992). From closet to mainstream: Upscale gay magazines flood the newsstand. *Newsweek*, June 1, p. 62.

Otnes, C., Ruth, J., & Milbourne, C. (1993). I like you, I like me: The influence of gender, romantic involvement and self-acceptance on Valentine's Day gift exchange. Presented at the February 1993 American Marketing Association's Winter Educators' Conference, Newport Beach, CA.

Otnes, C., Ruth, J., & Milbourne, C. (1994). The pleasure and pain of being close: Men's mixed feelings about participation in Valentine's Day gift exchange. *Advances in Consumer Research*, 21, 159-164.

Poe, D. (1977). The giving of gifts: Anthropological data and social psychological theory. *Cornell Journal of Social Relations*, 12(1) (Spring), 47-63.

Sherry, J. (1983). Gift-giving in anthropological perspective. *Journal of Consumer Research*, 10, (September), 157-168.

Wallendorf, M. & Arnould, E. (1991). "We gather together: Consumption rituals of Thanksgiving day," *Journal of Consumer Research*, 18 (June), 13-31.

Desire and Deviate Nymphos:
Performing Inversion(s)
as a Lesbian Consumer

sidney matrix

Syracuse University

SUMMARY. This paper uses a personalist methodology to discuss my experience of being a lesbian consumer of pop-culture representations of lesbianism. It details, through cultural and feminist/lesbian theory, film theory, and performance criticism, my confusing and contradictory postmodern-feminist-lesbian-theorist response to and desire for what I read as lesbophobia inscribed all over a postcard photo of the cover of a lesbian 1950s pulp novel. I discuss my position as a lesbian looking at a lesbian looking and note the obvious elements of lesbo/homophobia present in this cultural artefact: the trivialization of lesbian desire; the stereotyping of lesbian women; the censorship or erasure of the possibilities of healthy same-sex desire; the prefiguration of the male voyeuristic gaze turning lesbian sex into a spectacle for male pleasure.

The paper aims to underline the critical strategies of lesbian experience, the required negotiations in a hostile culture, and the ways that cultural criticism in the academy shape and prefigure my responses to lesbophobic performances in mass media. I question the

---

sidney matrix is a graduate student working in the fields of lesbian life-writing and personalist lesbian cultural theory and criticism. Correspondence should be addressed to: P.O. Box 7205, Syracuse, NY 13203. E-mail: *smatrix@mail box.syr.edu*

[Haworth co-indexing entry note]: "Desire and Deviate Nymphos: Performing Inversion(s) as a Lesbian Consumer." matrix, sidney. Co-published simultaneously in *Journal of Homosexuality* (The Haworth Press, Inc.) Vol. 31, No. 1/2, 1996, pp. 71-81; and: *Gays, Lesbians, and Consumer Behavior: Theory, Practice, and Research Issues in Marketing* (ed: Daniel L. Wardlow) The Haworth Press, Inc., 1996, pp. 71-81; and: *Gays, Lesbians, and Consumer Behavior: Theory, Practice, and Research Issues in Marketing* (ed: Daniel L. Wardlow) Harrington Park Press, an imprint of The Haworth Press, Inc., 1996, pp. 71-81. Single or multiple copies of this article are available from The Haworth Document Delivery Service [1-800-342-9678, 9:00 a.m. - 5:00 p.m. (EST)].

nature of my pleasure in lesbophobic fictions and detail the process of reversing discourse in the Foucauldian sense. As I identify with the representations, however inaccurate, however fictional, I must invert or *queer* the lesbophobic message, finding pleasure in the very discourses that oppress me, stereotype me, tolerate me, target me. *[Article copies available from The Haworth Document Delivery Service: 1-800-342-9678.]*

It takes two to love: They swap mates for wild thrills and uncurbed desire. Could they return to the path of unconventional morality?

–from *Deviate Nymphos* by Eamon Jeffy

I was playing hooky from a large-scale conference being held in a small town that bored me by wandering aimlessly up and down the main street. Far from home on a summer weekend, I walked about in the sunshine, skipping presentations, daydreaming, thinking of sending a note through the mail to my lover. Browsing through a drugstore, I spun a wire rack of postcards. Images spinning around, including cartoon caricatures of movie stars in compromising positions, Bart Simpson and Marilyn Monroe with bubbles over their heads to indicate their telling a dirty joke, a lot of penises and breasts, and on the back of each card, the series title "Postmoderns" something-or-other. Postmodern postcards sitting beside the vitamins, shampoo and chocolate bars in a drugstore display. Turning the rack, fingering the cards, thinking of my lover and feeling lonely.

And then suddenly there was only one card: two women, lounging in lingerie, posed together, seducing each other, and looking at me from under bouffant hair with catlike, heavily made-up eyes, drawing me in with their gaze. I gripped it with both hands like a life-raft; stood there staring at it, consuming it all at once, ravenously, and then bit by bit, slowly, carefully, taking in every detail: the pastel satin push-up bra, the tousled tresses, the curves of their bodies, long red nails, slippery shiny silk pillows, and her eyes, her eyes. LESBIANS! In that drugstore, on that main street, in that small town, where I thought I was the only one. I found two lesbians and searched fruitlessly for more. Greedily, I bought every copy of the card on the rack, and felt like I'd unearthed a small treasure, something very rare.

to have the card is to have/be the women
looking at her looking at me looking at her

In this essay I explore and problematize my experience as a lesbian consumer of a postcard depicting the cover of a lesbian pulp novel, circa

1950, with the title *Deviate Nymphos*. I read my purchase-experience in various ways, reflecting the conflicting and contradictory performances that being a lesbian consumer requires me to act out. I unpack the dynamics of my purchase in terms of its significance as a postcard, as an erotic or pornographic portrait of lesbian sexuality, and as representative of a genre of literature: textual lesbian experience in pulp-novel form. The term "postmodern" is both the title of the series of postcards from which *Deviate Nymphos* comes, and a useful description of my narrative strategy, since postmodern is a concept that calls to mind an excess of significations, resistant to static definitions, closure and containment. Postmodernism, as I understand it, is a relatively fluid and discontinuous body of ideas that transgresses the boundaries which often separate academic discourse from popular culture. I write as a lesbian academic who also crosses these boundaries, about pleasure and perversion around the purchase of mass culture representations of lesbianism.

CONTEXT: LESBIAN PULPS AND LESBIAN HERSTORY

> I had to find reflections of myself to be assured that I was a valuable human being and not alone in the world. (Lynch 1990)

In small towns, in drugstores, on spinning wire racks, lesbian pulps such as *Deviate Nymphos* offered textual lesbian representation in pop culture, and presumedly lesbians bought them with the same eagerness that I felt in that drugstore, spinning that wire rack, holding those postcards in my hand. Libby Smith argues that these novels "were crucial to lesbians during those years, simply as a recognition of their existence" (Smith 1984). Documenting and constructing a slice of a lesbian culture, lesbian pulp fiction combined fiction and "fact" about inverted women to educate, to narrate, and to excite lesbian readers. Lillian Faderman notes,

> The pulps, with their lurid covers featuring two young women exchanging erotic gazes or locked in an embrace, could be picked up at newsstands and corner drugstores, even in small towns, and they helped spread the word about lesbian lifestyles to women who might have been too sheltered otherwise to know that such things existed. Lesbians bought these books with relish because they learned to read between the lines and get whatever nurturance they needed from them. Where else could one find public images of women loving women? (Faderman 1991)

Lesbians learned to read between the lines and be nurtured by these public images of women loving women. "Lesbians (like most members of stigmatized groups) learn very quickly to read life" (Zimmerman 1993). But it wasn't a novel that I held in my hand in the drugstore that day, it wasn't even the cover of a novel but just a representation of lesbian representation, a seductive sign (postmodern simulacra) pointing to post/ past genres of lesbian textuality. A postcard which I instinctively turned over in my hands and searched over for text. Text! Text! Where were the pages that should have followed that "cover," and what did the absence of those pages signify? As a postmodern lesbian consumer should I be post-pulp fiction by now?

For me to be nurtured by this fictional image of women loving women, I had to read between extra-textual lines, read the portrait as a text in itself. But there were other lines for me to negotiate between, lines that I imagine separate lesbian erotica from pseudo-*lesbian* pornography, and the lines separating my private and uncensored lesbian fantasies/desires/pleasures from the public/political lesbian feminist theorist in me who knows, "sex is presumed guilty unless proven innocent" (Rubin 1992).

PLEASURE IN THE PURCHASE: LESBIAN REPRESENTATION

In researching the context of production of the novel pictured on my postcard, I learn that, "the lesbian pulp industry [of the 1950s was] dominated largely by male authors, and written for a voyeuristic male audience" (Walters 1989). This insight calls to mind the 'lesbian' spreads in contemporary magazines like *Penthouse* and *Hustler*, women posed erotically with each other, who, like the women on the *Deviate Nymphos* card/cover, cast their seductive poses and gaze for a heterosexual male consumer, a masculine spectator. I can't leaf through a "girlie" magazine without feeling that my desire is treacherous to the lesbian feminist in me, and, perhaps more interestingly, that my desire is trespassing on male erotic territory.

In situations like these, I see myself as a lesbian consumer, consuming representations of lesbian women drawn for the male voyeur. And, re/turning to the postcard, I read/see elements of what I would call lesbo/homophobia inscribed there: the trivialization of lesbian desire; the stereotyping of lesbian women; the censorship or erasure of the possibilities of same-sex desire as anything but deviant; and most significantly, the prefiguration of the male voyeuristic gaze turning lesbian sex into a spectacle for male pleasure. My guilt over desiring the postcard images has much to do with the lesbo-trivialization I read there, but it is more complicated. I am, admittedly, not overwhelmed by guilt.

Beyond guilt, beyond desire, beyond intrigue, I cannot overlook the fact that the postcard is part of a tradition of male authorship and production of representations of lesbianism. Similarly, I cannot overlook the fact that the postcard represents a novel which inspired similar confusing emotions for generations of lesbian women before me.

> There was a newspaper store where regular vigilance turned up books I was petrified to take to the cashier. Their ludicrous and blatantly sensational cover copy were both my signals and my shame ... these books I would savour alone, heart pounding from both lust and terror of discovery, poised to plunge the tainted tome into hiding. (Lynch 1990)

The sensational cover copy is also both *my* signal and *my* shame, and thus, to unpack my conflicting emotions as a lesbian consumer, I think about the dynamics of the double-edged nature of my fantasies and desires invested in this card, this purchase. In the portrait/postcard I experience(d) a kind of distorted mirroring/mis-reflection of lesbian erotics with which I still identify. I am seduced by the card, by the lesbian looking at me and all that she promises/(mis)represents. I am drawn to the card precisely and paradoxically because I recognize the lesbian reader address, the "textual elements which suggest lesbians as the intended audience" and the targeted consumer (Henderson 1992). But are the elements of lesbian reader address actually inherent in the production of the postcard, or am I effecting an inversion, reading an/other version of these lesbian postures? I am reading between the lines when I read/look at the postcard depicting two women in various stages of undress (undressing for each other/for me) and take pleasure in this, and when, simultaneously, I read/over-look the word "deviant" and the male author's name, and the knowledge that I am occupying a spectator's position presumed to be male. Or is it that simple?

> Even pornographic representations as textualized fantasy do not supply a single point of identification for their viewers, whether presumed male or female. (Butler 1990)

I am exploring "how the pleasures of spectatorship might operate differently" when women exchange erotic gazes (Stacey 1989). I am a lesbian looking at a lesbian looking. A differential lesbian:equation (Brossard), a different lesbian:economy of desire, leaves me wondering not so much about gendered viewing positions, but more about the place that I am called to take up in relation to myself and the reflection of my lesbian selves in this postmodern postcard portrait. I bought it, but do I buy it, and what if I do? What is the nature of my pleasure in lesbophobic fictions?

Lesbian pulp by men, for men? "But lesbians too are consumers," Danae Clark reminds me, although "lesbians have not . . . been targeted as a separate consumer group within the dominant configuration of capitalism" (Clark 1993). Perhaps not as separate or special, but certainly my position as a lesbian consumer was also anticipated by the producers of this cover, or the producer of the novel behind this postcard, perhaps even by the marketer of this postcard? Certainly, Clark reassures me, "the appropriation of lesbian styles or appeal to lesbian desires can also assure a lesbian market" (Clark 1993). Was it assured that I would fall for the woman's gaze? Was it assured that generations of lesbians before me would be captured by those gazes, seduced into those performances on covers, in spinning racks, at drugstores? I think about the cultural context rooted as it is in a "history of struggle, invisibility, and ambivalence that positions the lesbian subject in relation to cultural practices" within which my performance as a lesbian consumer/spectator occurs (Clark 1993). A small town, a massive women's studies conference where my paper is the only lesbian one, a hotel room where I stay for three nights alone and far from my lover. Isolation. Desperation, and the desire for a lesbian link, representation, even a postmodern one will do, because I am a lesbian who is accustomed to reading oppositionally, just off to the side of the beaten "path of conventional morality" (Jeffy).

> Lesbians are accustomed to playing out multiple styles and sexual roles as a tactic of survival and thus have learned the artifice of invention in defeating heterosexual codes of naturalism. (Clark 1993)

Inventing (/inverting) a lesbian moment in my purchase, I read into the postcard "certain subtextual elements that correspond to experiences with or representations of gay/lesbian subculture" even when I am far from any lesbian community that I recognize (Clark 1993). As a strategic reader, I enact a reverse discourse in the Foucauldian sense, as I identify with the potentially lesbophobic postcard representation, however inaccurate, however fictional, finding pleasure in the very discourses that oppress me, stereotype me, tolerate me, target me (Dollimore 1987). This is a performance of lesbian consumerism in excess of the text, a performance of excess (de Lauretis 1984). More than the pleasure I felt holding the lesbians in my hand, more than the guilt I felt later when I decided not to mail the postcards to another lesbian woman. More like an anxiety over lesbian representation, and questions about authenticity and deviant lesbian plea-sures/desires.

> In a community whose members are wary of images–particularly sexual ones–that somehow refer to us but which we perceive to be unintended for our pleasure, unmarked by other signifiers of lesbian identity. (Henderson 1992)

Is the desire that this "deviate" image inspired in me always and only an excess, unintended, unfigured in its production? Or have I been caught, a lesbian caught looking?

> The figure of the 'lesbian' produced in much lesbian-feminist dis-course is a monochromatic type whose sexual (or asexual) virtue is overwhelming. She is never 'caught looking' at or reading pornogra-phy. (Meese 1992)

And if I am looking, am I a voyeur if my pleasure is in the recognition of my lesbian selves in that erotic space, that postcard scene? Is it voyeur-ism if it is not the act of looking that turns me on, but more specifically the act of remembering my own lesbian pleasures? Are the women in the cover photo fetish objects for my "uncurbed desire," my "wild thrills"–or are they subjects who signify? In any case I am certainly caught-up in looking at these women looking at me. I am certainly catching myself looking at them as I write this piece with the postcard propped against my computer screen. Caught looking, my lesbian virtue up for grabs, and she grabs hold of my theory-trained mind again and again, I come to her.

STRATEGIES OF READING/CONSUMING POPULAR IMAGES OF LESBIANISM

Strategies of a lesbian consumer have everything to do with reading discourses and (mis)appropriating them, subverting them by inverting them (Dollimore 1987). I invert the prefigured response to the card, des-tined for male, voyeuristic eyes, and intervene into the inscribed sexolog-ical discourses of female inversion, perversion, pathology in the title *Devi-ate Nymphos* to write a new narrative on the postcard-as-text. Performing as a perverse reader and lesbian consumer, I undermine this discursive *heterotext* "by privately rewriting and thus appropriating it as [a] lesbian text" (Zimmerman 1993).

> Desire is not necessarily a fixed, male-owned commodity, but can be
> exchanged, with a much different meaning, between women. (Dolan
> 1987)

Male-authored erotic representations of lesbianism, such as the *Nymphos* postcard, open up the possibility for lesbian resistant readings, lesbian appropriations. The postcard and its discourses "acquire new meanings when they are used to communicate desire for readers of a different gender and sexual orientation" (Dolan 1987). Reading the image against the text of the card, reading outside (or between) the lines, the woman/woman desire inscribed in the portrait becomes a "sign that must be reread on the basis of different interpretive strategies" (Martin 1988). "They swapped mates for wild thrills and uncurbed desire. Could they return to the path of conventional morality?" Do the women in the postcard look like they *want* to return to anything except to the erotic scene which the spectator has interrupted?

Performing/posing as a lesbian consumer, I purchase perversion, buying into a version of this postcard that calls up/on all the excesses of lesbian erotics. The excess, the "(sem)erotics" of the postcard's inter- (or extra-) textuality–when I feel my insides clench with the pleasure and the excitement of stumbling across two women having sex in a drugstore! (Meese 1992) More than voyeurism, more than fetishization. "Lesbian sexual/textual pleasure exceeds the effects of representational content" (Meese 1992). Lesbian:(sem)erotics that I read, negotiate, re-read, re-member and re-write.

> If I desire a women, if a woman desires me, then there is the beginning of writing. (Brossard 1988)

"The moment of desire. I write our story, in my mind if not on paper. How I will have her, and, always, how she will take me" (Meese 1992). If the postcard was made by men for men and in the name of male pleasure–then my response to it is, not surprisingly, another instance of experiencing that which remains unthinkable/unimaginable in heterosexist pop culture: lesbian existence, woman to woman pleasure. She smiles at me. She knows. I know. He will never know. Whom does she really beckon, tease, with her gaze as she parts the heavy burgundy curtain so that I can see the woman reclining ready behind her? Who will be left as the frustrated voyeur when the curtain falls and the lingerie-clad women are hidden from view? In my imagination, in my remembering, I have been behind the curtain. The vision of her takes me back behind my own lesbian curtain, back to memories of my own lesbian performances. She knows. I know. He will never know.

IN/COMPLETION: THE LESBIAN LOOKING

Part of being a lesbian consumer of lesbophobic representations of our past is knowing how to translate. With the postcard in my hand I am not forced to pass as a male voyeur, nor am I the masculinized spectator. The explicit code of the postcard, of the lesbian pulp novel may be "always already phallic and patriarchal," that which e(xc)ludes me, and the prefigured position of the consumer may be male and heterosexual (Parker 1993). Yet, as a perverse lesbian reader/consumer, I translate these lesbophobic codes and enact a performance that is a making strange, a reconfiguration, perversion, inversion (Godard 1991).

In my strange performance, watching these women watching me, the relationship of looking, the prefigured gaze is upset. The woman who looks at me is not (only) an object of my desire, but also a f(r)iction of lesbianism. Lesbian to lesbian we share this secret gaze and erotic exchange. A performative f(r)iction that leaves me unsettled (as many powerful lesbian erotic experiences do) and points to the lesbian (sem)erotics in the card, subversion "as aberration and as trans-position" that leads to "a physical appreciation or response to the textual, when the sexual and the textual fuse" (Meese 1992). What do her eyes tell me, and what do mine reveal, standing here, in this drugstore with my guilty conscience, my knotted stomach, and perverse purchase in hand?

> For the female spectator there is a certain over-presence of the image–she is the image. (Doane 1982)

Mary Ann Doane asks, "what is there to prevent her from reversing the relation and appropriating the gaze for her own pleasure?" (Doane 1982). And what is there? Looking back to consider the context of my lesbian shopping spree, I realize that there was so much not there: my lover so far away, not a single other out lesbian at the conference, no women's bookstore where I could treat myself to a lesbian novel. What was there? The postcard, and I couldn't resist desiring it, perverting it, embracing it. My desire, always already prefigured as voyeurism or fetishism, "is precisely a pleasure in seeing what is prohibited in relation to the female body" (Doane 1982). The image on the postcard both "orchestrates a gaze, a limit, and its pleasurable transgression" (Doane 1982). Transgressing the limit, blurring the boundaries, touching her, who is touching her, who touches me, touches off something: lesbian re-memberings.

Seeing as never before–we write new things. Fiction and theory
coming together . . . Returning the gaze we are often afraid. We have
so seldom looked in each other's I/s, so often eavesdropped on our
own li(v)es. (Warland 1986)

As part of my performance as a lesbian consumer, always resisting
while simultaneously desiring, perhaps I enact a masquerade, passing as a
heterosexual shopper, with this joke card for a friend. The masquerade,
writes Doane, "[is] a type of representation which carries a threat, disarti-
culating male systems of viewing . . . What might it mean to masquerade
as spectator? To assume the mask in order to see a different way?" (Doane
1982). Beneath my masquerade is another kind of passing, I pass from
being a lesbian with strict ideas about what constitutes lesbophobic representation, to a guilty shopper, seduced, re/turning to a lesbian theorist
writing up experience in/through fiction:theory. Facing my desire, re-
thinking my need to reach out and touch another lesbian, the postcard and
its image, empower me, stir my imagination. This masquerade, then,
threatens the male voyeuristic gaze it is expected to attract, it allows me to
disrupt, transgress, undo. I pass over the law of the masculinist gaze, into a
space of lesbian-lookings. Re/turning the gaze: embodied rememberings
of lesbian experience in a *Deviate Nymphos* postcard, and *wild thrills* in a
lesbian (sem)erotic space.

REFERENCES

Brossard, N. (1988). *The Aerial Letter.* Marlene Wildeman (trans), Toronto:
Women's Press.
Butler, J. (1990). The Force of Fantasy: Feminism, Mapplethorpe, and Discursive
Excess. *differences*, 2. 105-125.
Clark, D. (1993). Commodity Lesbianism. In Abelove, H., Barale, M. A., &
Halperin, D. M. (Eds.), *The Lesbian and Gay Studies Reader.* New York:
Routledge, 186-201.
de Lauretis, T. (1984). *Alice Doesn't.* Indiana: Indiana University Press.
Doane, M. A. (1982). Film and the Masquerade: Theorizing the Female Spectator.
Screen, 23 (3/4), 74-87.
Dolan, J. (1987). The Dynamics of Desire: Sexuality and Gender in Pornography
and Performance. *Theatre Journal*, 39, 156-174.
Dollimore, J. (1987). The Dominant and the Deviant: A Violent Dialectic. *Critical
Quarterly*, 28 (1/2), 179-192.
Faderman, L. (1991). *Odd Girls and Twilight Lovers: A History of Lesbian Life in
Twentieth-Century America.* New York: Penguin.
Godard, B. (1991). Performance/Transformance: Editorial. *Tessera*, 11, 11-18.
Henderson, L. (1992). Lesbian Pornography: Cultural Transgression and Sexual

Demystification. In Munt, S. (Ed.), *New Lesbian Criticism*. New York: Harvester Wheatsheaf.

Lynch, L. (1990). Cruising the Libraries. In Jay, K. & Glasgow, J. (Eds.), *Lesbian Texts and Contexts: Radical Revisions*. New York: New York University Press.

Martin, B. (1988). Lesbian Identity and Autobiographical Difference[s]. In Brodzki, B. & Schenck, C. (Eds.), *Life/Lines*. Ithaca: Cornell University Press.

Meese, E. (1992). *(Sem)Erotics: Theorizing Lesbian: Writing*. Ithaca: New York University Press.

Parker, A. (1993). Under the Covers: A Synesthesia of Desire (Lesbian Translations). In Penelope, J. & Wolfe, S. J. (Eds.), *Sexual Practice, Textual Theory*. Cambridge, Mass: Blackwell.

Rubin, G. (1992). Thinking Sex: Notes for a Radical Theory of the Politics of Sexuality. In Abelove, H., Barale, M. A., & Halperin, D. M. (Eds.), *The Lesbian and Gay Studies Reader*. New York: Routledge.

Smith, L. (1984). Lesbian Pulp Novels, 1955-1968. Unpublished article, Department of History/Graduate Division, University of Pennsylvania.

Stacey, J. (1989). Desperately Seeking Difference. In Gamman, L. & Marshment, M. (Eds.), *The Female Gaze: Women as Viewers of Popular Culture*, Seattle: Real Comet Press.

Walters, S. D. (1989). As Her Hand Crept Slowly Up Her Thigh: Ann Bannon and the Politics of Pulp. *Social Text*, 8 (2), 83-101.

Warland, B. (1986). As Far As the I Can See. *Canadian Fiction Magazine*, 57, 92-96.

Zimmerman, B. (1993). Perverse Reading: The Lesbian Appropriation of Literature. In Penelope, J. & Wolfe, S. J. (Eds.), *Sexual Practice/Textual Theory: Lesbian Cultural Criticism*. Cambridge, Mass: Blackwell.

Communities, Commodities, Cultural Space, and Style

Anthony Freitas, MS

University of California, San Diego

Susan Kaiser, PhD
Tania Hammidi, BA

University of California, Davis

SUMMARY. This article explores the interconnections between queer communities and cultural space(s) in the context of style. Visibility issues and politics have become important to gay communities in the U.S. Gays and lesbians use clothing and appearance style to signal membership in or separation from specific cultures or com-

Anthony Freitas is a doctoral student in communication at the University of California, San Diego. Susan Kaiser is Professor of Textiles and Clothing and Associate Dean for Human Health and Development in the College of Agricultural and Environmental Sciences at the University of California, Davis. Tania Hammidi is Research Associate in Textiles and Clothing at the University of California, Davis. The authors would like to acknowledge Anna Abraham, Joan Chandler, Dora Epstein, Oscar Huidor, Jung Won Kim, Susan Kim, Melissa Myles, Carla Piedrahita, and Kimli Socarras for their assistance in interviewing. The authors also wish to express their appreciation to Dan Wardlow and the anonymous reviewers for the critical and constructive feedback they provided for an earlier draft of this piece. Correspondence should be addressed to Susan Kaiser, Division of Textiles and Clothing, University of California, Davis, CA 95616. E-mail: *kaiser@agdean. ucdavis.edu*

83

munities. Within commodity capital, the heuristic categories of 'sub-culture' and 'target market' describe space or spaces that gays and lesbians occupy, and often occupy differently, based on self position-ality within gay cultures, within commodity capital, and in relation to gender-specific discourse. Based on in-depth interviews with 60 lesbians and gays, this paper illuminates the ambivalences gays and lesbians express in embracing 'subculture' and 'target market' as categories to establish differences and fashion identities within the current cultural economy. *[Article copies available from The Haworth Document Delivery Service: 1-800-342-9678.]*

"VISIBILITY = LIFE." A 21-year-old lesbian consumer describes this equation on a T-shirt she owns and explains that the shirt was produced by The AIDS Coalition to Unleash Power (ACT UP). This equation expresses the urgent situation of individuals with HIV and AIDS, highlighting the critical, political nature of visibility in dominant culture. Without visibil-ity, it is all too easy for others to deny a disease that they do not see. Still another layer of meaning may be assigned to this shirt–one of identity politics within lesbian and gay (L&G) communities.[1] As a cultural text, this T-shirt is just one of many examples illustrating the interconnections between communities and cultural space(s).

In this paper, we examine these interconnections in the context of style, recognizing that this T-shirt is not only a symbol of community, but also a commodity. We draw on in-depth, qualitative interviews with L&G con-sumers to illustrate two concepts that traditionally have been used to frame analyses of diverse consumer groups: target markets and subcultures. We interrogate this binary and hope to open a third conceptual space that is neither neatly stitched nor cleanly sealed. This third space lies in between, yet overlaps, the other two spaces. It recognizes the links between com-modity and symbolic values of style. As with any inquiry, our "lenses" color the questions we ask and the interpretations we develop. Our lenses are grounded in the study of style, clothing, and appearance. We pursue this study with a commitment to problematize sexual categories and to acknowledge the multiple, shifting character of sexual and other identities (see Stein & Plummer, 1994). Our approach has been to strive to capture individuals' rich descriptions of the meaning(s) of style(s) in their social worlds. In recognition that "there is no clear window into the inner life of an individual" and that "any gaze is always filtered through the lenses of language, gender, social class, race, and ethnicity" (Denzin & Lincoln, 1994, p. 12), we have employed an analysis that can best be described as negotiated and interpretive. That is, by reading and re-reading interview transcripts, engaging in an interpretive dialogue, and discussing theoretical and personal standpoints, we have negotiated a shared understanding that informs our analysis of styles and cultural spaces.

To be gay or lesbian is to be marked by the larger culture, on the one hand, and invisible, on the other. Visibility has become important to the G&L communities, because it provides a space in which to live as gays and lesbians. Although these communities have "lived" for quite some time (D'Emilio, 1983), there has been a continual struggle in the last 25 years (since Stonewall) to inhabit a wider and more comfortable space. This desire for a larger space comes in part from the extreme diversity of the L&G communities. This diversity calls for an increase in options and outlets–in short, for more ways to experience and express everyday life.

By being visible, activists believe that spaces will expand, and lesbians and gays will have more room to position themselves in response to mandatory heterosexuality. These spaces may assume the form of concrete, community-constructed environments such as bars, clubs, stores, and neighborhoods, in which sexual expression may or may not be restricted. Yet they may also be abstract, transitory, or "experiential" spaces in which one feels comfortable expressing or acknowledging her/his sexuality. Such "experiential spaces" may range from recognizing another gay or lesbian in a public place, to hearing a news report about gays or lesbians, seeing a same-sex embrace on television, or catching a glimpse of a homoerotic advertisement.[2] While these latter spaces are less geographical or fixed than community-constructed environments, they are no less "real" in their consequences. They are temporary, always moving and subject to expansion or closure at any time, but while there, they provide refuge and confirmation of same-sex desire and culture. They are spaces that are cultural and symbolic and that open from the use of codes and styles. They are collective spaces that allow for multiple modes of expression and room to roam. They are mobile or mythical spaces that derive from and allow for feelings of difference, or queerness.[3]

These spaces may open from the "inside," the "outside," or the "borders."[4] Herein lies the complexity. In the context of advanced capitalism, cultural spaces need to be analyzed critically and creatively to acknowledge not only who exercises agency within the space(s), but also who profits or benefits from the space(s).[5] In the process, questions such as the following must be addressed: Who is allowed to occupy these spaces? Who controls their borders? And how are they supported?

Citizenship in the G&L communities, like in any community, may be marked through the deployment of style. In other words, communities may use style to signify membership, separation from a more general culture, and expression of common feelings and values. *Camp*, for example, has been characterized as being created by gays (especially men) to provide "a larger space in which to move, loosened from the restraints of the dominant society" (Bergman, 1991, p. 103). However, the borders are not impermeable, and the styles cultivated by a group or community are not exclusive to it. Other groups may borrow or imitate, or members of the group may share the styles with other groups to which they belong. As styles become more widely circulated, it becomes more and more difficult for a group to claim authorship of a style. Within a capitalist context, authorship and the associated myth of origins assume value and importance. Therefore, although some gays and lesbians like to see styles thought to have originated in their cultures diffuse into the wider culture, some want credit or acknowledgment. This desire is, of course, not new or exclusive to the lesbian and gay communities; people of color have long sought recognition for their contributions to style–visual and otherwise–in "mainstream" western culture (hooks, 1992).

Issues of authorship and diffusion converge with the ambivalent desire by many G&L consumers to be not only accepted by, but also distinct from, mainstream culture. Given the assumption that ambivalence fuels style change (Davis, 1992; Kaiser, Nagasawa & Hutton, 1991), this ambivalent desire likely provides an aesthetic and political base for L&G style. And capitalism is pleased to comply.

If gay and lesbian communities did indeed result from capitalism's freeing of labor and undermining of the material necessity of the nuclear family (D'Emilio, 1983), then cultural discourses within and beyond the communities enable interrogation of the pervasiveness and "naturalness" of both heterosexuality and capital. As Hebdige has pointed out, ideology "by definition thrives *beneath* consciousness. It is here, at the level of 'normal common sense', that ideological frames of reference are most firmly sedimented and most effective, because it is here that their ideological nature is most effectively concealed" (Hebdige, 1979, p. 11). Thus "queer common sense" may lead to ambivalence towards both heterosexual norms and capital. D'Emilio (1983) and Clark (1991) suggest that the relationship of L&G communities to capital, for example, is neither clear nor direct. In her essay "Commodity Lesbianism," Clark (1991) specifies the process by which lesbians are both resistant to and complicit with commodity capital. As the money in the gay and lesbian communities becomes itself a commodity, the community becomes described more as a target market than as a community. But there is more to the story of style. The politics and aesthetics of style constitute a form of cultural capital that does not rely entirely upon monetary value (Bourdieu, 1984). Cultural capital becomes a metaphor for the relationship between the G&L communities and dominant heterosexuality.

In addition to discussing the creation of cultural (community) spaces, we recognize the need for increased conceptual and methodological spaces drawing from both critical and empirical methods. We agree with MacCannell's (1992) call for a social science that is "simultaneously empirically tough and speculative" (p. 308). The strategies used by lesbians and gays to create and occupy communities through complex margin-center relations bear resemblance to contemporary debates over inter-disciplinary-disciplinary relations within the academy–relations involving diverse philosophies of science and criticism.[6,7]

We believe that style–especially clothing and appearance style–provides heuristic possibilities for understanding the interdependencies among issues of visibility, identity, community, and cultural spaces.[8] We explored these issues by framing our discussion around two analytical categories and the standpoints they represent: target market and subculture. This framing enabled us to see the meanings these categories hold for G&L consumers and to delineate the contexts in which these categories become useful.

As stated earlier, this paper involves a negotiated interpretation of a series of in-depth interviews with 36 women and 24 men residing in Northern California, most of whom identified as lesbian or gay.[9,10] The interview format was open-ended and focused on personal gay/lesbian clothing and appearance styles. Participants ranged in age from 19 to 50, with a mean age of 28 years.[11] Respondents self-identified ethnicity in an open-ended manner.[12] The majority of those interviewed (n = 36) described themselves as ethnically White and of European descent (13 men, 23 women); seven identified as Asian/Asian American (6 men, 1 woman), seven as Jewish (1 man, 6 women), six as Chicano/a or Latino/a (3 men, 3 women), three as African American (1 man, 2 women), and one woman did not respond to the question.

Many of the respondents were students pursuing undergraduate or graduate degrees (17 women, 14 men); the remainder worked as professionals in service industries (6 women, 4 men), office administration (2 women, 2 men), research (5 women), management (3 women), counseling (2 women, 2 men), and architecture (1 man). Two respondents were unemployed (1 woman, 1 man). Informants were recruited through posted flyers and word-of-mouth. They were paid five dollars for participation in the one-and-a-half to two-hour interview. Informants chose the locations for their interviews, usually at their homes, at local cafes or public spaces, or at the university. The interviews were recorded on audiotape and were later transcribed verbatim.

The majority of interviews were conducted in Northern California and represent some of the diversity within that population; however, we acknowledge the impossibility of fully representing views within the lesbian and gay communities. Moreover, we recognize that Northern Californian L&G consumers may maintain a privilege of expression not necessarily available in other areas. Other factors influencing the study include a relatively small sample size and a sampling method that may have limited variability in age, occupation, and level of education.

TARGET MARKET

Wanna reach a market with half a trillion bucks to spend? According to recent *Advertising Age* figures, that's how much spending power the gay and lesbian community has today. *Overlooked Opinions*, a Chicago market research firm, puts the figure at $514 billion in earnings. Average gay household income in this country is $55,430–compared with $32,144 per year in straight households . . . Advertising with us puts you right in front of some of America's most affluent consumers . . . What are you waiting for? You wanna make some money, or what? (*Victory! The National Gay Entrepreneur Magazine*, 1994)

I guess I just wanted to see a commercial
Not for any particular product
Just sort of a romantic commercial
For jeans, perfume, . . . I don't know . . . hair care products . . .
Anyhow–the "stars" would be lesbians, 2 of them . . .
(That would make *me* the target market)
30 years (almost) of television for me, & I've never been the target market
30 years of pretending . . .
It certainly can't be that we aren't "pretty" enough to be in mainstream media
After all, we comprise so much of the talent that portrays the part of the heterosexual on TV.
(Franchini, 1994)

[D]esigned to bridge the gap between Corporate America and the Gay and Lesbian community. . . . (Unity Expo, 1994)

Target markets become culturally constructed spaces containing both market and community value. In the process, the concepts of consumer and citizen can become conflated (Evans, 1994), and access to markets and consumer goods begins to mean not only visibility, but also political and economic clout.[13] Hence, it becomes increasingly important to ask how representations–visual, electoral, and economic–are achieved in the contemporary cultural moment. If markets are defined by their incorporation of "the norms and practices of advantaged groups" and by their devaluation of "the products and enterprises of identifiable minorities" (Evans, 1994, pp. 39-40), then does the targeting of lesbian and gay consumers signal a granting of citizenship to sexual aliens in the capitalist state? How has the struggle for equal access to laws come to mean equal access to consumer goods and services? How are the symbols of queerness exchanged in the marketplace, and what capital do they hold? What exchange value, symbolic and monetary, do they carry? And, how do symbolizing "queer" and participation in the marketplace coincide?

In the last few years, market researchers have determined that queer communities, and gay males specifically, have more discretionary income than the population in general (Schwartz, 1992). Moreover, it is estimated that this community numbers at least 25 million people and "consists of many consumers who are affluent, highly educated, and brand loyal" (Solomon, 1994, p. 309). Still other studies suggest that gay and lesbian household incomes are lower than those of heterosexual households (Tuller, 1994). Nevertheless, described as DINKs (double income, no kids), gay and lesbian households are seen as lucrative market sources. Accordingly, corporations have begun to develop products and advertising campaigns to attract these consumers. Corporations such as Absolut and Stolichnaya vodkas were early advertisers in gay press (Solomon, 1994).[14] This type of targeting taps into the economic capital of the market by using G&L cultural media as a conduit, without "labeling" the product through advertising imagery as being specific to the G&L market.

Calvin Klein developed an extensive market in the community by using "gay window advertising" (Clark, 1991). This method uses ambiguous images to attract G&L consumers without coding the advertisement in such a way as to exclude a heterosexual reading as well:

> "Gayness" remains in the eye of the beholder: gays and lesbians can read into an ad certain subtextual elements that correspond to experiences with or representations of gay/lesbian subcultures. If heterosexual consumers do not notice these subtexts or subcultural codes, then advertisers are able to reach the homosexual market along with

the heterosexual market without ever revealing their aim. (Clark, 1991, p. 183)

Hence, Calvin Klein underwear ads highlighting young, lean and muscular male models can target gay male consumers without closing the larger market window. The (homo)erotic imagery of these ads may also appeal to women who buy underwear for the men in their lives.

In our interviews, one White, 19-year old gay male targeted by the "window" in Calvin Klein ads describes his emotions as follows:

> It is like there is kind of a satisfaction . . . This ad is targeting me, and it was made for me and people like me, so that we will buy this product. And so in a way that is kind of flattering, and I guess it shouldn't be, because they just want our money. But still . . . recognize that they have to target us. We are not just going to buy. They need to ask for it.

This comment suggests a conscious, if not critical, awareness of the relationship between cultural visibility and target marketing. That is, to be acknowledged as having cultural capital becomes meaningful in the democratic sense. Ambivalence, however, emerges from the recognition that there is a price tag associated with such visibility. The questions become: How much is this visibility worth? And who pays for and profits from it? While the political aspects of consumption may not interest or concern some lesbians and gays, for others this is a priority. (For example, a boycott of the Bank of America resulted from its reinstatement of funding to the Boy Scouts of America who deny membership to openly gay scouts or scout leaders; Coward, 1992.)

These questions bring us back to the concepts of citizenship and cultural capital. As Evans (1994) notes, the right to participate in society and the right to consume become indistinguishable in contemporary life. The presence of advertisements can easily be misread as support for the community, resulting in "casting a ballot" in the marketplace through a product choice. Indeed, some corporations manage to create a space for themselves within the queer community and, in some instances, gain reputations as supporters, based on sponsorship of events or charitable donations (e.g., Apple Computer, VISA sponsorship of the 1994 Gay Games). Yet as happens in other underrepresented communities, there is no guarantee that the money earned from the community will stay in the community. It may be transferred to firms who prioritize corporate profits over community viability.

As the profit potential associated with the G&L community's economic and political capital becomes more evident to marketers, it appears that the gay window shade becomes more receptive to marketing advances. Recently, IKEA (an international home furnishings chain) developed the first television commercial featuring a gay male couple as one of many diverse "lifestyles and life-stages." (Other ads in the campaign include a family in the midst of adoption, a divorced woman, and a family moving to a new state.) The television commercial shows two affluent white–straight acting, straight appearing, but presumably gay–males shopping for a dining room table and, simultaneously, suggesting their gayness through expressions of commitment to one another. Rather than intending the commercial to be targeted to the G&L "niche market," IKEA's advertising firm developed their inclusive campaign to appeal to consumers dubbed "wannabes": consumers who are moving up the ladder, have a sense of style, and live in double-income households with either no children or one child (Gallagher, May 1994).

Regardless of IKEA's intent and the consequences of the commercial, this example illustrates the emerging role of today's gay white male as the 'new model intellectual' of consumer capitalism, at the forefront of the business of shaping and defining taste, choice, and style for mainstream markets" (Ross, 1988, p. 8). The lack of such visibility beyond the context of an affluent, style-appreciating white gay male couple, however, does little to counter problems of racism, sexism, and classism.

Relative to this concern, we noted a certain self-reflexivity among some of our interviewees, who pointed to the need to interrogate classist images of gayness. One male noted that gay men seem to wear "nicer jewelry" than straight men and then critically noted the "probably classist" stereotype associated with such a perception. Another male expressed concern about status symbolism within the gay community:

> If you want to impress someone, you wear a Polo shirt or you wear an Armani, so that you can show that you have money and that you have status and that you have power and whatever else so that people know something about you from what they are reading from your clothes. And I think sometimes people just dress that way, so that they can attract people. (Chicano male, 24)

Clark (1991, p. 181) describes how lesbian consumers traditionally have not been targeted "either directly through the mechanism of advertising or indirectly through fictional media representations," because advertisers have perceived them both as lacking in economic power and as inaccessible or "unknowable." However, Clark also notes that advertisers for the fashion industry have begun to capitalize on the recent trend of younger, urban lesbians, in particular, to experiment openly with the possibilities of fashion and beauty, rebelling against what she describes as the "lesbian-feminist credo of political correctness that they perceive as stifling" (1991, p. 185). The emergence of "life style" lesbianism may be in part a response to gay window advertising. Nevertheless, there is more to "lipstick lesbians" or "style nomads" than boredom with the idea that a "natural look" exists. Fashion, it seems, becomes an assertion of personal freedom as well as political choice (Clark, 1991, p. 185). And fashion advertisers have begun to capitalize on this assertion through "lesbian window advertising," as they have noted the increasing affluence and visibility of the predominately White, educated, middle-class and mostly childless segment of the lesbian population.

Since the publication of Clark's essay, lesbians have (arrived at) a degree of visibility and celebrity never before afforded to them by the larger culture. Several women's fashion and mainstream magazines have run articles on "Lesbian Chic" (e.g., Kasindorf, 1993; "Sexual Politics," 1993). In addition, Cindy Crawford and k.d. lang share the cover of *Vanity Fair* ("k.d. lang cuts it close," 1993), and *Newsweek* ("Pride and Prejudice," 1993) features a cover story on lesbians around the time of Roberta Achtenberg's appointment to the position of Assistant Secretary of Fair Housing and Equal Opportunity in the Department of Housing and Urban Development.

One female in our study noted the increased visibility that goes along with media coverage and the increased willingness of younger lesbians to be visible:[15]

> Twenty years ago, you didn't see [visible lesbians] as much. . . . I will say [that there is] more acceptance of lesbians within [the women's movement today]. That is how visibility will come. People [will] know that there are others. I think it is easier to be out at a younger age. It is easier to ask questions at a time in your life when you are seeing styles and buying clothes. I think that contributes a lot. (White Jewish female, 22)

Our interviews suggest a wide range of clothing budgets and appearance styles among gay and lesbian consumers. Purchasing practices ranged from thrift store purchases to the purchase of $1100 designer leather jackets, and from relatively infrequent to weekly shopping excursions. Particular catalogs, magazines, and retail stores were identified with regularity. Foremost among these was The Gap, which markets unisexual styles. A number of individuals commented on the good fit of the jeans and the variety of separates within the store, offering numerous opportunities for mixing and matching.

> Generally I like to wear jeans and a shirt and a vest. Well, I am kind of funny, and I don't think this has to do with my sexual orientation at all. I like to match colors. I like to have socks that match my sweaters, and The Gap is great with that, and I really like to have socks to match. So that is my main thing . . . I have always felt different, and I think part of that is my sexual orientation–part of it, and maybe my artistic orientation. I like to look like a mixture. (White female, 42)

> The Gap–because I can afford it, and nice proletariat clothing. Jeans and T-shirts, and you don't have to worry about it, and you figure out things, and you don't have to try things on any more. I just go and grab it and use it. (White female, 25)

One of our colleagues characterizes Gap clothes as a kind of "Grr-Animals for adults."[16] The Grr-Animals label from Healthtex offered a kind of aesthetics indoctrination for children. It helped them to develop ensembles by matching specific animal tags on tops and bottoms. Without the animal tags, The Gap seems to offer a similar promise: ease in coordinating an ensemble. At the same time, it offers room for experimentation among consumers who "value individualistic, unique experiences" (Solomon, 1994, p. 457).

Collective patronization of large fashion marketers to develop gay and lesbian "looks" raises the critical question: Are gays and lesbians a community, a target market, or more likely, a little bit of both? In addition, questions also arise pertaining to the motives of large corporations to back gay and lesbian publications, like Time Warner (Carmody, 1994), or to support queer-positive TV and film. Clearly, segments of the community become target markets for both gay and non-gay owned businesses (e.g., IKEA). But when other (right-wing) groups threaten to boycott advertisers, do corporate-sponsored stages of G&L visibility come tumbling down?[17] Or, will these corporations have provided the G&L community enough seed money and encouragement to keep the momentum going? And what happens when these ventures are not profitable, such as the 1994 Gay Games (Gallagher, October 1994)? In addition, are these corporations, so eager to tap the mythical gold mine of the gay and lesbian consumer, willing to institute business practices that help the G&L communities and protect them from discrimination?

In contrast to a "target market" analysis focusing on visibility politics in the context of economic capital, a "subcultural" analysis of the G&L community highlights such politics and others through a nexus of subversion, aesthetics, and communication. A target market, heuristically and metaphorically, crystallizes from the outside looking into the community or from the inside looking around at the possibilities. In either case, the intent is to capitalize economically. A subcultural analysis, in contrast, emanates from the inside looking out at dominant culture and defining itself creatively (if not ambivalently) in relation to it. It may derive from an external intellectual critique of margin-center cultural relationships or from a social deviance perspective. Such an analysis, it seems, focuses more directly on the question of cultural capital in the political sense, without the overriding filter of economics. In many ways, non-commercial and politically subversive aspects of life are prioritized over the links of the G&L community to capitalism.

SUBCULTURE

In matters of grave importance, style, not sincerity, is the vital thing. (Oscar Wilde, *The Importance of Being Earnest*)

There is more fun in art and more art in fun than many of us will even now allow. (Babuscio, 1993, p. 19)

A second cultural space can be designated as *subcultural*. Such a space hinges on the perception that an insider/outsider membership binary exists, and privileges symbolic over monetary exchange value. In a subcultural approach to style, members code and signify their outsider status (a status gained either through self-definition or ostracism), which allows for the emergence of a distinct collective subculture. This culture "creates and recreates itself–politically and artistically–along with, as well as in reaction to, the prevailing cultural norms" (Bronski, 1984, p. 7). According to Hebdige (1979), the key point of analysis is "the status and meaning of revolt, the idea of style as a form of Refusal" (p. 2), and part of this revolt revolves around broken codes and meaning(s) that are continually in dispute. On an ongoing basis, a subculture develops strategies that enable resistance and self-identification in the face of repression by the dominant culture:

The subculture finds ways to respond to this repression. It hides, recreates itself, takes secret or coded forms, and regroups to survive. (Bronski, 1984, p. 3)

In the 25 years since the 1969 Stonewall riots, the G&L subculture has taken a turn toward increased political visibility and viability, along with the articulation of a culture based upon distinctive analyses, experiences, and perceptions (Bronski, 1984, p. 13). The dramatic art of "passing" (Babuscio, 1993) as heterosexual is a central component of shared gay experiences.[18] Passing fosters a heightened awareness and an appreciation for disguise (Babuscio, 1993, p. 25). In short, it is part of the gay history upon which the contemporary subculture has been constructed. The result is a cultural sensibility that expresses "itself by implying rather than stating, by indicating with appearance what it was not allowed to express with context" (p. 57).[19]

Through this sensibility, salience shifts "from what a thing *is* to how it *looks*, from *what* is done to *how* it is done" (Newton, 1979, p. 107). Hence, aesthetic *detail* and style's subtle *gestalt* comprise the conceptual and symbolic field of the gay sensibility. The important principles are "arrangement, timing, and tone" (Babuscio, 1993, p. 21). A number of the G&L individuals we interviewed pointed to the significance of "*how* it is done." This *how* refers to the abstract, attitudinal and visual gestalt:

> It is not so much in the clothes they wear but how they wear it. It is more abstract than that, and I can't explain it. It is just the attitude. I think it is a combination of a lot of things. The hairstyle. The clothing combined with the attitude make it a trademark of gay male and lesbians. (23-year old, Filipino/Asian American male)

> Seems to me that lesbians tend to stand up a little straighter. Better posture. Sort of like an assurance of where their toes are and an awareness of where their personal space is. (African American female, 43)

> There is an attitude toward style, . . . and I think it definitely reflects people knowing that they are different from the norm and feeling that that difference has been stigmatized, and now wanting to reclaim that as a positive thing . . . (our) material community and gay culture . . . (having) access to these codes and sensibilities. (White male, 32)

The *how* of style also refers to the details which serve to change the cultural contexts in which appearances are read. Such aesthetic details–for instance, a particular shoe with a particular style, a bandanna–decenter appearance style as a cultural text with a hegemonic reading, redirecting our attention to its subversive reading, to the margins and the meaning(s) to which they refer (see Barthes, 1974; Rudd, 1992). Through connotation, meaning becomes situated *alongside* rather than *within* (Viengener, 1993, p. 286).

> We pay attention to the smallest details and make sure everything is in its place and taken care of and presented properly. Whether . . . you want the grunge look or the elegant [look]. (Latino male, 21)

> I pay attention to things that look different. Not traditional stuff. Things that catch my eye. I don't typically like the average women's stuff, so I look for things that have a different pattern or a nicer material. Interesting pattern, interesting colors. (Jewish female, 24)

> When you wear a certain color bandanna on your right pocket, it says something to someone who knows what you are wearing. When you wear a leather arm band on your biceps on your right side, it says something else than if he is wearing it around his neck. If you are wearing button-front 501s and you have the top one unbuttoned, it says something differently than if you have your bottom button unbuttoned. People who are into that language and into that communication will know what you are saying to them by which button you have unbuttoned. . . . The combination of articles that either men or women wear–like the idea of maybe one or two earrings for a man, and he is also wearing Doc Martens, . . . very short cutoffs that are faded, and white socks sticking out of the boots and a ribbed tank T-shirt and maybe a flannel shirt that is cut off at the shoulders. That whole look definitely says gay to me. (Chicano male, 28)

In addition to G&L sensibilities and codes of communication, our informants made reference to their use of political symbols in personal appearance. There were frequent references to gay pride T-shirts and jewelry (e.g., freedom ring necklaces, pink or black triangle earrings, gay pride pins). A white male sales representative wears a "100% dyke" T-shirt. Another male describes his "controversial" Madonna T-shirt in the context of what it represents:

> A year ago I went for the very first time . . . to see the Pride Parade in San Francisco . . . It brings back memories of that . . . very interesting weekend. The weekend that I bought that shirt. It basically symbolizes my gayness. (White male, 20)

The G&L students often made reference to their feelings about wearing visible signs of gayness on the campus. One female noted that she wears her gay pride earrings and buttons a lot, but she puts the latter "on the back, and I don't really see people's reactions." She also described wearing:

> A T-shirt that says "I am not gay, but my girlfriend is." . . . Another one that says "Read my lips." . . . I am kind of ashamed to say this, but it is true . . . I am not always feeling strong enough to wear it on campus. I get a lot of nasty looks. Actually, I wear the "Read my lips" T-shirt, but a lot of people don't get it, so I am safe. . . . But I also think I am a walking billboard, because I get called "sir" a lot. (White female, 22)

Another student described his experiences and feelings as follows:

> Sometimes I do wear my T-shirts with gay rights and ACT UP T-shirts and "Come out, come out, whoever you are." [I feel] powerful only in the sense that I know I am educating people, because I am being visible. (Latino male, 21)

But this visibility is often coded for "perceivers who matter," in the knowledge that most heterosexuals on campus "won't get it." For example, some males reported interest in getting a tattoo on their ankles, which would not be visible on a regular basis:

> Something that means something to me significantly that I wouldn't mind having on me forever. I want something to deal with my [gay] fraternity–our letters or our mascot on our ankle. (Filipino/Asian male, 23)

> The universal gay male sign. The circle and the arrows [two of them interconnected] with the inverted triangle in one and the peace symbol in the other. I will probably have the circle and peace sign in standard ink and probably the triangle pink. (White male, 23)

Some interviewees also had body piercings and often commented that "you know it's there" and "so if the topic comes up, you know what kind of people you are dealing with" (White, Jewish female, 22).

Symbols such as leather jackets and Doc Marten boots were commonly identified. The latter were especially common among the lesbians interviewed, whose descriptions often reveal the subtleties of aesthetic and symbolic detailing relative to issues of visibility and community:

> I have been wearing black Doc Martens for probably six or seven years now, and those have been a part of me, and I have recently

changed to the ones with the yellow laces . . . I didn't realize it 'til afterwards that the yellow stitching around the side of Doc Martens are part of the lesbian uniform . . . I don't know any lesbians that wear the ones without the yellow stitching, but all the ones without the yellow stitching are straight . . . Every now and then I like having certain things that are easily identifiable as being part of the community. And that is one of them. That and my black leather jacket. (White female, 25)

I wear Doc Martens. I have two pairs. I have a black pair and a green pair. Both high tops. I get new steel toes every year . . . It is important for dykes to be included and say we have a community, and in order to be included in that community, there are certain clothing rules for different dyke communities . . . I think for the community to accept you or include you they like you to wear their uniform, and I think that is true in the straight world as in the dyke world. (White female, 29)

Other symbols included accessories, often with an emphasis on how they are worn in addition to what they symbolize.

I have a patch that I am very proud of. The Gay Olympics. I have that patch. I was there at the very first Olympics . . . My patch is on Velcro. So I like to transfer that a lot. (African American female, 43)

I put a purple bandanna in my pocket. I think for me the color purple is very woman-oriented and powerful. (22, White female)

There was also evidence of "bricolage" in the form of the inventive use of materials not originally intended for the purpose of accessorizing (Hebdige, 1979). One male noted how he could transform metal hoops and "pieces of black rubber," along with other items:

Ornamentation is a good feeling . . . It is actually bicycle tubing that I glued together. I used to wear these knit white cotton . . . made for packing material. They fit my wrist, and I used to wear a whole bunch of them. (White, Jewish, 29)

Another male also identified pleasure as a major theme in his appearance management. While teaching in Tokyo, he had bleached out the "tail" in his hair and dyed it in various shades of purple or pink. His students were very accepting, "so that gave me great pleasure." Stressing the theme of using pleasure and style to balance seriousness, he noted the value of "obviously frivolous" acts of appearance management in bringing "levity and enjoyment" to others. One female made a similar point relative to the need for "play" and fun:

> I think clothing is so political, and beauty is so political. I wish it could be like playful and for fun. (White female, 29)

Being "part of the community" seems to entail a blend of a responsibility to be identifiable, on the one hand, and a freedom to be creative, on the other.

> I think if you feel you are a part of the greater lesbian community, it is important to look like you identify with that community . . . I think you are more welcomed if you look like you identify. (African American female, 27)

> What I like about lesbian and gay style is that there doesn't seem to be a box, and there are a lot of different styles that you can choose from, which is cool. When I walk down the street, I think I can pretty much tell the lesbians from the non-lesbians. And I think they are a lot more trendy than the heterosexual women. (White female, 46)

But one woman noted,

> I have never found lesbian community . . . I refuse to be conventional for lesbians, either. I don't like the lesbian police–if you will, and the way in which fashion ideas are supposed to go together in a very limiting way . . . There is this critical gaze of "How can you like the Grateful Dead if you are a feminist?" I have had many lesbians ask me that . . . I don't want to meld myself into one metal. I want to stay all the different parts. (White female, 45)

Establishing differences and fashioning identities, within and beyond the G&L communities, are dynamic and symbolic processes that operate within a cultural economy. When the symbolism of the community becomes framed as the basis for a target market from an "outside" perspective, the styles become divorced of the meaning(s) they once held. This is also true of subcultural community styles that diffuse into mainstream fashion (see Kaiser, 1990, and Solomon, 1994, for reviews of the literature on fashion diffusion). Hence, Doc Martens become popular not just among ACT-UPers and Queer Nationals but among teens and middle-class people of any sexual orientation. And the style takes on new or more vague meanings. Based on the perspectives expressed in our interviews, the issue is not so much that meaning has become diluted or that a symbol has been stolen, as it is that manufacturers are selling the product as "cool" or "hip" without reference to its meaning. Our interviewees noted that symbols are continually stolen from L&G cultures, who, in turn, continually create and re-create "looks."

> They rip us off. If we look fabulous, they take it away from us. It is true for disco, and it is true for all the great looks of our eras . . . It is fine with me, because we will come up with a new one. We are clever. We are fabulous. It will take me two seconds to come up with a new look. (White male, 26)

Since the 1960s, the cultural economy of gay sensibility has signaled an "important break with the style and legitimacy of the old liberal intellectual" toward an ethos linked to pop culture. This ethos is based, in part, on a "commitment to the new and everyday" through style that "already contains the knowledge that it will soon be outdated" (Ross, 1988, p. 13).

It is this sense of *becoming* through visual expression that has led some writers to describe contemporary gay sensibility or camp as a "poststructuralist mode *par excellence*" (Bergman, 1991, p. 105).[20] As such, it not only deconstructs dominant cultural forms, but also continually shapes and reshapes their forms and meanings

> toward a new and ultimately stabler sense of what the serious and nonserious are. (Long, 1989, p. 56)

In so doing, camp style enables the G&L subculture to appropriate the laughter of a "society that laughs at the wrong things" (Long, 1989, p. 56).

The appropriation works in the other direction as well. Camp style has become part of what it means to be straight as well as gay in accordance with the postmodern canon (Blau, 1982-1983; Case, 1993). Part of the irony in this appropriation of camp style by dominant culture is the ability of the G&L subculture(s) to experience style's pleasure and cultural capital only "at the expense of others, [because] . . . 'taste' is only possible through exclusion *and* depreciation" (Ross, 1988, p. 16). This is even achieved within the context of gay window fashion advertising, which affords opportunities for lesbian consumers/readers to claim an "unarticulated space as something distinct and separable from heterosexual (or heterosexist) culture," a culture not "privy to the inside jokes that create an experience of pleasure and solidarity with other lesbians 'in the know'" (Clark, 1991, p. 188). These "inside" lesbian readings of cultural texts mark a shift in the long tradition within the lesbian subculture to separate politically from heterosexual definitions of fashion and beauty (Clark, 1991). The downside, of course, is the extent to which dominant culture welcomes lesbians "as consuming subjects but not as social subjects" (Clark, 1991, p. 192).

Social subjectivity also factors into G&L relations. As Wilson (1990) has noted, subcultures (e.g., punk, hippie) are often framed around male experiences and subjectivities. Historically and culturally, lesbians have been framed as "female versions of male homosexuality" (Rich, 1980, p. 649). Yet, Ross (1988, p. 23) has argued that "the subaltern position" of lesbian culture has enabled the construction of a "more successful 'liberation culture'." Still, such differences as women's lack of economic privilege and cultural visibility relative to men (Rich, 1980; Sedgwick, 1993) point to the need for a critical analysis of gender relations within and beyond the G&L community. As Smith (1993) points out,

> thinking narrowly of gay people as white, middle class, and male, which is just what the establishment media want people to think, undermines consciousness of how identities and issues overlap. (Smith, 1993, p. 101)

The postmodern and anti-essentialist media discourse that allows for "inside" readings is certainly democratic. But is it necessarily accepting?

TOWARD A CONTEXTUAL UNDERSTANDING

Consumers' readings, purchases of commodities, and creations of "looks" need to be contextualized in light of larger modes and means of production, distribution, and consumption. Rather than reaching for any universalizing and harmonizing "happy endings" to the relation between G&L subculture(s) and dominant culture, it may be more beneficial to become as creative and critical in the use of particulars as is the G&L community in the context of style.

Meanwhile, there exists another dilemma: naming. As we framed our discussions around the concepts of "target market" and "subculture," we became conscious of the need to become liberated from the "binary prison" (Barthes, 1974). In fact, the diversity of fashion preferences and subjectivities evidenced in our interviews suggests the arbitrary and simplified nature of the two concepts. In this connection, we believe it is important to point out some of the conceptual and practical difficulties of the terms. The concept of subculture implies, if not accepts, that one cultural practice is "above" others. It suggests that we all subscribe to a larger culture, which is autonomous of the multiple subcultures to which individuals belong. This seems to us to reify the marginal status of the "lesser" cultures. Typically, the subcultural concept has been readily invoked in academic literature embodying an ethos of resistance and social change (e.g., Hebdige, 1979). Yet this concept may, in fact, promote self-fulfilling prophecies within the value and meaning systems of the G&L community. That is, inasmuch as G&L sensibility revolves around a sense of hope (Long, 1989), its conceptualization is not complete in the subcultural context.

There were repeated references in the interviews to "the community" but rarely to "the subculture." Similarly, the term "target market" is obviously one used among individuals with a particular standpoint and motivation. Rarely will the term be used among consumers within a community per se. Stemming from a marketing perspective, the target market concept is based on a capitalist, profit-motivated ideology. Clearly, it falls short of capturing the creative and subversive energies within the G&L community, especially in the context of postmodern life, wherein "to consume is to produce again" (Baudrillard, 1975).

We do not believe the solution to the target market versus subculture dichotomy is to harmonize or obscure the two. But we do think it is important to recognize the everyday social realities experienced by *individuals* such as those whose voices we heard. And we sense that they are quite conscious of the fact that their social realities intersect in diverse and cross-cutting ways with the world of commodities. But does, as Evans (1994) suggests, "consumerism direct our energies to the purchase of private pleasures and happiness" (p. 25)? Or, does the ongoing search for a link between playfulness and seriousness in everyday life lead us to seek modes of expression through style? The interviews suggest a fairly conscious, critical and creative reflexivity on the part of these members of the G&L community. This reflexivity needs to be continually articulated and problematized, as do the community's expressive dynamics and relation to capital. This reflexivity involves a recognition of the fact that both of the heuristic devices we have examined (target market and subculture) create space or spaces that lesbians and gays can occupy. These spaces have their costs and risks, however. And in a community as diverse as the gay and lesbian community, what is labelled as a risk by some may be seen as a benefit by others.

The use of codes and styles creates a rich and varied space for members of a constituency. It marks a territory for queer nationals or IKEA and

Gap customers. More subtly, it defines itself through the stitching on Doc Martens, the detail in a denim shirt, or the homoeroticism in a Calvin Klein ad. These spaces allow for alternative and sometimes confrontational expression. They assume form through style and attention to detail. However, these regions have no secured frontiers, and the symbols that mark them require frequent alteration and negotiation/renegotiation. This lack of security allows for the development of sign systems and interpretive skills by members of each constituency.

Yet both the territories and the ciphering systems come at a cost. They have developed in relation to a homogenizing and hegemonic system: a system in which the attention to detail and the dual citizenship of the closet become the threads for emotional, psychic, and physical survival. Today, in the context of global capitalism, this stylistic and geographic property carries additional costs. As soon as the L&G community is "known," it becomes a new territory for global capital to exploit. As soon as its codes are cracked, its images are easily appropriated by those with different political agendas. But if the community is not known and visible, how can the need for equal protection be claimed? How can it insist on the credit due for stylistic authorship and originality? There cannot be a "happy ending" to the story of style, because there *is* no ending, no closure. The issue, instead is: How can the L&G community negotiate a meaningful space within capitalism? Open territories are subject to colonization and expansion from within as well as from "joint ventures." Should lesbians and gays attempt to control access to the ever-new stylistic spaces they create? If so, how?

Creating and negotiating stylistic spaces are ongoing processes that blur the boundaries among community, commodity, style, and politics. A community can and does become a consumer culture, and vice versa. This culture need not be characterized as "sub." It has its own value and meaning systems, but it connects with those of other contiguous and intersecting cultures. There is not one consumer culture, but many. And within each of these, we need to understand consumption as more than that for which we pay. It is *both* that *and* the symbols and meanings used to define and construct everyday life.

NOTES

1. We use the term L&G (or G&L) throughout this paper, recognizing the contested and contextual nature of this and other terms, both within and beyond communities. We intend G&L to be an inclusive term, but one that needs to be used with attention to particularities and individual subjectivities. In addition, we are aware that this paper may not adequately address the positions of bisexual and

transgender individuals. As Evans (1994) suggests, the sexual discourses of these groups may be the most potent of discourses, and we hope future work will explore these discourses further.

2. Kisses between same-sex individuals, of course, are rarely shown on television.

3. We do not mean to imply, however, that this feeling of difference is essential or that all gays and lesbians share these feelings.

4. It has been argued that there is always a space "outside," for that is how the "inside" defines itself (Foucault, 1977). While homosexuals have occupied this space for some time, who occupies the space is a function of which borders the "inside" perceives as important.

5. For further discussion of the relationships between lesbian and gay cultures and capitalism, see Clark (1991), D'Emilio (1983), Evans (1994), and Ingraham (1994).

6. In our study, the term "community" was frequently used to describe the space(s) that lesbians and gays as a whole occupy.

7. For a thorough discussion of this debate, see the articles dedicated to exploring the relationship between queer theory and sociology, in *Sociological Theory*, July 1994, edited by Steven Seidman.

8. The discussion of style, however, is not meant to be restricted to apparel.

9. To the question "What is your sex?", 33 women described themselves as female; 24 men described themselves as male. Three individuals used terms which incorporated their gender and sexuality without assuming the biologically-determined categories of "female" and "male." Phrases such as "earth butch mama" and "female most of the time" and "MTF (male-to-female) of dubious sexuality" were used. For this paper, we use the terms "male" and "female" as signals of the informants' representation, because they were most often used in conversation.

10. To the question "How do you describe your sexuality?", 28 women and 23 men described their sexuality as homosexual, using such terms as gay, lesbian, dyke, fag, or queer. Five women and one man described themselves as bisexual, and three women did not offer a response.

11. The women's ages ranged between 19 and 50 years, with a mean of 29. The men's ages ranged from 19 to 40, with a mean of 25.

12. Race is a difficult and increasingly problematic descriptor; hence, we chose to ask subjects about their ethnicity. However, because the language of race is so embedded in our culture, responses were often framed in terms that do not distinguish between race and ethnicity.

13. The double-edged nature of visibility politics is a related, critical issue that needs to be explored in further depth (Phelan, 1993). We hope this paper and the voices of the G&L consumers that it presents will begin to inform a debate that incorporates attention to the issue of symbolic consumption in the dual contexts of community coalescence and commodity capitalism.

14. It should be noted that in comparison with the general public, gays and lesbians report higher numbers of drinking problems (McKirnan and Peterson, 1989).

15. Similar to the IKEA ad, media attention focuses almost exclusively on a "socially-acceptable" lesbian: predominately professional, white, upper-middle class.

16. We are indebted to Dora Epstein for this clever insight.

17. Consider, for example, Fox TV's edit of the male-to-male kiss in response to threats by the American Family Association to boycott major advertisers such as Burger King.

18. See Judith Butler (1990, 1993) for more about performativity, performance theory, and performing gender roles.

19. Since the aesthetic movement of the 1880s espoused by Oscar Wilde and others, the concept of "art for art's sake" has been associated with and attributed to the gay community. This association has often been an elitist one, based in part on the cultural figure of the "dandy," the antithesis of the middle-class, capitalist work ethic (Bronski 1984). Nevertheless, the conditions and requirements of capitalism, to a large extent, provided the L&G community with the economic and geographic means to coalesce in the twentieth century (D'Emilio 1983). Hence, a paradox seems to exist in the history of the subcultural community in relation to capitalism.

20. Camp can probably be characterized as the epitome of the gay sensibility. See Bergman (1993) for a review of the complexities associated with camp and style.

REFERENCES

Babuscio, J. (1993). Camp and the gay sensibility. In Bergman, D. (Ed.), *Camp grounds: Style and Homosexuality*. Amherst, MA: University of Massachusetts Press.

Barthes, R. (1974). *S/Z*. Translated by R. Miller. London: Jonathan Cape, Ltd.

Baudrillard, J. (1975). *The Mirror of Production*. Translated by M. Poster. St. Louis, MO: Telos Press.

Bergman, D. (Ed.) (1993). *Camp Grounds: Style and Homosexuality*. Amherst, MA: University of Massachusetts Press.

_____. (1991). *Gaiety Transfigured: Gay Self-Representation in American Literature*. Madison, WI: University of Wisconsin Press.

Blau, H. (1982-1983). Politics and the presentation of self: Disseminating *Sodom. Salmagundi*, 58 & 59, 221-251.

Bourdieu, P. (1984). *Distinction: A Social Critique of the Judgment of Taste*. Translated by R. Nice. Cambridge, MA: Harvard University Press.

Bronski, M. (1984). *Culture Clash: The Making of Gay Sensibility*. Boston, MA: South End Press.

Butler, J. (1990). *Gender Trouble: Feminism and the Subversion of Identity*. New York, NY: Routledge.

_____. (1993). *Bodies That Matter: On the Discursive Limits of "Sex."* New York, NY: Routledge.
Carmody, D. (1994). Time Inc. Considering starting a magazine for gay readers. *New York Times* (Jan. 24), p. D8.
Case, S. E. (1993). Toward a butch-femme aesthetic. In Abelove, H., Barale, M. A., & Halperin, D. (Eds.), *The Lesbian and Gay Studies Reader.* New York, NY: Routledge.
Clark, D. (1991). Commodity lesbianism. *Camera Obscura*, 25-26, 180-201.
Coward, C. (1992). After intense pressure, Bank America reverses its stand against the Boy Scout ban. *The Advocate* (September 22), p. 21.
Davis, F. (1992). *Fashion, Culture, and Identity.* Chicago, IL: University of Chicago Press.
D'Emilio, J. (1983). Capitalism and gay identity. In Snitow, A., Stansell, C., & Thompson, S. (Eds.), *Powers of Desire: The Politics of Sexuality.* New York, NY: Monthly Review Press.
Denzin, N. K. & Lincoln, Y. S. (1994). Introduction: Entering the field of qualitative research. In Denzin, N. K. & Lincoln, Y. S. (Eds.), *Handbook of Qualitative Research.* Thousand Oaks, CA: Sage Publications, Inc.
Evans, D. (1994). *Sexual Citizenship: The Material Construction of Sexualities.* London: Routledge.
Foucault, M. (1977). *Discipline and Punish: Birth of the Prison.* Translated by A. Sheridan. New York, NY: Pantheon.
Franchini, F. (Director) (1994). *Fell* [Film]. San Francisco, CA: Dackell Productions.
Gallagher, J. (1994). IKEA's gay gamble. *The Advocate* (May 3), 24-27.
_____. (1994). Million dollar mess. *The Advocate* (Oct. 4), 24-26.
Hebdige, D. (1979). *Subculture: The Meaning of Style.* London: Methuen.
hooks, b. (1992). *Black Looks: Race and Representation.* Boston, MA: South End Press.
Ingraham, C. (1994). The heterosexual imaginary: Feminist sociology and theories of gender. *Sociological Theory*, 12 (2), 203-219.
Kaiser, S. B. (1990). *The Social Psychology of Clothing: Symbolic Appearances in Context.* New York, NY: Macmillan.
Kaiser, S., Nagasawa, R., & Hutton, S. (1991). Fashion, postmodernity and personal appearance: A symbolic interactionist formulation. *Symbolic Interaction*, 14, 165-185.
Kasindorf, J. (1993). Lesbian chic: The bold, brave new world of gay women. *New York Magazine*, 26 (19), (May 10), 30-37.
Long, S. (1989). Useful laughter: Camp and seriousness. *Southwest Review*, 74, 53-70.
MacCannell, D. (1992). *Empty Meeting Grounds: The Tourist Papers.* London: Routledge.
McKirnan, D. & Peterson, P. (1989). Alcohol and drug use among homosexual men and women: Epidemiology and population characteristics. *Addictive Behavior*, 14, 545-553.

Newsweek (1993). Pride and prejudice: Lesbians come out strong. (June 21). pp. 56-60.

Newton, E. (1979). *Mother camp: Female impersonators in America.* Chicago, IL: University of Chicago Press.

Phelan, P. (1993). *Unmarked: The Politics of Performance.* London: Routledge.

Rich, A. (1980). Compulsory heterosexuality and the lesbian existence. *Signs: Journal of women in culture and society,* 5, 631-660.

Ross, A. (1988). Uses of camp. *Yale Journal of Criticism,* 2, 1-24.

Rudd, N. A. (1992). Clothing as a signifier in the perceptions of college male homosexuals. *Semiotica,* 91 (1/2), 67-78.

Schwartz, J. (1992). Gay consumers come out spending. *American Demographics* (April), 10-11.

Sedgwick, E. (1993). Epistemology of the closet. In Abelove, H., Barale, M. A., & Halperin, D. (Eds.), *The Lesbian and Gay Studies Reader.* New York, NY: Routledge.

Smith, B. (1993). Homophobia, why bring it up? In Abelove, H., Barale, M. A., & Halperin, D. (Eds.), *The Lesbian and Gay Studies Reader.* New York, NY: Routledge.

Solomon, M. (1994). *Consumer Behavior: Buying, Having and Being.* Boston, MA: Allyn & Bacon.

Staff. (1994). *Victory! The National Gay Entrepreneur Magazine, 1* (May), p. 4.

Stanley, L. & Wise, S. (1993). *Breaking Out Again: Feminist Ontology and Epistemology.* London: Routledge.

Seidman, S. (Ed.) (1994). *Sociological Theory,* 12 (2).

Stein, A. & Plummer, K. (1994). "I can't even think straight": "Queer" theory and the missing sexual revolution in sociology. *Sociological Theory,* 12 (2), 178-187.

Tuller, D. (1994). Gays, lesbians listed as 6% of population. *San Francisco Chronicle* (June 10), p. A3.

Unity Expo. (1994). *Girlfriends: The magazine of lesbian enjoyment* (July), p. 2.

Vanity Fair (1993). k.d. lang cuts it close. 56 (8) (August), 94-99, 142-146.

Viengener, M. (1993). Kinky escapades, bedroom techniques, unbridled passion, and secret sex codes. In Bergman, D. (Ed.), *Camp grounds: Style and Homosexuality.* Amherst, MA: University of Massachusetts Press.

Vogue (1993). Sexual politics: Goodbye to the last taboo. 183 (July), 86-92.

Wilson, E. (1993). Fashion and the postmodern body. In Ash, J. & Wilson, E. (Eds.), *Chic Thrills: A Fashion Reader.* Berkeley, CA: University of California Press.

Wilson, E. (1990). All the rage. In Gaines, J. & Herzog, C. (Eds.), *Fabrications: Costume and the Female Body.* New York, NY: Routledge.

Appearance
and Self-Presentation Research
in Gay Consumer Cultures:
Issues and Impact

Nancy A. Rudd, PhD

The Ohio State University

SUMMARY. Individuals present themselves to others through a variety of verbal and non-verbal behaviors. Appearance represents a non-verbal behavior which consumes a significant amount of our time, effort, and thought. We create and monitor our appearances in relation to cultural standards of attractiveness, relying on a wide range of appearance products and services to do so. The purpose of this paper is to examine the impact of appearance and self-presentation among gay consumers, to discuss issues relating to conducting gay consumer research, to discuss implications for marketing strategies, and to suggest recommendations for further research on specific aspects of appearance management as they may affect marketing to gay consumers.

Two studies are reported herein. The first study examines differences in perception among homosexual men when viewing a stimulus person dressed in six distinctly different modes of expression.

Nancy A. Rudd is Associate Professor of Consumer & Textile Sciences at The Ohio State University. Correspondence should be addressed to: Department of Consumer and Textile Sciences, 265 Campbell Hall, 1787 Neil Avenue, Columbus, OH 43210. E-mail: *rudd.1@postbox.acs.ohio-state.edu*

[Haworth co-indexing entry note]: "Appearance and Self-Presentation Research in Gay Consumer Cultures: Issues and Impact." Rudd, Nancy A. Co-published simultaneously in *Journal of Homosexuality* (The Haworth Press, Inc.) Vol. 31, No. 1/2, 1996, pp. 109-134; and: *Gays, Lesbians, and Consumer Behavior: Theory, Practice, and Research Issues in Marketing* (ed: Daniel L. Wardlow) The Haworth Press, Inc., 1996, pp. 109-134; and: *Gays, Lesbians, and Consumer Behavior: Theory, Practice, and Research Issues in Marketing* (ed: Daniel L. Wardlow) Harrington Park Press, an imprint of The Haworth Press, Inc., 1996, pp. 109-134. Single or multiple copies of this article are available from The Haworth Document Delivery Service [1-800-342-9678, 9:00 a.m. - 5:00 p.m. (EST)].

Social impressions of the stimulus person were different on 15 pairs of characteristics, with certain modes of dress resulting in greater consistency of response and others resulting in greater variability of response. The second study explores differences in aesthetic responses between homosexual and heterosexual men with respect to 14 apparel style categories and 3 fragrance categories. It was found that homosexual men had significantly different responses to innovative, trendy variations in 6 categories of dress, while both homosexual and heterosexual men had similar responses for classic, traditional variations in style categories that might constitute a basic college campus wardrobe (jeans, casual shirts, casual pants, underwear, and coats). Scent preferences also differed between the two groups of respondents. Homosexual men preferred floral, sweet fragrance categories and oriental, spicy categories, while heterosexual men preferred woody, green fragrance categories.

These studies suggest that different appearance aesthetics may operate for homosexual and heterosexual men, findings that may have implications for marketing strategies and for understanding the importance of appearance in socialization and self-presentation. Issues relating to conducting consumer studies such as these are discussed, including approval from institutional review boards, sample selection and setting, and measurement. Marketing strategies are discussed relative to target market, product, promotion, distribution, and pricing. Finally, recommendations are offered for further research relating to appearance and self-presentation among gay consumers. *[Article copies available from The Haworth Document Delivery Service: 1-800-342-9678.]*

INTRODUCTION

We use cognitive categories to make sense of the world around us. In fact, the process of categorization is a built-in mechanism for human beings to distinguish, classify, and organize the wide range of people, objects, and phenomena they experience in life. Through categorization we exaggerate differences between groups and lessen differences within groups (Linville, 1982). Cultural categories are cognitive heuristics that permit individuals to classify and identify particular behavior and events (e.g., dress, traditions) and people according to a pre-existing conceptualization of the world (McCracken, 1986). These categories are constructed in specific cultural and historical moments. Categories are linked to gender, physical appearance and ability, age, social class, and ethnicity (Kaiser, 1990). Appearance helps to solidify these cultural coordinates of meaning. In other words, one's appearance can identify oneself as a distinct member of a cultural category.

Cultural identification strongly impacts on individuals' lives and leads to distinctions among people that can result in differential social position (e.g., prestige, privilege, and power) (Kaiser, 1990). How identity is expressed to others can be critical to emphasizing or deemphasizing cultural membership. For example, dress and appearance can be used to distinguish oneself clearly as a member of young, attractive, upwardly mobile cultural categories. Alternatively, a different collection of apparel items and appearance could create an image signifying membership in a less powerful group (older adults, working class). Thus, presenting oneself through appearance can help to clarify or blur boundaries between certain categories.

We present ourselves to others through a variety of verbal and non-verbal behaviors. Appearance is one mode of non-verbal behavior, which we manage through a collection of strategies including apparel and accessory selection, cosmetic and grooming procedures, and modification of body form and size (e.g., dieting, exercising, weight training, surgical implants or reconstruction). We actively create and monitor our appearance in relation to cultural standards of attractiveness. These appearance standards are learned through socialization and are revised as we compare ourselves to other members of our own social group (Richins, 1991; Tesser, 1980). Clothing and other appearance products are used to enhance our appearance with the ultimate goal of obtaining the benefits ascribed to attractive persons (Bloch & Richins, 1992).

Given its controversy, the male homosexual culture has been a somewhat elusive social culture to study. In fact, it is probably more appropriate to think of the gay consumer culture as comprising several distinct subcultures. Core characteristics of any subculture are: a distinctive vocabulary and manner of expression, and "style, dress, and folk ways" that may differ from those in the general culture. Thus, the homosexual population may encompass several subcultures, each one having a distinctive mode of expression. This may be particularly true in large urban areas. In fact, Johnson (1993) suggests that mainstream marketers should concentrate on those urban gay consumer cultures with above-average incomes, implying that these individuals influence the buying decisions of other gay consumers irrespective of culture, and a greater number of heterosexual consumers who borrow from gay culture.

The purpose of the current paper is four-fold: (1) to share information, gleaned through research, about the impact of appearance and self-presentation among gay consumers, (2) to discuss issues related to conducting research in gay consumer cultures, (3) to discuss implications for marketing strategies, and (4) to suggest recommendations for further market research of gay consumer cultures. Given the scant literature on marketing to homosexual consumers, it is hoped this paper will serve as a catalyst to marketing researchers and instructors. Finally, this writer hopes to underscore the point that the social psychology of appearance can be extended to any cultural subgroup. By including cultural minorities as part of a marketing strategy we become both inclusive of others and more profitable in our businesses.

MARKETING OF APPEARANCE PRODUCTS TO GAY CONSUMERS

Meaning is socially constructed and reconstructed through appearance. Self-presentation through appearance may allow homosexual men to proclaim both personal and social identity, and thus achieve a strong sense of identity within a larger culture that may stigmatize or marginalize them. Several factors supporting the viability of marketing to gay consumers include size, buying power, lifestyle characteristics (such as travel and entertainment), and the culturally prescribed social importance of apparel and grooming aids. Exact figures concerning the size of a homosexual market segment vary from 14 million (Johnson, 1993) to 25 million gay men and women (Miller, 1992b), of which approximately two-thirds are estimated to be male. However, certain urban areas (e.g., New York, San Francisco, Los Angeles, and Washington, D.C.) contain a greater proportion of gays and lesbians–15% to 22% of the city population (Stabiner, 1982). Market research suggests that the gay community is a powerful buying market. Simmons Market Research Bureau (Miller, 1990) reported that the average income of readers of eight gay newspapers in 1988 was $55,430, compared to a national average of $32,114; households earning over $100,000 constituted 12% of their readership, compared to 2.5% of households in the general population reported by the Census Bureau (Miller, 1990). Overlooked Opinions, a market research firm dedicated to tracking homosexual consumers, cites a higher median level of education for gay consumers (15.7 years) than for the general population (12.7 years) (Schwartz, 1992.) It is assumed that most gay consumers do not have children and therefore do not have the additional expenses associated with them, resulting in a higher level of discretionary income. It is important to note that these surveys are polls of openly gay men and probably do not include incomes and other demographic information of closeted homosexual men or homosexual men currently married to women. Urban white professionals may also be over-represented in such surveys.

Several pieces of evidence suggest the spending power of gay consumers equals or exceeds what heterosexuals spend on equivalent services (e.g., entertainment, dining out, travel, exercising at private clubs) and material goods (liquor, clothing, fragrances, books, greeting cards, and compact discs). See Davis, 1993; Elliott, 1990; Miller, 1990; and Miller 1992a for a complete review. Gay consumers have also been characterized as being brand loyal (Rodkin, 1990) and image conscious in fashion and luxury products (Levin, 1993; Miller, 1990). These very psychographic characteristics have prompted such mainstream apparel marketers as Banana Republic, Benetton, Calvin Klein, and Perry Ellis to directly appeal to gay consumers through advertising campaigns in the last few years (Levin, 1993).

Appearance has been found to be an important factor in homosexual socialization (Marmor, 1980), both in terms of attraction and communication. Homosexual men have been found to strongly value aspects of physical appearance such as body build, grooming, attractiveness, and dress (Kleinberg, 1980; Lakoff & Scherr, 1984). Reasons cited for a focus on appearances among gay men include the relation of appearance and sexual behavior (Hagen, 1979; Symons, 1979), the socially conditioned attraction of some homosexual men to a narrow range of body types which results in an increased focus on physical attractiveness over other personal characteristics (Clark, 1977), and the threat of rejection if a man does not live up to some socialized standard of attractiveness himself (Sergios & Cody, 1985/86).

SELF-PRESENTATION OF HOMOSEXUAL IDENTITY

The homosexual identity is just one of several identities incorporated into an individual's self-concept (Troiden, 1989), and may be presented to others in varying degrees. One's sexual identity may be a self-identity, a perceived identity, a presented identity, or all three together (Cass, 1984a). *Self-identity* operates when an individual sees himself as gay. *Perceived identity* occurs in social settings in which the individual believes others perceive him as gay. *Presented identity* results from presenting oneself as gay in specific social contexts. Clearly, the most fully integrated identity is one in which self-identity, perceived identity, and presented identity are consistent (Troiden, 1989). Roach-Higgins and Eicher (1992) suggest that, as individuals experience interactions with others, they develop predictions of what others' reactions toward them will be. If the predictions are accurate, a gay man's self-identity will agree with his identity as perceived by others. Moreover, social interaction is evaluated as satisfactory when the presenter and perceiver are at similar places of identity achievement.

Homosexual identity formation occurs in stages (Cass, 1984b; Troiden, 1989), often occurring within a setting of social stigma, undoubtedly affecting both the formation and the expression of identity. Typical stages of identity formation include: (1) sensitization, usually occurring before puberty, when individuals have general feelings of marginality and perceptions of being different from same-sex peers; (2) identity confusion, usually during adolescence, when thoughts of possible homosexuality cause inner turmoil and uncertainty; (3) identity assumption, during or after adolescence, when homosexuality is accepted as a self-identity and a presented identity at least to others of the same sexual orientation; (4) commitment, adopting homosexuality as a way of life, and presenting that identity publicly (although the degree of disclosure may vary) (Troiden, 1989). Identity synthesis occurs when an individual has self-identified as homosexual, has presented that identity to others, and is content to have that gay identity perceived by others (Cass, 1984a).

Identities are socially constructed. Some of the scholarship on the social construction of gay identity has included interpretation of texts, cultural codes, signifying practices, and social attitudes toward homosexuality (Escoffier, 1992). Cultural codes and signifying practices have particular relevance to appearance management. Therefore, two studies will be discussed which investigate the existence of a semiotic code and an aesthetic code that may operate to some degree within gay consumer cultures.

SEMIOTIC CODES

Appearance may serve as a sign system that exists within the gay community, as well as within any other community or subculture. A study was conducted to explore the existence of an underlying code that links specific appearance signs in some manner and thereby constitutes meaning among gay men. As previously discussed, clothing is a cultural sign system that serves a communicative function. It is used on a daily basis by individuals, groups, and entire cultures to create specific impressions and subsequently to interact with one another based on those impressions. Kaiser (1990) suggests that we continually "negotiate" meaning through our appearances and interactions. Interaction is constantly negotiated between the sender and receiver of appearance messages, as symbols acquire new meanings and thus suggest new responses. The present study focused on (1) whether gay men would prefer to interact socially with a stimulus person in one particular appearance style; (2) whether gay men preferred appearances in others that closely resembled their own appearance styles; and (3) whether agreement existed among gay men on characteristics perceived in six stimulus appearances. Forty homosexual men (a convenience sample recruited from a campus, gay student organization) participated in the study. Respondents completed (1) a psychographic measure of sexual and sociopolitical attitudes, personality characteristics, and openness of sexual identity, and (2) a person perception measure of the stimulus appearances. Respondents used a seven-point Likert scale to rate the appearances on 15 bipolar, person-perception adjectives adapted from Conner, Peters, and Nagasawa (1975). These adjective pairs were:

- conservative/liberal
- homosexual/heterosexual
- extroverted/introverted
- attractive/unattractive
- friendly/hostile
- masculine/feminine
- impulsive/cautious
- sociable/unsociable
- lively/reserved
- analytical/artistic
- down to earth/pretentious
- worldly/naive
- responsible/irresponsible
- trustworthy/untrustworthy
- willingness/unwillingness to interact socially

After viewing the slides again, subjects indicated with which one of the six appearances they would be most likely to interact socially. The nature of this likely social interaction was not defined any further, thus allowing each respondent to define it as he wished.

The six appearance manipulations were based on visual personality typologies identified by Fischer (1977), Kron (1986), McJimsey (1973), Snezek (1986), and Von Furstenberg (1978). These typologies had distinct visual characteristics and represented points along a visual continuum. Face validity of these appearance manipulations was established through focus interviews with homosexual men and then with a panel of experts who were familiar with the typologies and who came to agreement that selected images represented the six types. A pretest (Johnson, 1989) verified that the six appearances were accurate interpretations of the six points along the continuum. Because the meaning of clothing signs may change over time, the resulting choices were a somewhat conservative interpretation of contemporary styles. Slides of each clothing appearance were taken, with variables such as background, lighting, distance from the camera, and facial expression of the model held constant. The resulting appearance styles included:

- Dramatic   black pants and turtleneck, iridescent green jacket with contemporary styling (representing striking, sophisticated, high fashion appearance).
- Athletic   jeans, brown cotton rag sweater (casual, natural appearance).
  natural
- Classic   grey slacks, white turtleneck, traditional navy blazer (conservative, refined appearance).
- Romantic   white pants, pastel striped sweater (luxurious, soft appearance).
- Gamin   grey pants, black and red lumberjack shirt (carefree, informal appearance).
- Ingenue   baggy black overalls with rolled legs, white tee shirt with humorous motif (trendy, detailed appearance).

(Refer to Rudd, 1992; for additional information.)

Findings on the psychographic measure revealed that both sexual and socio-political attitudes ranged from moderate to slightly liberal. In self-identifying their personality types, 11 respondents each self-selected classic and ingenue typologies; gamin and dramatic were chosen by 7 each; romantic was selected by 3 men; athletic/natural was selected by 1 subject. It should be noted that all subjects reported the degree to which they expressed their sexuality. These frequency data suggest that respondents were moderately to somewhat open in expressing their sexual orientation to others.

The stimulus person was perceived much differently when dressed in each of the six appearance styles. Table 1 compares mean scores for all six appearance styles on each set of adjectives. On certain adjective pairs, the six appearances were seen as much more distinct, as indicated by mean ranges of 3-4 points (i.e., 2.88 to 3.87). These pairs included conservative/liberal, homosexual/heterosexual, extroverted/introverted, attractive/unattractive, impulsive/cautious, lively/reserved, and analytical/artistic. For example, the athletic variation was perceived as the most conservative, while the ingenue variation was perceived as the most liberal. The ingenue variation was perceived as the most homosexual in appearance, while both the gamin and the athletic variations were perceived as most heterosexual. On other adjective pairs, the six appearance styles were not perceived much differently from one another, as indicated by mean ranges of .95 (friendly/hostile) to 1.7 (trustworthy/untrustworthy). Respondents expressed the most desire to interact socially with the stimulus person when dressed in the classic variation, which was also the appearance style most often reported as being held by the respondents themselves. The controlled setting of the experiment may have led to this perception of willingness to interact, since perception

TABLE 1. Mean Responses to Appearance Styles on Bi-Polar Adjectives (rated 1-7)

Conservative–Liberal		Homosexual–Heterosexual		Extroverted–Introverted	
D	4.80	D	3.18	D	3.45+
A	2.53+	A	5.10	A	4.45
C	5.00*	C	2.68	C	3.36
R	3.65	R	3.80+	R	3.98
G	2.60	G	5.30	G	5.43
I	6.40	I	1.83	I	2.40

Attractive-Unattractive		Friendly–Hostile		Masculine–Feminine	
D	2.93	D	3.78	D	3.48
A	3.78	A	3.30	A	2.58
C	2.65	C	3.85	C	3.58+
R	4.33	R	2.90	R	4.20
G	5.53	G	3.45	G	3.10
I	4.20	I	3.25	I	5.08

Impulsive–Cautious		Sociable–Unsociable		Lively–Reserved	
D	3.85	D	3.28	D	3.95+
A	5.30+	A	3.70	A	5.13+
C	3.60	C	3.23	C	3.83
R	4.08	R	3.65	R	3.85*
G	5.25	G	4.88	G	5.30
I	2.23	I	2.83	I	2.35

Analytical–Artistic		Down to earth–Pretentious		Worldly–Naive	
D	4.93	D	3.93	D	2.83
A	2.75	A	2.73	A	4.45
C	5.00	C	4.98*	C	3.00+
R	3.80	R	3.73+	R	4.45
G	2.35	G	2.63	G	5.18
I	5.78	I	4.40+	I	3.50+

Responsible-Irresponsible		Trustworthy–Untrustworthy		Willing–Unwilling to Interact	
D	3.18	D	3.58	D	3.20
A	2.88	A	3.20	A	3.90
C	3.95	C	3.73	C	2.93
R	3.78	R	3.40	R	4.43
G	3.20+	G	3.20+	G	5.10
I	5.25+	I	4.90	I	4.08

D = dramatic, A = athletic/natural, C = classic, R = romantic, G = gamin, I = ingenue.
* = significant chi square values related to sexual attitudes
+ = significant chi square values related to sociopolitical attitudes

tends to lean toward safe ground when social context or other interpersonal communication is unavailable to the perceiver.

Of all six variations, the ingenue received the most extreme ratings overall. It was perceived as most liberal, homosexual, extroverted, feminine, impulsive, sociable, lively, artistic, irresponsible, and untrustworthy.

The dramatic variation had fewer extreme responses. The gamin and athletic variations were rated similarly on many of the variables, suggesting little difference in the appearance messages of those appearance variations based on the scales used.

Chi square tests of independence indicated that only in a few instances did sexual attitudes affect perception of specific variables. For the athletic typology, holding liberal or conservative sexual attitudes affected ratings on the conservative/liberal appearance variable (chi square = 9.60, p = .047) and the down-to-earth/pretentious variable (chi square = 9.725, p = .045). For the romantic typology, attitudes affected ratings on the lively/reserved variable (chi square = 10.320, p = .035). Socio-political attitudes affected ratings of specific variables in more cases, with significant chi square values found for 2 variables on 4 slides and 3 variables on 2 slides. However, 2 to 3 variables out of a possible 15 variables for each slide meant that these attitudes really played no substantial role overall in the perception of appearance variations. Those appearances for which significant values were noted are as follows:

- Athletic   —conservative/liberal (chi square = 10.730, df = 4, p = .03)
             —impulsive/cautious (chi square = 12.395, df = 4, p = .015)
             —lively/reserved (chi square = 9.955, df = 4, p = .041)
- Classic   —masculine/feminine (chi square = 10.812, df = 4, p = .029)
             — worldly/naive (chi square = 6.042, df = 4, p = .049)
- Ingenue   —down-to-earth/pretentious (chi square = 13.333, df = 4, p = .010)
             —worldly/naive (chi square = 10.551, df = 4, p = .032)
             —responsible/irresponsible (chi square = 6.784, df = 4, p = .034)
- Dramatic   —extroverted/introverted (chi square = 10.628, df = 4, p = .031)
             —lively/reserved (chi square = 11.085, df = 4, p = .026)
- Romantic   —homosexual/heterosexual (chi square = 9.804, df = 4, p = .044)
             —down-to-earth/pretentious (chi square = 10.115, df = 4, p = .039)
- Gamin   —responsible/irresponsible (chi square = 11.784, df = 4, p = .019)
             —trustworthy/untrustworthy (chi square = 17.243, df = 4, p = .002)

Some implications are suggested by the study. First, there seems to be evidence that, as in most subcultures or communities of any type, a semiotic code operates within this particular community as well. Respondents were more consistent than inconsistent in attributing similar meaning to each of the six appearances. Second, respondents often identified with the stimulus person on some level as indicated through comments suggesting that the stimulus person had similar taste or dressed as they themselves did. Third, comments by respondents suggested that the nature of the social setting would affect how they viewed the characteristics of the appearance. In fact, many respondents desired additional information about social context to help them in interpreting meaning, offering that bars, parties, and informal settings are perceived differently than work or professional settings. The slides showed the stimulus person against a white, photographic studio background rather than in any particular social context. Other comments suggested that gay men may prefer two separate wardrobes, one for the gay social scene and one for office or everyday interaction with heterosexuals.

If, even to a small degree, an appearance code operates to constitute meaning among homosexual men, then it is necessary to study aesthetic responses to particular elements used in presenting oneself to others through appearance. Are there qualitative characteristics that can help define apparel shopping behavior, preferences for particular styles of appearance, or preferences for certain types of fragrance? What are the parameters, if any, of an aesthetic code that may operate among homosexual men? Elliott (1990) believes that homosexual men are considered to be a trend-setting subculture that influences other consumers. Other authors concur (Martin, 1993; Wilson, 1993), citing examples of imagery that have crossed over into mainstream imagery.

AESTHETIC CODE

To examine the extent to which differences in aesthetic responses to appearance may exist between homosexual men and heterosexual men, another study was undertaken. The variables examined were responses to various apparel style categories and fragrance categories. Apparel shopping behavior was another variable that was studied. Descriptive data were collected through a questionnaire from a purposive sample of 47 self-identified homosexual men and 48 self-identified heterosexual men attending a major midwestern university. The instruments used included a section on shopping orientation and store patronage, a clothing style preference section containing line drawings of 14 apparel style categories representing 3 aesthetic types (innovative/trendy, classic/traditional, and casual/relaxed), and a fragrance section that included fragrance usage questions and 15 fragrances that respondents were asked to evaluate.

The apparel style categories included sweaters, jeans, dress shirts, dress pants, sportcoats, casual shirts, casual pants, outerwear jackets, underwear, dress shoes, casual shoes, coats, socks, and ties. Fragrance preferences were measured via a scent test of 15 fragrances representing 3 industry categories (woody, green; Oriental, spicy; floral, sweet). To arrive at the apparel categories, 6 experts in fashion merchandising/design were given 83 photographs of men's fashion taken from several issues of *GQ*. Each person used the Q-sort method to sort the photographs into the 14 categories and the 3 aesthetic types; the most consistent photographs were kept. Photographs were transposed into line drawings using the same male figure in order to keep pose and size of model constant, a visual methodology substantiated by Whisney, Winakor, and Wolins (1979). With the assistance of a men's fragrance buyer, cologne samples were selected that represented equal numbers of fragrances in each of the 3 categories. Blotter paper cards were saturated with each of the fragrances and stored in glassine envelopes to keep scents from blending. Cards were given to subjects in groups of 5 and evaluated at different times throughout the administration of the questionnaire to avoid scent fatigue. A pretest of the instrument was given to 5 homosexual men and 5 heterosexual men to determine content validity (Snezek, 1986). The aesthetic types were readily distinguishable, as were the fragrances.

Shopping behavior varied between homosexual and heterosexual men. Homosexual men spent more time shopping (t = 2.75, p = .0072), enjoyed shopping more (t = 5.29, p = .0001), and viewed shopping as a means of gathering fashion information without necessarily intending to purchase (t = 2.27, p = .026). They also spent more on apparel annually than did heterosexual respondents (chi square = 23.21, df = 3, p = .0001).

Overall, homosexual respondents stated they were more likely to prefer innovative/trendy styles (M = 3.62) than were heterosexual respondents (M = 2.19), a difference that was significant (chi square = 15.54, df = 4, p = .0004). With respect to apparel aesthetics, Table 2 indicates that there was no singular aesthetic type (innovative/trendy; classic/traditional; casual/relaxed) that was consistently preferred across all 14 apparel style categories by respondents of one sexual orientation or the other. Homosexual men did prefer innovative/trendy styles more often than heterosexual men, who almost never preferred trendy styles (5 categories versus none). There were some clear differences within style categories. For example, few differences in response existed between homosexual and heterosexual men for jeans, casual pants, casual shirts, underwear, and coats. The classic/traditional aesthetic type was consistently preferred, perhaps because most men perceive these items to constitute a basic campus wardrobe and

TABLE 2. Clothing Style Preferences of Homosexual and Heterosexual Men

Style	Group*	Trendy		Traditional		Casual	
		N	%	N	%	N	%
Sweaters	Ho (N = 47)	18	38.3	11	23.4	13	27.7**
	He (N = 48)	11	22.9	21	44.7	13	27.1
Jeans	Ho	6	12.7	28	59.6	8	17.0
	He	8	16.6	32	66.6	5	10.4
Dress Shirts	Ho	18	38.3	6	12.7	19	40.4
	He	5	10.4	12	25.0	30	62.5
Dress Pants	Ho	25	53.2	8	17.0	13	27.7
	He	11	22.9	18	37.5	12	25.0
Sport Coats	Ho	16	34.0	14	29.8	13	27.7
	He	8	16.6	21	43.8	16	33.3
Casual Shirts	Ho	17	36.2	21	44.7	4	8.5
	He	6	12.5	31	64.6	5	10.4
Outer Jackets	Ho	32	68.1	7	14.8	2	4.2
	He	15	31.3	18	37.5	5	10.4
Casual Pants	Ho	6	12.7	20	42.5	13	27.7
	He	0	0	24	50.0	16	33.3
Undergarments	Ho	14	29.9	28	59.6	3	6.3
	He	7	14.5	21	43.8	11	22.9
Dress Shoes	Ho	14	29.8	8	17.0	21	44.7
	He	15	31.3	6	12.5	24	50.0
Coats	Ho	8	17.0	29	61.7	5	10.6
	He	6	12.5	35	72.9	4	8.3
Socks	Ho	14	29.8	12	25.5	19	40.4**
	He	1	2.1	21	43.8	19	39.6
Neckties	Ho	24	51.1	9	19.1	11	23.4
	He	9	18.8	19	39.6	13	27.1
Casual Shoes	Ho	10	21.3	17	36.2**	18	38.3
	He	1	2.1	17	35.4	26	54.2

* Does not include "don't wear" and "none of the above" responses.

**Differing percentages are due to differences in Ns in two samples.

thus serve more utilitarian purposes than expressive purposes. Insignificant chi square values were found for jeans and coats. Casual pants, casual shirts, and underwear had significant chi square values due to disagreements in the evaluation of the trendy aesthetic variation, which homosexual men preferred more than did heterosexual men. Fisher's Exact probabilities were computed to confirm chi square probabilities if cells had expected counts less than 5. For casual pants, chi square was 6.66 (df = 2, p = .036, Fisher's Exact p = .036); for casual shirts, chi square was 7.295 (df = 2, p = .026, Fisher's Exact p = .027); for underwear, chi square was 7.52 (df = 2, p = .023, Fisher's Exact p = .024).

However, within style categories that were not perceived to constitute a basic wardrobe, there were clear differences in aesthetic preferences. For example, homosexual men preferred the innovative/trendy aesthetic style in the following categories:

- dress pants (chi square = 9.07, df = 2, p = .011, Fisher's Exact p = .011)
- dress shirts (chi square = 11.66, df = 2, p = .003, Fisher's Exact p = .003)
- outerwear jackets (chi square = 12.18, df = 2, p = .002, Fisher's Exact p = .001)
- ties (chi square = 10.46, df = 2, p = .005, Fisher's Exact p = .0046)
- socks (chi square = 13.57, df = 2, p = .001, Fisher's Exact p = .0007)
- casual shoes (chi square = 8.81, df = 2, p = .012, Fisher's Exact p = .011).

Heterosexual men preferred casual/relaxed styles in these style categories. No significant differences were found for categories of sport coats, sweaters, and dress shoes. That is, both heterosexual and homosexual men preferred these equally (see means in Table 2).

Differences were also noted with respect to fragrance aesthetics. Significant differences were found in fragrance usage. Homosexual men used cologne daily (chi square = 8.97, df = 4, p = .05), while heterosexual men used it occasionally (chi square = 17.51, df = 4, p = .05). Significant differences were also noted in which categories of fragrance respondents felt more attractive and sexually appealing. Homosexual men identified floral/sweet fragrances, while heterosexual men identified woody/green fragrances (chi square = 11.56, df = 2, p = .05). There was no statistical difference for average number of fragrances worn (M = 5 for homosexual men, M = 4 for heterosexual men). Floral/sweet and Oriental/spicy fragrances were preferred by more homosexual men, while heterosexual men preferred woody/green fragrances (chi square = 114.65, df = 2, p = .05). By and large, fragrances preferred by homosexual men were not preferred by heterosexual men, and vice versa. (See Rudd & Tedrick, 1994, for a more complete analysis of data.)

Conclusions from this study suggest that some homosexual men may prefer more novel, trendy or creative ways in which to present themselves than do some heterosexual men, both in apparel styles and in fragrance. This finding supports opinions in the literature that gay consumer cultures may lean toward a more image-sensitive, fashionable, distinguishing presentation of themselves to others (Johnson, 1993; Levin, 1993; Marmor,

1980; Stabiner, 1982). However, the literature to date does not suggest how such images are operationalized, if they are. There is great room for studying how narrow or broad any aesthetic codes may be within various gay consumer cultures, and what specific characteristics of appearance may be related to stages of identity formation.

ISSUES RELATED TO CONDUCTING RESEARCH ON GAY CONSUMER CULTURES

Several issues have arisen in conducting these research studies on gay consumer cultures. While these concerns may apply to the study of nearly any consumer culture, these specific experiences and considerations surfaced when studying gay consumer cultures in the studies reported here.

Institutional Review Board Approval and Confidentiality/Risk

Most colleges and universities have institutional review boards that oversee the conducting of research, ensuring that the investigators abide by established ethical practices, do not cause any undue risk to the participant, and inform research participants about the nature of their responses (e.g., anonymous versus confidential) and how data will be stored. In larger universities, there may exist two separate review boards, one for the review of behavioral and social science research projects and another for review of clinical and natural science research projects. Typically, the principal investigators submit a complete research prospectus for the project, including the study's purpose and hypotheses, a theoretical basis for executing the research, methodology (sample size and selection, data collection procedures), and a clear description of procedures to be implemented that ensure the safety of the participants. Copies of intended instruments or measurement procedures and copies of oral and written directions are submitted in the approval packet.

In addition to maintaining standards of rigor and ethical conduct, this process provides investigators with feedback and validation of the methodology. Having colleagues outside of one's discipline carefully read and discuss one's proposal often results in suggestions that may strengthen the study. Another advantage is that subjects may be more likely to participate if they know that the study has been reviewed and approved. However, occasionally as a condition of approval, these committees may suggest changes to the wording of questionnaires or to the methodology itself that may reduce some perceived risk, yet weaken the quality of information gathered. Therefore, one must be careful to state exactly why some questions must remain somewhat personal, and be prepared to justify why any perceived risk can be countered through such strategies as not identifying respondents by name or other identifying information, or by allowing subjects to withdraw from the study at any time without penalty.

Sample Selection and Settings

To find enough homosexual subjects for a statistically sound analysis may require creative thinking. For example, a stratified sampling frame does not exist for homosexuals. Therefore, a completely random sample (i.e., one most desirable for inferring sample to populations) is not possible. Organizations such as university gay and lesbian alliance organizations or community organizations/centers that go by names such as lambda societies or Stonewall unions may provide settings with large sample size. However, unless the investigator is an active member of such organizations, they may be somewhat difficult to access. A procedure that has proven useful is to first write a letter to the organization leader(s) or center director(s) stating the research goals of the study and why this particular sample is important. Enclosing a brief prospectus of the research proposal, along with a letter indicating institutional board approval, is helpful. After the initial letter, a follow-up phone call will usually lead to a meeting of the organization leaders in which any questions can be answered. These meetings may allay any fears or misconceptions about the motivations of the investigator, and often result in great cooperation.

Mailing lists for gay consumer publications may seem to be a likely source if the research requires a mail survey; these are not only difficult to acquire, but they are quite expensive when they do exist. If time is of the essence, they are not very practical. It may take about 3-4 weeks to acquire a mailing list, then send the mailing; allowing sufficient response time (2-3 weeks), the entire process may require 5-7 weeks.

One technique that has proven effective in some cases is the "ripple" or "snowball" technique of subject selection, whereby a small number of gay consumers that the researcher may know individually will then ask 5 of their friends to participate, who in turn may ask 5 of their friends, and so on. It should be noted here that subjects recruited by this method are likely to be quite homogenous and systematic biases for data collected through this fashion are a likely outcome. While the snowball sampling technique may result in a substantial sample size, which would be suitable for a questionnaire to be distributed through some central point, it does not seem to work favorably for focus group interviews or an experimental research design that requires all subjects to meet in one location at a specified time.

Gay bars or clubs may be satisfactory settings for locating subjects, but they typically are not appropriate for actual data collection. Thus, arrangements may be warranted for data collection elsewhere. It may be appropriate to collect data in such settings if one is making observations about individual or group behavior with respect to appearance cues, but the investigator should have a detailed and accurate coding system and employ trained research assistants to assist with data collection. It may also be appropriate to conduct brief interviews with patrons, but they should be conducted in a quiet place away from the main activities in the bar or club. It may also be appropriate to hand out questionnaires, along with a return stamped envelope; however, response rate may not be as strong as desired.

Measurement–Sexual Orientation, Gay Identity; Response Issues

Sexual orientation is somewhat easier to measure than gay identity because it may rely on nominal or ordinal level scales. A nominal level scale classifies items into discrete groupings that have no relationships of magnitude to one another. If one were to ask respondents to identify their sexual orientation (homosexual or heterosexual), they would be classified into two groups; sexual orientation would therefore be a dichotomous variable, representing 2 discrete points on a nominal level scale. Alternatively, an ordinal level scale classifies items into groups according to differences in magnitude, but without assuming equal intervals between the groups. The Kinsey scale (The A. Kinsey Institute, 1974), is such a scale, with 7 designations ranging from exclusively homosexual to exclusively heterosexual, with bisexuality existing as middle responses. In this case, sexual orientation is treated as a continuous variable with many values between the end points of the scale. Shively, Jones, and DeCecco (1984) provide a thoughtful overview of how sexual orientation has been defined both conceptually and operationally in the research literature on this topic, concluding that wide variation exists in both conceptual and operational definitions.

Gay identity is not as easy to measure because it is a more complex concept, referring to the degree to which an individual is comfortable with his orientation as well as the degree to which he has accepted it as a self, perceived, and presented identity (Troiden, 1989). Yet, gay identity may be a more cogent variable in some studies than sexual orientation, so there are indeed ways to establish identity with some degree of confidence. Some would argue that gay identity exists only at the point when one's homosexual identity is actively presented to others and when affiliation with the gay community occurs (Cass, 1984a). Cass (1984b) presents a useful theoretical model that identifies 16 cognitive, behavioral, and affective dimensions of development that distinguish various stages of homosexual identity formation. She has developed a self-administered Stage Allocation Measure which relies on one-paragraph descriptions of attitudinal and behavioral characteristics along each of six stages of development. Troiden (1989) has developed a model based on four stages of development. The difficulty in measuring stages of identity formation lies in operationalizing the theoretical models. It may be easier to ask a series of probing questions to arrive at a subject's relative identity formation than to ask subjects to read through descriptions and self-select.

As in any methodological approach requiring self-report data, the risk exists that subjects will respond in a socially desirable way, or the way in which they believe the researcher or society wishes them to respond. In focus group interviews, subjects may feel particularly vulnerable since their responses are heard by all members of the group. These responses, of course, may not wholly represent the subject's feelings. Therefore, care must be taken to encourage complete responses by suggesting that there are no wrong answers, or that subjects must be sure to give their first and fullest responses, regardless of how they perceive others to feel about the topic.

DISCUSSION AND IMPLICATIONS

From this stream of research on appearance and self-presentation among gay men, there are several implications related to marketing strategy. Five specific aspects of marketing strategy will be discussed: target market, product, promotion, distribution, and pricing.

Target Market

Rather than targeting all gay men as one market segment with similar characteristics, needs, desires, attitudes and lifestyles, it seems much more prudent for marketers to clearly delineate various gay subcultures in order to design products and provide services that satisfy specific needs. Humphreys and Miller (1980) discuss the concepts of subcultures and scenes, both of which are smaller units of culture than the whole. Such smaller cultural groups exist within particular geographic or social parameters and have a distinctive value system and manner of expression. These authors point out that skills shared within subcultures are geared to providing assistance in earning a living, while skills shared within scenes tend to contribute only to recreational development (p. 144). Within gay culture, there may exist various business and professional subcultures as well as various scenes that are typically organized around recreational or social activities, including clubs and bars, performing groups, and political activist groups. Any one of these subcultures or scenes could provide rich data with respect to consumption needs and use of goods and services. For example, Moore (1994) has identified a categorization of gay club dress in a midwestern city, including leather, trendy, preppy/classic, club kid, and drag. Each of these categories has a rather specific set of expectations for dress. The gay community in this midwestern city also hosts an annual Halloween party and has hosted several female illusionist pageants. Thus, there exists in this locale a distinct market for ball gowns, provocative lingerie, wigs, and evening shoes and accessories in larger sizes than many women may wear. One costume rental company caters to these consumer needs. By comparing consumption patterns within and between different gay subcultures and scenes, this company has positioned itself rather lucratively to meet specific needs. Conversely, a much larger company in this same city has several retail divisions which could easily claim some market share by carrying larger size lingerie and evening wear, yet it has not considered that these markets exist.

It should be recognized that several gay subcultures do exist, particularly in metropolitan areas. They dress differently, act differently, attend different social events, and may wish to consume different goods and services. By identifying these narrower target markets, marketers can develop successful, highly targeted marketing strategies that appeal to each group. Market research firms can be helpful in identifying particular demographic and lifestyle characteristics of each group. These research firms can help big businesses to attract gay dollars with alternative approaches, and also encourage gay businesses or cooperatives to be more competitive in reaching customers.

Product

From the studies discussed, there are some clear implications for appearance products (apparel, fragrance) and services targeted to gay consumer cultures. While there is evidence to suggest that some gay men are more likely to be fashion innovators and fashion opinion leaders, it would be foolish to suggest that all marketers who wish to reach gay consumers do so through product mix that is very innovative and trendy. Because other gay consumers have tastes that run to the classic/traditional or to the casual/relaxed, it would be wise to specialize in one of these aesthetic styles if one is located in a particular geographic setting (e.g., campus strip mall, or perhaps an established gay neighborhood) or carry merchandise representing a mix of aesthetic styles if one is located in a non-specific locale. It would also be of benefit for specialty businesses to carry items for specific social events that are popular among gay consumer cultures (e.g., female illusionist pageants and performances). Gay dance clubs may promote particular modes of appearance that are sometimes categorized as outrageous or avant-garde; these present possibilities for specialty retailers.

In department store retail operations, product style categories could be mixed together in departments according to similar aesthetic categories (innovative/trendy, classic/traditional, casual/relaxed) instead of separating products into departments by style categories (suits, shirts, pants, coats, etc.) If the consumer has a more innovative/trendy preference, for example, he may be more motivated to shop in one or two departments that are located next to each other and that have a range of trendy apparel items in many product categories than to walk from department to department to find similar trendy items to constitute a complete outfit. Cologne could also be displayed together with this total concept, thereby suggesting a range of woody/green fragrances that might accompany a rugged outdoor look in apparel, or Oriental/spicy fragrances that might accessorize an elegant, dramatic, high fashion appearance.

Appearance services could be marketed with the same approach. For example, the idea of a "grand salon" which caters to hairstyling, manicures, pedicures, facials, styling of facial hair, body waxing, massages, and aromatherapy might be targeted to gay consumer cultures. If gay men spend more time shopping and enjoy it more than heterosexual men, it is likely that they would also spend time in establishments offering complete appearance services. Other strategies that could be used to attract gay men who enjoy shopping might include self-improvement seminars that focus on wardrobe planning or personal color analysis.

Promotion

Promotion issues focus on developing advertising, sales promotion, public relations, publicity, and other marketing communications campaigns to reach target audiences. If one examines product images being marketed to gay consumers, there are several issues that arise. Advertising images can be studied from the standpoint of describing (qualifying) the image itself, counting (quantifying) the frequency of particular products in particular publications or the saturation of product categories across publications, and examining the gatekeeping role of the product photographer or even the editorial staff in determining what products will be advertised and in what manner. Sutyak (1994) examined images of fashion products from Benetton and Banana Republic in issues of *Out*, concluding that the products were portrayed in a different manner than for mainstream publications such as *Interview* and *Vanity Fair*. Both Benetton and Banana Republic appeared to be less concerned with advertising the actual product in the gay publications and more concerned with appealing to some level of social consciousness among readers. However, it should be noted that many factors may enter into decisions about which ads run where. For example, Benetton may decide to put its advertising dollars into a multi-page ad in *Vanity Fair* because it will reach more consumers, and run fewer ads in *Out*. Editors of magazines with larger circulation may refuse a particular advertising image, and it may then be placed in a gay publication which may welcome advertising dollars with fewer restrictions on images. Other issues surrounding the representation of images focus on how masculinity is defined and represented differently in response to patterns of consumption. See Triggs (1992) for a complete review of masculine images in fashion over the past decade.

A firm's promotional decisions do not always need to differentiate between homosexual and heterosexual consumers, a finding supported by the research studies reported in this paper. Certain types of apparel (jeans, casual pants, casual shirts, underwear, coats) may be targeted to all men without specific promotional strategies. A jeans/pants company that can use one strategy to reach both homosexual and heterosexual consumers can be effective in sales and market share gains, while saving the company marketing and advertising dollars. Yet, evidence suggests that other categories of apparel such as dress pants, dress shirts, outerwear jackets, ties, socks, and casual shoes may benefit from sales promotions or advertising targeted directly to gay consumers. For categories with no clear distinction in preferences between homosexual and heterosexual men (sweaters, sport coats, dress shoes), promotional strategies could perhaps create more distinct patterns of consumption.

An interesting point of discussion is for firm branding strategies. Those firms that sell branded goods (i.e., "Guess" jeans, Rolex watches) could modify their brand names for the gay market and create separate brand identities or images. This might result in greater sales. Yet, if they maintain their existing brand identities and aggressively pursue gay consumers, heterosexual consumers might stop purchasing the items, resulting in declining sales.

Distribution

Where and how marketers make their products available to gay consumers is a critical consideration in marketing strategy. Because gyms and athletic clubs are important social scenes for some gay men (Moore, 1994), specialty retail operations housed in these facilities would likely prove to be profitable. These locations would also make private labeling a good risk and would most likely not require additional promotion.

In most cities of any size, one finds certain neighborhoods with higher concentrations of gay men, so specialty stores might be logically positioned there. In mega-malls that serve wide geographic areas, mall management would be well advised to include stores that cater apparel products and services to gay men. Of course, even some small stores in out-of-the-way places are successful via word-of-mouth advertising.

Seasonal distribution is another strategy that may be successful. Halloween and New Year's parties and balls that are held in many cities provide a need for formal evening wear and accessories, particularly in large women's sizes for those who attend in drag appearance. While there may not be enough business all year long to sustain a large-size women's shoe store, for example, a shoe store that would stock large sizes from September to January (and make that fact known in local gay business directories) would probably be patronized by gay consumers. Costume rental businesses, especially those who carry wigs in addition to evening wear, would also do well with this type of seasonal business.

Catalog distribution is an alternative worth exploring. While there are only a few nationally distributed catalogs, there is room for other national retailers to compete in the market. Even smaller retailers, or cooperatives, might consider joining forces to publish and distribute catalogs on a regional level.

Pricing

Marketers may question whether or not pricing strategies or price levels should differ for gay consumers. The answer would surely depend on the perceived quality of the goods, prestige of the retailer, market demand for the goods, and nature of the goods themselves. Another point to consider is that there are many socio-economic levels of gay consumers just as there are among non-gay consumers. Yes, certain demographics may indicate that gay consumers may have higher disposable incomes than the general population, but that doesn't justify price gouging. Most groups of consumers soon recognize if they are being taken advantage of. However, it may well be that tastes in jewelry, fragrance, and other personal grooming products, and certain apparel categories are sufficiently different between homosexual and heterosexual men that higher prices can be commanded. The research literature indicates that gay men place more emphasis on personal grooming, including cosmetic products, fragrance, and tanning, so high end products that promise more benefit or that have an element of status attached may command more sales. In fact, higher prices may even become a criterion for luxury or quality goods among some consumers. Even consumers on the lower end of the economic scale may go beyond their means to purchase a $40 cologne if they know it carries social prestige (e.g., Drakkar Noir).

Additional studies are needed to determine the extent to which homosexual and heterosexual men differ in their willingness to purchase particular apparel and appearance products at certain price points. Some specialty items such as wigs, lingerie, ball gowns, and high heels might require additional fabric or workmanship to fit a larger or non-standard female size, thus justifying a higher price than that asked for traditional women's sizes. This is typically true for women's apparel that is classified as large size; an additional $5.00 over the cost of a standard size garment is included. Female illusion artists often require theater makeup to serve as foundation to cover beard growth and this makeup is often more costly than regular foundation sold at cosmetics counters. They may also use a greater quantity of makeup than women (e.g., thickly applying pancake stick makeup), resulting in more frequent and more costly purchases.

FURTHER RESEARCH RELATING TO APPEARANCE AND SELF-PRESENTATION AMONG GAY CONSUMERS

Results from the studies mentioned herein have given rise to several suggestions for additional study, some of which have already been implemented in their early stages. Briefly, these ideas include:

1. An examination of the relationship of body image, appearance behaviors, and self-esteem among gay men. With the confirmed findings of increased interest in appearance among homosexual men versus heterosexual men, it would be of interest to study specific aspects of perceived body image among gay men, how that perceived image directs particular appearance behaviors (including food, exercise, and weight training behaviors), and how self-esteem may be affected. A study of these variables is currently underway, using both quantitative and qualitative instruments. Body image is being measured by the Multidimensional Body Self-Relations Questionnaire (Brown, Cash, & Mikulka, 1990); self-esteem is being measured using the Rosenberg Self-Esteem Scale (1965); appearance behaviors are being measured using both quantitative checklists and open-ended response questions.

2. An exploration of the importance of appearance among specific gay subcultures, such as female illusion competitors, patrons of various gay bar scenes, gay political activist groups, gay performing groups such as choirs, and gay professional groups. Through specific investigations we can gain a fuller understanding of the role that appearance plays in group conformity and in presenting group identity to others.

3. A study of body size/build and personal appearance in relation to initiating interaction with others. By examining these factors as they suggest the type of attention sought from others or the type of attention given by others, we may be able to better understand attitudes toward dress in sexual harassment cases or in cases of intimidating or hostile work environments.
4. An experimental study of the effect of store atmospherics on purchase behavior. By studying the use of such elements as lighting, fragrance, merchandise positioning, and use of certain types of store fixtures, retailers can more accurately appeal to certain shopping behavior preferences among both gay and non-gay consumers. McCullough (1993) has conducted a pilot study of these variables.

The time is ripe for critical investigation of consumer issues related to all consumer cultures, including gay consumer cultures. Of particular importance to the rather sparse literature that exists would be the importance of materialism and cultural expression, the effect of various marketing strategies on purchase behavior, the nature and impact of various advertising strategies, identity formation and the social presentation of self, and appearance management motivations and behaviors within specific subcultures. Through scholarly inquiry into issues such as these, we can bring more accurate and sensitive target marketing strategies to specific consumer cultures. The more clearly we understand the needs, desires, attitudes, lifestyles and psychographic characteristics of any consumer culture, the better we can both design and deliver satisfactory products and services to those individuals.

REFERENCES

Alfred C. Kinsey Institute for Sex Research, The (1974). *Sex Behavior.* Philadelphia: Author.

Bloch, P. H. & Richins, M. L. (1992). You look "Mahvelous": The pursuit of beauty and the marketing concept. *Psychology and Marketing*, 9, 3-15.

Brown, T., Cash, T., & Mikulka, P. (1990). Attitudinal body image assessment: Factor analysis of the Body-Self Relations Questionnaire. Unpublished manuscript, Old Dominion University, Norfolk, VA.

Cass, V. C. (1984a). Homosexual identity: A concept in need of definition. *Journal of Homosexuality*, 9, 105-126.

_____ . (1984b). Homosexual identity formation: Testing a theoretical model. *The Journal of Sex Research*, 20, 143-167.

Clark, D. (1977). *Loving Someone Gay.* Milbrae, CA: Celestial Arts.

Conner, C., Peters, K., & Nagasawa, R. (1975). Person and costume: Effects on the formation of first impressions. *Home Economics Research Journal*, 4 (1), 32-41.

Davis, R. (1993). Sky's the limit for tour operators. *Advertising Age*, 34 (January 18), 36-37.

Elliott, S. (1990). Advertisers bypass gay market. *USA Today* (17 July), B1-2.

Escoffier, J. (1992). Generations and paradigms: Mainstreams in gay and lesbian studies. *Journal of Homosexuality* 24 (1-2), 7-26.

Fischer, H. (1977). *Gay Semiotics: A Photographic Study of Visual Coding among Homosexual Men*. San Francisco: NFS Press.

Hagan, R. (1979). *The Bio-Sexual Factor*. New York: Doubleday.

Humphreys, L. & Miller, B. (1980). In Judd Marmor (Ed.), *Homosexual Behavior*. New York: Basic Books, Inc.

Johnson, B. (1993). The gay quandary: Advertising's most elusive, yet lucrative, target market proved difficult to measure. *Advertising Age*, 64 (Jan. 18), pp. 29 & 35.

Johnson, M. (1989). How clothing affects the perceptions of homosexual males. Unpublished honors thesis, The Ohio State University, Columbus, OH.

Kaiser, S. B. (1990). *The Social Psychology of Clothing: Symbolic Appearances in Context*. New York: Macmillan Publishing Co.

Kleinberg, S. (1980). *Alienated Affections: Being Gay in America*. New York: St. Martin's Press.

Kron, J. (1986). A few daring dressers risk sneers to push menswear into the future. *The Wall Street Journal* (March 11), p. 31.

Lakoff, R. & Scherr, R. (1984). *Face Value, the Politics of Beauty*. Boston: Routledge & Kegan Press.

Levin, G. (1993). Mainstream's domino effect: Liquor, fragrance, clothing advertising ease into gay magazines. *Advertising Age*, 64 (Jan. 18), 30 & 32.

Linville, P. W. (1982). The complexity-extremity effect and age-based stereotyping. *Journal of Personality and Social Psychology*, 42, 193-211.

Marmor, J. (1980). Clinical aspects of male homosexuality. In Judd Marmor (Ed.), *Homosexual Behavior*. New York: Basic Books, Inc.

Martin, R. (1993). The gay factor in fashion. *Esquire Gentleman* (Spring), 135-140.

McCracken, G. (1986). *Culture and Consumption: New Approaches to Symbolic Character of Consumer Goods and Activities*. Bloomington, IN: Indiana University Press.

McCullough, J. (1993). Fashion involvement and valuation of store atmospherics as predictors of in-store shopping behavior among male consumers. Unpublished master's thesis, The Ohio State University, Columbus, OH.

McJimsey, H. (1993). *Art and Fashion in Clothing Selection*. Ames, IA: Iowa State University Press.

Miller, C. (1990). Gays are affluent but often overlooked market. *Marketing News*, 24 (December 24), p. 2.

_____. (1992a). Two new firms market exclusively to gays. *Marketing News*, 26 (July 10), p. 8.

_____. (1992b). Mainstream marketers decide time is right to target gays. *Marketing News*, 26 (July 10), pp. 8 & 15.

Moore, M. (1994). Gay club dress. Unpublished paper, The Ohio State University, Columbus, Ohio.

Richins, M. L. (1991). Social comparison and the idealized images of advertising. *Journal of Consumer Research*, 18, 71-83.

Roach-Higgins, M. E. & Eicher, J. B. (1992). Dress and identity. *Clothing and Textiles Research Journal*, 10 (4), 1-8.

Rodkin, D. (1990). Untapped niche offers markets brand loyalty: Gay consumers favor companies that don't exclude them. *Advertising Age*, 61 (July 9), p. S2.

Rosenberg, M. (1965). *Society and the Adolescent Self-Image*. Princeton, NJ: Princeton University Press.

Rudd, N. A. (1992). Clothing as signifier in the perceptions of college male homosexuals. *Semiotica*, 91 (1/2), 67-78.

Rudd, N. A. & Tedrick, L.S. (1994). Male appearance aesthetics: Evidence to target a homosexual market? In DeLong, M. & Fiore, A. M. (Eds.), *Aesthetics of Textiles and Clothing: Advancing Multi-Disciplinary Perspectives, 200-211.* Monument, Co: International Textiles and Apparel Association.

Schwartz, P. (1992). Gay consumers come out spending. *American Demographics*, 14, 10-11.

Sergios, P. & Cody, J. (1985/86). Importance of physical attractiveness and social assertiveness skills in male homosexual dating behavior and partner selection. *Journal of Homosexuality*, 12 (2), 71-84.

Shively, M., Jones, C., & DeCecco, J. (1984). Research on sexual orientation: Definitions and methods. *Journal of Homosexuality*, 9 (2/3), 127-136.

Snezek, L. (1986). Clothing preferences and shopping behavior of male homosexual and heterosexual college students. Unpublished master's thesis, The Ohio State University, Columbus.

Stabiner, K. (1982). Tapping the homosexual market. *New York Times Magazine* (March), 34-41.

Sutyak, P. (1994). Gearing up for gay marketing. Unpublished paper, The Ohio State University, Columbus, Ohio.

Symons, D. (1979). *The Evolution of Human Sexuality.* New York: Oxford Press.

Tesser, A. (1980). Self-esteem maintenance in family dynamics. *Journal of Personality and Social Psychology*, 39, 77-91.

Triggs, T. (1992). Framing masculinity. In Ash, J. & Wilson, E. (Eds.), *Chic Thrills–A Fashion Reader.* London: Pandora, 25-29.

Troiden, R. (1989). The formation of homosexual identities. *Journal of Homosexuality*, 17 (1/2), 43-73.

Von Furstenburg, E. (1978). *The Power Book.* New York: Holt, Rinehart, and Winston.

Whisney, A., Winakor, G., & Wolins, L. (1979). Fashion drawings versus photographs. *Home Economics Research Journal*, 8, 138-150.

Wilson, E. (1993). Interface: The boundary between body and dress. Style, Fashion and the Negotiation of Identities. Unpublished conference proceedings, University of California, Davis, CA.

"Excuse Me, Sir?
May I Help You and Your Boyfriend?":
Salespersons' Differential Treatment
of Homosexual and Straight Customers

Andrew S. Walters, PhD

University of California, San Francisco

Maria-Cristina Curran, BA

SUMMARY. An experimental field study was conducted to investigate differential treatment of same-sex versus opposite-sex couples. Over a period of four months, three couples (1 female-female, 1 male-female, 1 male-male) entered each of twenty retail stores. All

Andrew S. Walters is Research Fellow at the University of California, San Francisco. The current study was conducted while Dr. Walters was affiliated with the Department of Psychology at the University of Georgia. Maria-Cristina Curran is a recent graduate of the University of Georgia and is a graduate student in counseling. The authors gratefully acknowledge Peter Anderson, Michael Buchman, Kelly Dickson, Steve Lloyd, Dawn McLaughlin, and Jennifer Yarnell for serving as confederates. The authors also wish to thank Terri D. Fisher and Gail M. Williamson for their valuable comments and assistance in reviewing an earlier version of this manuscript. Address correspondence regarding this article to Andrew S. Walters, Division of Clinical Epidemiology, The Center for AIDS Research, 74 New Montgomery Street, San Francisco, CA 94105.

[Haworth co-indexing entry note]: "'Excuse Me, Sir? May I Help You and Your Boyfriend?': Salespersons' Differential Treatment of Homosexual and Straight Customers." Walters, Andrew S., and Maria-Cristina Curran. Co-published simultaneously in *Journal of Homosexuality* (The Haworth Press, Inc.) Vol. 31, No. 1/2, 1996, pp. 135-152; and: *Gays, Lesbians, and Consumer Behavior: Theory, Practice, and Research Issues in Marketing* (ed: Daniel L. Wardlow) The Haworth Press, Inc., 1996, pp. 135-152; and: *Gays, Lesbians, and Consumer Behavior: Theory, Practice, and Research Issues in Marketing* (ed: Daniel L. Wardlow) Harrington Park Press, an imprint of The Haworth Press, Inc., 1996, pp. 135-152. Single or multiple copies of this article are available from The Haworth Document Delivery Service [1-800-342-9678, 9:00 a.m. - 5:00 p.m. (EST)].

135

couples were trained confederates. Multiple measures unequivocally showed differential treatment for heterosexual and homosexual couples. Heterosexual couples were assisted by staff in significantly less time than were homosexual couples, who often were not assisted and who were more likely to be repudiated. Results are discussed in terms of the sociopolitical climate for homosexuals. *[Article copies available from The Haworth Document Delivery Service: 1-800-342-9678.]*

The extent to which individuals exhibit negative attitudes or behavior toward others on the basis of sexual orientation remains an under-researched but critical area of study. For example, the current sociopolitical debate over "special rights" (endorsed by the Religious Right) versus "equal rights" (endorsed by gay and lesbian groups, human rights advocacy groups, the ACLU) rests on the assumption that gays are denied the same treatment as heterosexuals. In the past two years, legislation attempting to prohibit discrimination on the basis of sexual orientation has been impeded by conservative constituencies, and publicly-sanctioned discriminatory policies have been blocked only by court order.

The cultural climate available to lesbians, gay men, and bisexuals in most arenas of American society is negative, if not hostile. Basic civil liberties are routinely denied to homosexuals or persons perceived to be homosexuals. Although domestic partnership ordinances–a nonlegal recognition of relationship status–are highly publicized (Richardson, 1993), they remain proportionately rare and have been challenged in most states or municipalities that have sought to implement them. Nine states and the District of Columbia have enacted statutes protecting the rights of homosexuals in equal access to credit, employment, housing, and public accommodation (California, Connecticut, Hawaii, Massachusetts, Minnesota, New Jersey, Rhode Island, Vermont, and Wisconsin). In most other areas of the country, homosexuals are not guaranteed equal access to housing (Carman, 1992; Marchetti, 1989; Mehler, 1989), employment (e.g., Stewart, 1994), insurance and benefits (Anderson, 1992; Associated Press, 1989; Purdy, 1990; Thompson & Andrzejewski, 1988), and basic human rights (Higuera, 1989).

Early research on homosexuality sought to identify personality characteristics of persons who report homonegativism (also referred to as homophobia). Research has consistently found that homonegative individuals express authoritarianism (Larsen, Reed, & Hoffman, 1980) and political conservativism (Whitley, 1987) and strongly endorse traditional definitions of family and sex roles (Millham & Weinberger, 1977; Newman, 1989; Weinberger & Millham, 1979; Whitley, 1987). They are less sexually permissive and more likely to report sexual guilt and erotophobia (Dunbar, Brown, & Amoroso, 1973; Ficarrotto, 1990; Mosher & O'Grady, 1979).

Moreover, although they have less personal contact with lesbians and gay men (Herek & Glunt, 1993) and hence a predictably confined experience with homosexuality, homonegative individuals believe that homosexuality is a voluntary form of deviancy (Whitley, 1990), report greater dislike for homosexuals of their own sex (Gentry, 1987), and describe homosexuals according to stereotypes (Page & Yee, 1985). Finally, homonegative individuals are likely to perceive homosexuals as quite dissimilar from themselves even when they are not (Shaffer & Wallace, 1990).

Experimental studies have provided strong evidence for the pervasive attitudes against homosexuals (Kite & Deaux, 1986; Seligman, Howell, Cornell, Cutright, & Dewey, 1991) as well as elucidating stable traits that characterize homonegative individuals (see Herek, 1984, for a thorough review of earlier studies). Information gleaned from these studies has been useful for developing strategies for homosexuality education and professional training (e.g., Walters, 1994; Walters & Phillips, 1994). However, because nearly all of these studies have been conducted under laboratory conditions with college students as subjects, they are limited in several ways. First, results obtained from laboratory studies may not be representative of how individuals respond outside of experimental conditions. This is especially likely when subjects are asked to "project" how they think they would react in certain situations. Second, recruiting subjects from introductory psychology classes consisting almost entirely of first- and second-year students (i.e., 18-19 years old) may be particularly problematic when studying attitudes and behavior toward homosexuals. For example, Herek and Glunt (1993) have found that knowing or being friends with a homosexual is consistently associated with reduced homophobia. As students progress through college, they may become acquainted with lesbians and gay men–a situation that is less likely to have occurred among freshmen and sophomores. Furthermore, establishing a gay identity is itself a developmental process. Most gay students accept their sexual orientation in their junior and senior years of college (Remafedi, 1987). Thus, an indirect result of studying only younger students is that attitudes and indeed, personal identities, may not yet be fully developed.

We are aware of only one experimental study that investigated differential treatment of homosexuals and heterosexuals in a natural (i.e., non-laboratory) setting. Gray, Russell, and Blockley (1991) had either a male or female confederate approach shoppers and ask them for change. In half of the trials, the confederate wore an unmarked T-shirt; in the other half, the confederate wore a pro-gay T-shirt. As predicted by the researchers, results showed that help (as measured by listening to the request and physically looking for change) was offered significantly less frequently to the ostensibly pro-gay confederate. This effect was not attenuated by sex of the confederate, sex of the subject, or whether a justification (i.e., "Excuse me. I need to make an important phone call. Have you got change for a pound, please?") accompanied the request for change. Gray et al. (1991) concluded that the ubiquitous negative attitudes toward homosexuals have clear behavioral correlates.

The present study adds to previous research by examining discriminatory behavior toward homosexuals in a naturalistic setting. Specifically, we investigated how gay male, lesbian, and heterosexual couples were treated as customers in retail stores. Similar to the Gray et al. (1991) study, our central interest was in willingness to help gay-identified persons in a shopping environment. Unlike Gray et al., the confederates in our study were couples, and rather than ask shoppers for help (change), we investigated how retail employees–who are paid to assist customers–would treat homosexuals. We reasoned that if the *appearance* of homosexual status resulted in differential treatment of couples by employees paid to be respectful and courteous of customers, then a clear relationship must exist between attitudes and expressed behavior.

Three hypotheses guided the current study. First, we predicted that confederates posing as a heterosexual couple would be helped by sales associates in less time than would either gay male or lesbian couples. Previous literature documents more cultural dislike for gay men than for lesbians (Berrill, 1990; Berrill & Herek, 1990; Lehne, 1992). Thus, it was conceivable that staff assistance could vary between gay and lesbian couples as well. Given the scant research in naturalistic settings, however, we made no a priori hypotheses between these conditions. Second, we predicted that the quality of interaction with couples would depend on their perceived status as homosexuals or heterosexuals. Specifically, we hypothesized that staff would respond to the presence of homosexual couples by staring, laughing, pointing at, and talking about them. Similarly, we predicted that gay and lesbian couples–but not straight couples–would both perceive that staff looked uncomfortable with their presence and would report an overall less positive experience in the stores. Our third hypothesis was that discriminatory behavior would exist contrary to store policy and manager expectations.

METHOD

Confederates

Six senior psychology majors (three males, three females) served as confederates and for their participation, received one semester hour of academic research credit. Students were screened by the first author to assess their comfort in assuming (i.e., acting) the role of a gay man or lesbian. All students expressed interest in participating in field research and reported feeling comfortable acting as a member of either a heterosexual or homosexual couple. An additional female undergraduate student observed confederates on each site visit. To the best of our knowledge, all students identify themselves as heterosexual. Students were Caucasian and ranged in age from 23-28.

Physical attractiveness of confederates was judged by two independent raters (1 male, 1 female) on a scale of 1 = very unattractive to 10 = very attractive. Male [$M = 7.67$, $SD = 1.60$, Range 5-9] and female [$M = 7.88$, $SD = 1.25$, Range 5-9] confederates did not differ in attractiveness [$F = 0.40$, ns]. Students wore innocuous clothing (e.g., jeans, a college sweatshirt/polo shirt) at each site visit. Thus, the appearance and dress of our confederates appeared quite ordinary (e.g., no one wore a Queer Nation T-shirt) and inoffensive.

Participating Stores

Prior to the start of the study, managers from 20 retail stores were contacted and asked to participate in a study titled "Experiences of Mystery Shoppers." Managers were informed that six local residents (our confederates) would enter their stores as customers once over a period of four months and would rate the store on several criteria, including employee behavior and customer relations. Managers also consented to a follow-up interview with the first author and were assured that the name of their store would not be publicized without their additional consent. The follow-up interview served the dual purpose of determining managerial/company policies and expectations of employee behavior and as a debriefing session about the true nature of the study.

All stores included in the study were located in the same indoor mall. Stores were chosen based on three criteria: (1) a manager or owner from each store agreed to participate in the study, signing a consent form permitting confederates to enter their store as "mystery shoppers" and agreeing to a follow-up interview at a later date; (2) the size of each store favored employee-customer interactions (for this reason large department stores–whose sales associates oversee a larger portion of floor space–were excluded from the study); and (3) a variety of stores were represented (included were 11 clothing, 3 athletic, 2 music accessory, and 4 shoe stores).

Data were collected between September and December, 1993. Store visits were randomly determined as to the month, day, and time of day with the exceptions of Mondays and Tuesdays (managers often stated that stores are less busy on these days and fewer sales associates are available to work) and after 7:00 p.m. (to avoid interfering with student work schedules). For example, a gay couple would be randomly chosen to enter a particular store on a Wednesday afternoon in late September, a heterosexual couple to enter the same store at noon in mid-October, and a lesbian couple to enter the store at 6:00 p.m. on a Wednesday in early December. For another store, the heterosexual couple could be assigned to enter the store first (e.g., a Thursday in late October at 11:00 a.m.), the lesbian couple to visit the same store the next day at 4:00 p.m., and the gay couple to enter at 2:00 p.m. three weeks later.

Procedure

The first author was on-site during each visit and made an unobtrusive, cursory check of the participating stores to ensure that each was open and appeared as busy as it did on other site dates. We felt that this procedure was necessary to assure that no store had attracted an inordinate number of shoppers that could disrupt the typical ratio of sales associates to shoppers (e.g., a clearance sale). The first author then met the confederates in a mall restaurant at a pre-arranged time.

Confederates for each store were randomly assigned to a homosexual or heterosexual couple. Three males and three females were each assigned a number (1, 2, 3). For each store, one male and one female confederate were randomly assigned to comprise the heterosexual couple. The remaining two males and two females comprised the gay and lesbian couples, respectively. Confederates were unaware of the dyad type (heterosexual or gay, heterosexual or lesbian) they were assigned until the first author announced it several minutes before the couple was to enter the store. By randomly re-assigning confederate roles for each store, we eliminated systematic bias due to personality or individual difference variables specific to the confederates themselves. To summarize, each confederate was randomly assigned to a couple, the order in which couples visited stores was also randomly determined, and confederate roles were reassigned for each of the 20 stores. Thus, one gay, one lesbian, and one straight couple entered each store but no confederate entered the same store more than once.

One other student (the second author) was present as an observer in each store before, during, and after couples' visits. The observer was responsible for (1) insuring that the couple followed the script accurately, (2) clocking the time employees took to approach and offer help to couples, and (3) observing and recording comments made by the staff after couples departed.

The observer entered a store several minutes before the confederate couple and browsed inconspicuously, as if shopping. If the observer was approached by a sales associate she responded by saying, "I'm just looking for a blouse (CD/pair of shoes), thank you." In the several minutes that the observer was in the store without the couple, she was able to decline any assistance offered by staff and position herself facing the entrance of the store. Concealed in a pocket, the observer carried a stopwatch and starting timing when the confederates crossed the threshold of the store. She continued to browse while observing the employees' reactions to and behavior toward the couple. The moment the couple was approached by an employee and offered help, the observer stopped the watch.

All confederates were trained to follow the same script. They began holding hands before reaching the store. As they entered the store talking to one another and smiling, one member of the couple, like the observer, started a concealed stopwatch. Confederates identified the nearest sales associate, made eye contact with the employee, and then walked past salespersons and began to browse throughout the store. Confederates always displayed the same affectionate behavior regardless of pairing. At no time did confederates display additional affectionate behavior (e.g., hugging, kissing). If an employee approached the couple and asked if he/she could help them, the clock was stopped and one of the confederates said that he/she was looking for an article of clothing (CD/pair of shoes). After either being offered help and thanking the sales associate or waiting six minutes for an offer of help, the couple left the store. Confederates then reconvened with the first author in the mall restaurant and independently answered a questionnaire about their experience in the store.

As the couple began to leave the store, the observer casually walked toward the staff. While still appearing to look at merchandise, she was able to hear staff comments about the couple. Comments were mostly directed at other employees but were occasionally directed at other customers (including our confederate). Immediately after departing the store, the observer made a written record of these comments.

It is important to note here that both the observer and the confederates were trained to discriminate between sales associates' greeting behavior and an actual offer of help or exposition of merchandise. Manager interviews confirmed our suspicion that most stores situate an employee near the entrance of a store specifically to greet incoming patrons. The initial greeting by a sales associate did not constitute our definition of a helping response because their greeting was often tendered before they noticed the confederates were holding hands or was issued from an area of the store that did not permit them to identify the confederates as a couple (e.g., a table of merchandise blocked their view of the couples' hands). Thus, stopwatches were stopped only after employees first witnessed the confederates as a couple and then solicited their patronage.

Measures

In addition to the objective measure of time, each confederate independently completed a checklist immediately after departing each store. Confederates did not discuss their individual store experiences before completing the checklist. Couples were asked to confirm that they followed the script, their degree of assurance that members of the sales staff witnessed them as a couple, if they were helped within six minutes, and if they were helped, the level of assistance offered by a sales associate (1 = no offer of help, 4 = a second greeting, offer of help, and exposition of products). Couples also indicated whether they felt employees looked uncomfortable with their presence and rated their overall experience in the store (positive, neutral, negative). Finally, confederates were given the opportunity to write any specific comments about their experience in the store.

The observer also completed a checklist after each visit, recording the approximate number of customers present in the store when our confederates entered and the number of staff who were available to assist them. In addition, the observer verified that each couple followed the script, displayed the specified affectionate behavior, and if not assisted by sales staff within six minutes, departed the store. As mentioned above, the observer also reported comments made by staff about the couple after their departure.

Follow-up interviews were completed by the first author at the manager's convenience after one heterosexual, one gay, and one lesbian couple had visited all stores (i.e., sixty visits). Managers were asked about: (1) the characteristics or features they look for in hiring sales associates, (2) company policies/managerial expectations regarding the time by which staff are expected to offer an initial greeting to customers and a subsequent solicitation of service to them, (3) demographic variables describing their store's clientele (i.e., estimated percentages of customers by gender, race, and sexual orientation), and (4) their perceptions of how store employees address and attend to customers. Finally, managers were queried on store/company procedures regarding disciplinary action against employees who were found to mistreat or discriminate against customers.

Trial Procedure

In order to ensure that students were comfortable assuming their role as a member of a couple and to rehearse the sequence of events as prescribed, confederates visited four stores (2 clothing, 1 shoe, 1 music accessory) according to the procedures described above. These stores were located in a downtown area and were not associated with any of the stores in the mall. Although preliminary data collected from these pre-test stores suggested that heterosexual couples were treated in a more friendly and timely fashion, actual data from these stores were not included in analyses. Rather, the trial procedure was designed to familiarize confederates with their roles, and in fact, confederates assigned to the homosexual dyads displayed some discomfort initially. However, after the first few trials, the procedure ran smoothly and confederates were able to perform their roles comfortably.

RESULTS

Analyses were conducted at several levels. Initial tests were performed to determine whether the number of other customers present in stores was consistent across confederate dyads and if staff were available to help our couples. There were no significant differences in the number of customers present or the number of staff present, both X^2s (9) = 8.42, *ns*. Additional checks by the observer and both members of the couple revealed that in all cases actors followed the script, displayed affectionate behavior (holding hands, smiling, talking), and entered and exited the store appropriately. These data suggested to us that all protocols were consistent across stores and therefore, could be included in subsequent analyses.

The Time Variable

In order to test the reliability of timed responses, times collected by observer and confederates were compared. Paired *t*-tests yielded no significant differences, all *t*s < 1.85, *ns*. Correlations between observer and confederate were .92 in lesbian couples, .92 in straight couples, and .94 in gay couples. Because the two measures were nearly identical, only the time data collected by the observer were used in subsequent analyses.

The average time for sales associates to approach lesbian couples was 259 seconds (4 min. 18 sec.). Gay male couples were helped in slightly less time–231 seconds (3 min. 51 sec.). Heterosexual couples were helped in 82 seconds (1 min. 22 sec.). A repeated measures analysis of variance (ANOVA) revealed a significant difference by couple type, F = 36.58, p < .0001. Results of these analyses are illustrated in Figure 1. Planned comparisons (Winer, 1971) were used to test observed differences between

FIGURE 1. Mean Time (in Seconds) Lesbian, Gay, and Straight Confederates Were Helped by Sales Staff.

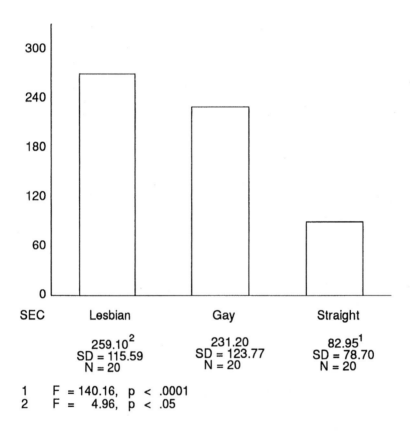

1   F = 140.16, p < .0001
2   F =   4.96, p < .05

groups. As predicted, heterosexual couples were helped in significantly less time than were homosexual couples F (2,17) = 140.16, p < .001. Although we made no a priori hypotheses about differences between gay male and lesbian couples, these analyses revealed that gay male couples were helped significantly more quickly than were lesbian couples, F (2,17) = 4.96, p < .05.

Additional analyses ruled out the possibility that observed effects were due to the order in which couples entered stores (e.g., if gay or lesbian couples entered stores in early December amid the rush of holiday shoppers whereas heterosexual couples did not). Neither the effect for order nor the order × couple interaction was significant, both *F*s < 0.39, *ns*. Thus, regardless of whether they shopped in September or December, heterosexual couples were always assisted in less time than homosexual couples.

Other Types of Discriminatory Treatment

Response time was not the only way in which our gay and lesbian couples were treated differently. Correlations were computed between confederate and observer ratings of five additional variables (staring, laughing, pointing, talking about, and being rude). Within gay and lesbian couples, considerable congruence was apparent in ratings of laughing, pointing, and rude treatment (all *r*s .40 or higher, p < .01). In other words, both confederates and observer reported that staff laughed and pointed at the couple in their presence. In addition, lesbian and gay couples consistently reported discourteous employee behavior, and these reactions were reported by the observer as well. Alternatively, significant relationships were not found in employees' staring at the couples or in talking about them. Although the observer did witness staff displaying these behaviors, they generally occurred outside of couples' presence.

The observer's ratings of five dimensions of staff demeanor are presented in Table 1. Note that at no time were heterosexual couples treated negatively by staff. In four categories (staring, laughing, pointing, talking), there were statistically significant differences between lesbian and straight couples. Gay couples differed significantly from lesbian couples in three categories (staring, talking, rude treatment). Lesbian and straight couples did not differ significantly in the amount of rude treatment they received by staff. However, there was a significant difference between the rude treatment displayed by staff toward gay males compared to either lesbian or straight couples. Thus, gay couples were treated more negatively than straight couples in all categories of behavior, and for one measure (rudeness) were treated more negatively than were lesbian couples. These data are consistent with and complement differences in time to offer help reported above.

Confederates' perceptions that staff looked uncomfortable also varied by couple type. Lesbian and gay couples did not report a significant difference in perception of staff discomfort (Lesbian *M* = 1.50, *SD* = .48, Gay *M* = 1.37, *SD* = .48, *t* [19] = 0.96, *ns*). Significant differences were found between the lesbian and straight (Straight *M* = 1.80, *SD* = .10, *t* [19] = −4.59, p < .0001) and gay and straight (*t* [19] = −5.78, p < .0001) couples. Finally, couples rated their overall experience in each store. Confederates in gay and lesbian couples reported no significant difference in their overall experience (Lesbian *M* = 1.82, *SD* = .59, Gay *M* = 1.82, *SD* = .71,

TABLE 1. Observer's Ratings of Sales Staff's Behavior Toward Couples

	Lesbian	Gay	Straight
Staring	45%[a]	75%[b]	0%
Laughing	25%[a]	35%[a]	0%
Pointing	15%[a]	30%[a]	0%
Talking	40%[a]	70%[b]	0%
Rude	10%	35%[a]	0%

Z tests were used to determine differences between dyad categories. Within each row, percentages not sharing a common superscript differ at p < .05 or better.

t [19] = .00). Straight couples' experiences in stores were more positive than were those of either lesbians (Straight $M = 1.30$, $SD = .44$, t [19] = 3.80, p < .001) or gays (t [19] = 3.68, p < .002).

Interviewing the Managers

In a follow-up interview with the managers, we obtained information on store policy and managerial expectations for staff. In all cases, managers stated that they were responsible for hiring sales staff. Generally, managers seek new employees who are friendly and attractive, have a "good personality," and are responsible. Employees in all 20 stores were trained by managers, and managers reported that any employee under her/his supervision had a thorough understanding of company/store and manager expectations for courtesy and full-service assistance to customers. According to managers, staff must greet entering customers immediately (ranging from 5 to 60 sec., the mean 25 sec.). Beyond the initial greeting, all sales associates were expected to approach customers and ask if they could be of help; in 17 stores, the expectation is that help should be offered to customers within 2 minutes, and in the remaining three stores, staff are expected to approach customers within 3 minutes.

Managers were asked to describe their clientele. For all stores combined, there was an equal distribution of male and female shoppers, although some stores cater to one gender more than another. Recall that stores were chosen for male and female shoppers. Racial composition across stores was also consistent, although again some stores reported more business by persons of color while others reported a higher percentage of White customers. When asked about the proportion of heterosexual vs. homosexual customers, 16 managers said flatly that no homosexuals shopped in their stores. The highest percentage given by a manager for nonheterosexual customers was 10%.

When asked if sales associates discuss customers or treat some customers differently than others, managers freely admitted that store employees are bound to talk about customers. In fact, 70% indicated that they had overheard their employees discussing specific customers negatively. However, in all of these cases managers were positive that in their store, such discussions occurred only in the back of the store or after hours. Inappropriate behavior simply did not exist among their staff while "on the floor." Thus, it appears that while managers assume staff will discuss customers, it is expected that impolite comments will not occur in the presence of customers.

Managers were asked also about the consequences of violating store or company policy in terms of politeness and respect for customers. Managers of all stores reported that they were responsible for confronting personnel about inappropriate behavior. However, of the twenty managers interviewed, only one reported that he would terminate an employee for rude or discourteous behavior. The remaining 19 managers commented more on the unpleasantries associated with disciplinary proceedings and expressed their hesitancy in confronting staff. Moreover, a formal system of discipline was not congruous across stores–even when asked what managers would do if they found an employee blatantly discriminating against a member of a minority group. Taken together, these descriptive data lead us to believe that in the retail stores we visited, it is quite possible that discrimination against homosexuals was implicitly sanctioned. That is, employees who perceive that managers are hesitant to confront employees may not associate inappropriate behavior with negative outcomes.

Finally, we inquired about the remuneration of staff. We wondered if staff who were paid on commission might be less likely to discriminate against homosexuals. For commission-based staff, a sale is a sale, and sales determine one's income. However, we found no difference in time to offer help according to method of payment–commission or hourly ($F = 1.37$, *ns*). That is, those sales associates paid on commission were just as likely to serve heterosexual couples quicker than lesbian or gay couples as were those who were not paid on commission.

DISCUSSION

In some respects, the results of this investigation are similar to previous experimental studies (e.g., Gray et al., 1991) showing societal prejudice against and discriminatory behavior toward homosexuals. However, the current study extends our knowledge about the ways in which homosexuals (or those perceived to be homosexuals) are mistreated. Recall that our confederates were heterosexual college students *posing* as members of homosexual or heterosexual couples. By virtue of their perceived status as homosexuals, the same individuals received poorer, less friendly, and more uncharitable service by sales associates. Perceived heterosexual couples were not slighted and were assisted by employees in significantly less time than were perceived gay or lesbian couples. In fact, one third of our homosexual couples were not assisted by staff at all during the six minutes they remained in the store. Alternatively, all heterosexual couples were helped.

The retail industry is fervidly competitive and dismissing any consumer population can result in dire consequences for retailers (Kelley, 1993; Rust & Zahorik, 1993). Retail managers typically recognize that customers who are treated unfairly are unlikely to return to retail stores (Bitner, Booms, & Tetreault, 1990). Nevertheless, employees' reluctance to help gay and lesbian couples and their demeanor toward them strongly suggest that homosexual customers are less valued than heterosexual customers and thus, deserve substandard treatment. In our investigation, only same-sex couples were stared and laughed at, pointed to, talked about, or treated rudely. Moreover, employees who work on a commission basis were equally as likely to resist helping homosexual couples as were hourly employees. We wonder if perhaps avoiding contact with same-sex couples is more important than earning a living.

Information gleaned from managers supported our hypothesis that employee behavior was contrary to formal policy and confuted their job description. Managers consistently stated that sales associates are expected to greet, approach, and help customers promptly. Our heterosexual couples were always helped within the parameters expected by managers of their employees. Gay and lesbian couples were not. These results suggest that sales associates comply with managerial expectations depending on whom they are required to help. Given that most managers expressed discomfort about confronting inappropriate employee behavior, staff seem to be implicitly allowed to select who they will or will not help. Furthermore, managers' estimates of the number of homosexual individuals who might shop in their stores was skewed. In fact, most managers found it particularly odd we would assume that gay and lesbian individuals shop.

Limitations and Implications

The research reported here is subject to several limitations. First, although care was taken to randomize all variables associated with confederates and store visits, we were unable to control for or manipulate sales associates' attitudes about homosexuality, sexual orientation, or work schedules. Thus, it is remains possible that other sales associates may have behaved differently.

The geographical location of the study (a college town in the Southeast) may also account for the high levels of observed discriminatory behavior. We recognize that across the country there are pockets of gay-friendly stores, and that in fact, anchor stores in larger cities often recruit staff to be responsive to a gay clientele; other service-industry stores intentionally employ a large percentage of gay staff. However, stores that specifically market to or welcome gay customers are less common, and we suspect our findings more accurately represent those from "typical" stores (i.e., those outside of large, urban areas). Nevertheless, replication in other regions seems warranted.

Another limitation to the current study is that neither observer nor confederates were blind to experimental conditions. However, several strategies were used to minimize systematic biases. For example, the pilot store visits ensured that confederates were familiar with and comfortable in their roles. Thus, it seems unlikely that staff responses were based on confederates' awkwardness or discomfort with their roles. In addition, the use of an observer who was not part of the stimulus couple and the high concordance rates between observer and confederate data strongly suggest that observations of sales staff behaviors were not systematically biased.

The broad purpose of this study was to determine if gays and lesbians are treated differently than heterosexuals in retail stores. Results indicate that homosexuals–at least when they are identified as members of a gay or lesbian couple–are treated substantially worse than are heterosexual couples. Given the generally accepted opinion that gay males are disliked more than lesbians, we were intrigued that our gay male couples were assisted by staff in significantly less time than were the lesbian couples. Staff demeanor toward male couples (as evidenced by staring at and talking about them and being rude), however, was more stigmatizing. Although our data do not address this discrepancy directly, we suspect that male couples were assisted in less time than female couples as an attempt to expedite their departure from the store. Comments overheard by (or sometimes directed to) our observer about gay couples suggested that male couples were particularly unwelcome in stores. For example, comments such as these were typical responses to gay male couples:

Did you see those two fruits? They were holding hands! I wasn't going to wait on them even if [*Manager's name*] saw me blow them off.

Those two guys who were just in here were together–like, I mean, a couple. That is just so gross. I didn't even know it until I saw they were holding hands. I just kept not looking at them.

In one store, several male employees gathered in SWAT-team formation and asked our male couple to leave. Although comments were made about lesbian couples, they tended to reflect more surprise than disgust. Further research is needed to identify the exact mechanisms underlying observed but unexpected differences in the treatment of gay and lesbian couples.

Individuals who oppose legislation to protect civil liberties for homosexuals argue that gay men and lesbians are treated no differently than heterosexuals (i.e., normal people) and are asking for privileged status. If the results from this study are any indication of how homosexuals are usually treated, then these arguments against equal protection for homosexuals are faulty. That is, if gays are treated so differently in as mundane an activity as shopping, it is reasonable to speculate that discrimination also occurs in other areas (e.g., housing, employment) as well. Our study illuminates the social acceptability of homonegativism. Retail employees–persons paid to be courteous to and solicitous of others–blatantly disregarded, ignored, or mocked our confederates posing as gays and lesbians. Perhaps even worse, it appears that such behaviors may be implicitly endorsed by those in positions of authority. The hesitancy of store managers in our study to confront discriminatory behaviors both sanctions and reinforces discrimination.

REFERENCES

Anderson, D. (1992). Woman galvanized by battle in court for injured lover. *Times Picayune* (June 7), p. B:1, 4.
Associated Press. (1989). In bias settlement, gay man can take companion on trip. *The New York Times* (Nov. 3), p. A:17.
Berrill, K. T. (1990). Anti-gay violence and victimization in the United States: An overview. *Journal of Interpersonal Violence*, 5, 274-294.
Berrill, K. T., & Herek, G. M. (1990). Primary and secondary victimization in anti-gay hate crimes: Official response and public policy. *Journal of Interpersonal Violence*, 5, 401-413.
Bitner, M. J., Booms, B. H., & Tetreault, M. S. (1990). The service encounter: Diagnosing favorable and unfavorable incidents. *Journal of Marketing*, 54, 71-84.
Carman, D. (1992). Bad taste of discrimination in past never more timely. *Denver Post* (Oct. 3), p. 1:1.
Dunbar, J., Brown, M., & Amoroso, D. M. (1973). Some correlates of attitudes toward homosexuality. *Journal of Social Psychology*, 89, 271-279.

Ficarrotto, T. J. (1990). Racism, sexism, and erotophobia: Attitudes of heterosexuals toward homosexuals. *Journal of Homosexuality*, 19, 111-116.

Gentry, C. S. (1987). Social distance regarding male and female homosexuals. *Journal of Social Psychology*, 127, 199-208.

Gray, C., Russell, P., & Blockley, S. (1991). The effects upon helping behaviour of wearing pro-gay identification. *British Journal of Social Psychology*, 30, 171-178.

Herek, G. M. (1984). Beyond "homophobia": A social psychological perspective on attitudes toward lesbians and gay men. *Journal of Homosexuality*, 10, 1-21.

Herek, G. M. & Glunt, E. K. (1993). Interpersonal contact and heterosexuals' attitudes toward gay men: Results from a national study. *Journal of Sex Research*, 30, 239-244.

Higuera, J. (1989). Human rights law doesn't cover gays, Arlington decides. *Washington Times* (January 24), p. 3:5.

Kelley, S. W. (1993). Discretion and the service employee. *Journal of Retailing*, 69, 104-126.

Kite, M. E., & Deaux, K. (1986). Attitudes toward homosexuality: Assessment and behavioral consequences. *Basic and Applied Social Psychology*, 7, 137-162.

Larsen, K. S., Reed, M., & Hoffman, S. (1980). Attitudes of heterosexuals toward homosexuality: A Likert-type scale and construct validity. *Journal of Sex Research*, 16, 245-257.

Lehne, G. K. (1992). Homophobia among men: Supporting and defining the male role. In Kimmel, M. S. & Messner, M. A. (Eds.), *Men's lives* (2nd ed., 381-394). New York: Macmillan.

Marchetti, D. (1989). Mt. Clemens housing bias angers gays. *Detroit News* (July 8), p. 1:5.

Mehler, N.H. (1989). Two males charge bias in housing. *Chicago Tribune* (August 16), p. 2:3.

Millham, J., & Weinberger, L. E. (1977). Sexual preference, sex role appropriateness, and restriction of social class. *Journal of Homosexuality*, 2, 343-357.

Mosher, D. L., & O'Grady, K. E. (1979). Homosexual threat, negative attitudes toward masturbation, sex guilt, and males' sexual and affective reactions to explicit sexual films. *Journal of Consulting and Clinical Psychology*, 47, 860-873.

Newman, B. (1989). The relative importance of gender role attitudes to male and female attitudes toward lesbians. *Sex Roles*, 21, 451-465.

Page, S., & Yee, M. (1985). Conception of male and female homosexual stereotypes among university undergraduates. *Journal of Homosexuality*, 12, 109-118.

Purdy, P. (1990). Is "lavender lining" practiced in Denver's insurance industry? *Denver Post* (April 1), p. 3:1.

Remafedi, G. (1987). Homosexual youth. *Journal of the American Medical Association*, 258, 222-225.

Richardson, L. (1993). Proud, official partners. *The New York Times* (August 1), pp. 37, 38.

Rust, R. T. & Zahorik, A. J. (1993). Customer satisfaction, customer retention, and market share. *Journal of Retailing*, 69, 193-215.

Sigelman, C. K., Howell, J. L., Cornell, D. P., Cutright, J. D., & Dewey, J. C. (1991). Courtesy stigma: The social implications of associating with a gay person. *Journal of Social Psychology*, 131, 45.56.

Shaffer, D. R., & Wallace, A. (1990). Belief congruence and evaluator homophobia as determinants of the attractiveness of competent homosexual and heterosexual males. *Journal of Psychology and Human Sexuality*, 3, 67-87.

Stewart, J. B. (1994). Annals of law: Gentleman's agreement. *The New Yorker* (June 13), 74-82.

Thompson, K. & Andrzejewski, J. (1988). *Why can't Sharon Kowalski come home?* San Francisco: Spinsters/Aunt Lute.

Walters, A. S. (1994). Using visual media to reduce homophobia: A classroom demonstration. *Journal of Sex Education and Therapy*, 20, 92-100.

Walters, A. S., & Phillips, C. P. (1994). Hurdles: An activity for homosexuality education. *Journal of Sex Education and Therapy*, 20, 198-203.

Weinberger, L. E., & Millham, J. (1979). Attitudinal homophobia and support of traditional sex roles. *Journal of Homosexuality*, 4, 237-253.

Whitley, B. E., Jr. (1990). The relationship of heterosexuals' attributions for the causes of homosexuality to attitudes toward lesbians and gay men. *Personality and Social Psychology Bulletin*, 16, 369-377.

_____. (1987). The relationship of sex-role orientation to heterosexuals' attitudes toward homosexuals. *Sex Roles*, 17, 103-113.

Winer, B. J. (1971). *Statistical Principles in Experimental Design* (2nd ed.). New York: McGraw-Hill.

Discrimination Against Same-Sex Couples in Hotel Reservation Policies

David A. Jones, MS

The Ohio State University

SUMMARY. Discrimination against same-sex couples in hotel reservations policies was investigated. Hotels and bed and breakfast establishments ($N = 320$) were sent letters from either a same-sex or opposite-sex couple, requesting weekend reservations for a room with one bed. Same-sex couples were granted significantly fewer reservations than opposite-sex couples, suggesting that there was indeed discrimination against same-sex couples. *[Article copies available from The Haworth Document Delivery Service: 1-800-342-9678.]*

Although considerable attention has been paid to studying attitudes toward gender, ethnic, and religious minorities, only recently have attitudes toward homosexuals been examined. There is little question that anti-homosexual prejudice exists (MacDonald, Huggins, Young, & Swanson, 1972; MacDonald & Games, 1974, Weinberger & Millham, 1979).

David A. Jones is a doctoral student in Counseling Psychology at The Ohio State University. The author gratefully acknowledges Dr. Michael Dawson for his guidance during the design phase of this study and Dr. Nancy Betz and Dr. Dan Wardlow for their helpful comments on a draft of this article. Correspondence should be addressed to: Department of Psychology, The Ohio State University, 142 Townshend Hall, 1885 Neil Avenue Mall, Columbus, OH 43210-1222. E-mail: *dajones@magnus.acs.ohio-state.edu*

[Haworth co-indexing entry note]: "Discrimination Against Same-Sex Couples in Hotel Reservation Policies." Jones, David A. Co-published simultaneously in *Journal of Homosexuality* (The Haworth Press, Inc.) Vol. 31, No. 1/2, 1996, pp. 153-159; and: *Gays, Lesbians, and Consumer Behavior: Theory, Practice, and Research Issues in Marketing* (ed: Daniel L. Wardlow) The Haworth Press, Inc., 1996, pp. 153-159; and: *Gays, Lesbians, and Consumer Behavior: Theory, Practice, and Research Issues in Marketing* (ed: Daniel L. Wardlow) Harrington Park Press, an imprint of The Haworth Press, Inc., 1996, pp. 153-159. Single or multiple copies of this article are available from The Haworth Document Delivery Service [1-800-342-9678, 9:00 a.m. - 5:00 p.m. (EST)].

While Smith (1971) and MacDonald and Games (1974) found that negative attitudes toward homosexuals were related to cognitive rigidity, authoritarianism, low tolerance for ambiguity, and status consciousness, Ficarrotto (1990) found that both sexual conservatism, as measured by an affective dimension of erotophilia-erotophobia, and social prejudice, as measured by racist and sexist beliefs, are independent and equal predictors of anti-homosexual sentiment.

Prejudice against homosexuals appears to have a geographic component as well, although urbanism, as opposed to geographic region, appears to be the variable of interest. By tapping attitudes toward the extension of civil liberties to such target groups as atheists, racists, militarists, communists, and homosexuals, Wilson (1985) concluded that urbanism is significantly and positively associated with tolerance.

To date, research on homophobia and anti-homosexual bias has focused on prejudicial attitudes and beliefs regarding homosexuals while little research has examined the discriminatory behaviors which those attitudes and beliefs produce. The present study examines discrimination against same-sex couples in hotel reservation policies. Hypotheses which will be tested are as follows:

Hypothesis 1:   Same-sex couples will be granted significantly fewer requests than opposite-sex couples.

Hypothesis 2:   Small hotels will grant significantly fewer requests than large hotels to same-sex couples.

Hypothesis 3A: Same-sex couples will be granted significantly fewer requests than opposite-sex couples in small hotels.

Hypothesis 3B: Same-sex couples will be granted significantly fewer requests than opposite-sex couples in large hotels.

Hypothesis 4A: Male-male couples will be granted significantly fewer requests than female-female couples.

Hypothesis 4B: Male-male couples will be granted significantly fewer requests than female-female couples in small hotels.

Hypothesis 4C: Male-male couples will be granted significantly fewer requests than female-female couples in large hotels.

METHOD

Subjects

Three-hundred-twenty hotels were randomly selected–160 with more than 50 rooms–from *Red Book: The Official American Hotel & Motel*

Association Lodging Directory, and 160 with 10 rooms or less from *Bed & Breakfast U.S.A 1992.* These hotels were then randomly assigned to each of four couple conditions–male-female with same last name, male-female with different last name, male-male with different last name, and female-female with different last name.[1]

Design

Reservation requests from four couple conditions–male-female with same last name, male-female with different last name, male-male with different last name, and female-female with different last name were sent to the 320 subjects, either large hotels (50 rooms or more) or small hotels (10 rooms or less). Thus, each of the eight conditions comprised 40 subjects (hotels).

Materials

Form letters requesting a reservation for a double room with queen or king-size bed for two consecutive weekend nights and asking for a response by mail were prepared, along with identical mailing envelopes. The form letters were identical except for the "gendered" first names (e.g., Brian, Diana) of the couple requesting the reservations.

Procedure

The reservation requests were mailed to the hotels approximately four weeks in advance of the reservation dates requested. Responses from the hotels were coded as follows: YES = request granted, request granted with deposit required, or request granted with exception (i.e., two rooms or two beds); NO = request denied or no response received.

Analysis

Chi-square analyses were performed for same-sex vs. opposite-sex couples across all hotels, for same-sex vs. opposite sex in small vs. large hotels, and for each of the eight individual couple type/hotel size combinations.

Results

In support of Hypothesis 1, significantly fewer requests were granted to the same-sex couple than to the opposite-sex couple, $x^2(1) = 7.92, p = .005$. The difference between the numbers of requests granted the two couple types

GAYS, LESBIANS, AND CONSUMER BEHAVIOR

was greater in small hotels than in large hotels, $x^2(1) = 5.58$, $p = .02$, and $x^2(1) = 2.58$, $p = .11$, respectively, supporting Hypothesis 2 (see Table 1).

In small hotels, the number of requests granted both the male-male couple and the female-female couple was significantly less than the number of requests granted the male-female-same-last-name couple, $x^2(1) = 3.81$, $p = .05$, and $x^2(1) = 4.71$, $p = .03$, respectively.

These data partially support Hypothesis 3A, but contrary to the original hypothesis, the difference between the number of requests granted the male-male and female-female couples and the male-female-different-last-name couple did not prove significant, $x^2(1) = 1.40$, $p = .24$, and $x^2(1) = 1.98$, $p = .16$, respectively (see Table 2). Among large hotels, the only support for Hypothesis 3B was the statistically significant difference found between the female-female couple and the male-female-different-last-name couple, $x^2(1) = 4.94$, $p = .03$, with the latter condition being granted the greater number of requests (see Table 3).

TABLE 1. Comparisons of "Yes" Responses to Requests for Room Reservations from Opposite-Sex and Same-Sex Couples

	Opposite-Sex Couples		Same-Sex Couples			
	N	%	N	%	$x2(1)$	$p =$
All Hotels	124	77.50	101	63.125	7.92	.005
Small Hotels	61	76.25	47	58.75	5.58	.02
Large Hotels	63	78.75	54	67.50	2.58	.11

TABLE 2. Comparisons of Small Hotels' "Yes" Responses to Requests for Room Reservations from Opposite-Sex and Same-Sex Couples

Opposite-Sex Couples				Same-Sex Couples					
Same Last Name		Different Last Name		Male-Male		Female-Female			
N	%	N	%	N	%	N	%	$x2(1)$	$p =$
32	80.00	29	72.50					0.63	.43
32	80.00			24	60.00			3.81	.05
32	80.00					23	57.50	4.71	.03
		29	72.50	24	60.00			1.40	.24
		29	72.50			23	57.50	1.98	.16
				24	60.00	23	57.50	.05	.82

TABLE 3. Comparisons of Large Hotels' "Yes" Responses to Requests for Room Reservations from Opposite-Sex and Same-Sex Couples

Opposite-Sex Couples				Same-Sex Couples					
Same Last Name		Different Last Name		Male-Male		Female-Female			
N		N	%	N	%	N	%	$x2(1)$	$p=$
30	75.00	33	82.50					0.61	.41
30	75.00			30	75.00			0.0	1.00
30	75.00					24	60.00	2.05	.15
		33	82.50	30	75.00			0.67	.41
		33	82.50			24	60.00	4.94	.03
				30	75.00	24	60.00	2.05	.15

Hypotheses 4A, 4B and 4C were not supported. Neither in the combined sample, nor in the small or large hotels was there a significant difference between the number of requests granted the male-male couple and the female-female couple, $x^2(1) = 1.32$, $p = .25$, $x^2(1) = .05$, $p = .82$ (see Table 2), and $x^2(1) = 2.05$, $p = .15$ (see Table 3), respectively.

Discussion

The present experiment investigated discriminatory practices against same-sex couples in hotel reservations policies. The results obtained supported the hypothesis that hotels would grant fewer reservations requests to same-sex couples than to opposite-sex couples, suggesting the presence of discrimination against such couples. The greater discrimination found in small hotels (bed and breakfasts) may be explained by the fact that the owner/operator of a bed and breakfast establishment almost always lives on the premises, rendering him or her more personally identified with the business, and thereby more likely to introduce personal prejudices into business practices. In addition, there may be an assumption that each guest has a relatively greater impact on every other guest in a small hotel, increasing the probability of discrimination based on projected personal beliefs, while in a larger hotel, the presumption of a certain degree of anonymity may decrease that probability.

The fact that a greater degree of discrimination was found against female-female couples than male-male couples may indicate that such couples indeed face greater discrimination. It may indicate an element of anti-female bias as well. However, the fact that smaller differences were found between the two same-sex groups than between the same-sex and opposite-sex groups suggests that the salient feature is the same-sex nature of the couple, and not gender per se.

There is at least one limitation to this study which may have bearing on its generalizability. While random selection and assignment of hotels for each of the eight couple/size conditions may have controlled for variables such as geographical location and urbanism and intervening variables (e.g., presence of a convention or high tourist season), it is unclear whether the relatively small cell sizes ($N = 40$) allow these effects to be ruled out with confidence. Also, the decision to combine the non-responses with the requests denied is debatable. Much thought was given to the issue of non-responses in the research design phase of this study. Indeed, the results would be somewhat different (less significant or not significant) if the "NO" category were separated into "request denied" and "no response received." However, it is assumed that hotels and bed and breakfast establishments are in business to make money and are therefore equally motivated to respond to all requests for room reservations. Furthermore, it is standard business practice to respond to written communication, whether or not the business is in a position to grant a request. Based on these criteria, the decision was made to combine the denials and non-responses into one category.

Whatever the reasons for the discriminatory behaviors found, at some point the impact on the victims of such discrimination must be addressed. While not being granted a hotel reservation may seem relatively insignificant in the larger scope of life experience, it may be indicative of a pattern of subtle discrimination against same-sex couples in a variety of settings. Word, Zanna, and Cooper (1974) have demonstrated that even subtle discrimination adversely affects both performance and self-esteem in its victims, creating a self-fulfilling prophecy in the eyes of the person who is discriminating.

Based on the implications of this study, future research should focus on areas in which discrimination against same-sex couples and homosexuals in general may have even more detrimental effects, such as housing, insurance, employment, execution of wills, and adoption of children. In addition to their use in further understanding the nature of prejudice and discrimination, such studies might well be cited in support of legislation to protect the rights of homosexual persons.

NOTE

1. A list of hotels and bed and breakfasts, along with their responses to the reservations requests, may be obtained from the author.

REFERENCES

American Hotel & Motel Association. (1986). Red Book: The Official American Hotel & Motel Association Lodging Directory. Walnut Creek, CA: Pactel Publishing.

Ficarrotto, T. J. (1990). Racism, sexism, and erotophobia: Attitudes of heterosexuals toward homosexuals. *Journal of Homosexuality*, 19, 111-116.

Macdonald, A. P. & Games, R. G. (1974). Some characteristics of those who hold positive and negative attitudes toward homosexuals. *Journal of Homosexuality*, 1, 9-27.

Macdonald, A. P., Huggins, J., Young, S., & Swanson, R. A. (1972). Attitudes toward homosexuality: Presentation of sex morality or the double standard? *Journal of Consulting and Clinical Psychology*, 40, p. 161.

Rundback, B. R. (1992). *Bed & Breakfast U.S.A. 1992*. New York: Penguin Books.

Smith, K. T. (1971). Homophobia: A tentative personality profile. *Psychological Reports*, 29, 1091-1094.

Weinberger, L. E. & Millham, J. (1979). Attitudinal homophobia and support of traditional sex roles. *Journal of Homosexuality*, 4, 237-246.

Wilson, T. C. (1985). Urbanism and tolerance: A test of some hypotheses drawn from Wirth and Stouffer. *American Sociological Review*, 50, 117-230.

Word, C. O., Zanna, M. P., & Cooper, J. (1974). The nonverbal mediation of self-fulfilling prophecies in interracial interaction. *Journal of Experimental Social Psychology*, 10, 109-120.

The Effect of Homosexual Imagery in Advertising on Attitude Toward the Ad

Subodh Bhat, PhD

San Francisco State University

Thomas W. Leigh, PhD

University of Georgia

Daniel L. Wardlow, PhD

San Francisco State University

SUMMARY. This study examines the differential impact that images in magazine advertising suggestive of either homosexuality or heterosexuality have on attitude toward the ad. Results support the hypothesis that homosexual imagery in advertising led to more positive attitude toward the ad among viewers more tolerant of homosexuality than among those less tolerant of homosexuality. Surpris-

Dr. Subodh Bhat and Dr. Daniel L. Wardlow are Associate Professors of Marketing at San Francisco State University. Dr. Thomas W. Leigh is Associate Professor and Terry Research Fellow in the Marketing Department at the University of Georgia. The authors are listed alphabetically. The authors wish to thank Professor Richard Nelson at San Francisco State University and to acknowledge support for portions of this research from a San Francisco State University Faculty Mini-Grant and from the Department of Marketing at San Francisco State University. Correspondence should be addressed to Daniel L. Wardlow, Department of Marketing, San Francisco State University, 1600 Holloway Avenue, San Francisco, CA 94132. E-mail: *dwardlow@sfsu.edu*

[Haworth co-indexing entry note]: "The Effect of Homosexual Imagery in Advertising on Attitude Toward the Ad." Bhat, Subodh, Thomas W. Leigh, and Daniel L. Wardlow. Co-published simultaneously in *Journal of Homosexuality* (The Haworth Press, Inc.) Vol. 31, No. 1/2, 1996, pp. 161-176; and: *Gays, Lesbians, and Consumer Behavior: Theory, Practice, and Research Issues in Marketing* (ed: Daniel L. Wardlow) The Haworth Press, Inc., 1996, pp. 161-176; and: *Gays, Lesbians, and Consumer Behavior: Theory, Practice, and Research Issues in Marketing* (ed: Daniel L. Wardlow) Harrington Park Press, an imprint of The Haworth Press, Inc., 1996, pp. 161-176. Single or multiple copies of this article are available from The Haworth Document Delivery Service [1-800-342-9678, 9:00 a.m. - 5:00 p.m. (EST)].

ingly, ads with heterosexual imagery were rated less favorably by viewers tolerant of homosexuality than by those less tolerant. *[Article copies available from The Haworth Document Delivery Service: 1-800-342-9678.]*

INTRODUCTION

Today's increasingly diverse markets and competitive pressures for incremental sales, market share, and profits have pushed marketers to extend their message to a wider variety of target audiences. Marketers have long targeted racial and ethnic audiences with advertising featuring members of the targeted group. This advertising has appeared in media targeted to selective audiences with appeals and themes that are unique to the group and presented in the appropriate language. As the racial and ethnic composition of the American population continues to diversify, more and more of this formerly selectively targeted advertising is placed in general circulation mass media. These diverse placements of ads create media crossover effects, where all manner of audiences may be exposed to advertising which is designed to appeal to a particular racial or ethnic group.

Most recently, marketers have begun to target the gay and lesbian audience with advertising that features gay or lesbian characters, uses appeals and themes unique to this minority market segment, and is placed in media targeted to gays and lesbians. The list of companies advertising in the gay media has grown to include Sony, Apple, Banana Republic, American Express, and the liquor brands of Carillon Importers (Absolut, Bombay Sapphire), among others. A few adventurous companies have begun to show images suggesting homosexuality in advertising to general audiences in the mass media. For example, in an American ad campaign it defines as "inclusive," Swedish furniture maker IKEA depicts a variety of realistic lifestyles including a couple grappling with middle age, a family with an adopted son, a gay male couple, and a divorced woman buying furniture for the first time. Images suggesting homosexuality have also appeared fairly extensively in mainstream fashion advertising for brands such as Calvin Klein, Benetton, and Banana Republic. Kmart Corporation ran a Father's Day television advertisement in 1993 which included character dialogue which many heard to imply a homosexual relationship between the two men depicted in the ad, although Kmart denied an intentional reference to homosexuality.

Given the themes which imply aspects of homosexuality now appearing in mainstream advertising, what are the possible implications for the viewers' attitudes toward that advertising? It has been well established that American public attitudes toward homosexuality have a substantial and sustained negative component (*San Francisco Chronicle*, June 20, 1994). If the desired effect of the advertising is ultimately some purchase behavior, advertisers must attempt to generate positive affective reactions to the brand through their advertising (Shimp 1981). Given the generally negative attitudes toward homosexuality in mainstream American society, why would an advertiser risk alienation of a substantial portion of a market to make a differential appeal to a very small segment (5.7% of the population; Yankelovich Associates data cited in the *San Francisco Chronicle*, June 10, 1994) such as homosexuals?[1] Or, do advertisers believe that the negative affect generated by the image depicting homosexuality fails to transfer to attitude toward the ad? In this study, we examine the question: what are the effects of homosexual imagery in advertising on individuals' attitude toward the ad?

REVIEW OF THE LITERATURE

Attitude Toward the Ad

Attitude toward the ad (A_{ad}) is a well-researched construct in the literature of marketing and advertising. A_{ad} is defined as "a predisposition to respond in a favorable or unfavorable manner to a particular advertising stimulus during a particular exposure occasion" (Lutz 1985). Early research in advertising tended to focus on cognitive responses to advertising, measuring such response functions as recall of ad content or significant copy points. During the 1980s, marketing researchers began to place reactions to advertising in a broader context, viewing A_{ad} as a summative or aggregate measure incorporating cognition, affective response, and evaluative components (Mitchell 1986; MacKenzie and Lutz 1989 among others) inspired by, and consistent with Fishbein and Ajzen's model of attitude formation (see Fishbein and Ajzen 1975 for an elaboration).

A_{ad} is an important concept to marketing managers, as it has been repeatedly linked to brand preference and brand choice in the academic literature (e.g., Shimp 1981). A_{ad} is generally viewed as a mediator of brand choice through attitude-toward-the-brand, and thus potentially is an influential determinant of a purchase decision (Batra and Ray 1985; Gardner 1985; Edell and Burke 1986; and Muehling and Laczniak 1988 among others).

While A_{ad} could be potentially influenced by a number of ad execution elements, visual imagery in advertising has been shown to be an important determinant of A_{ad} (Rossiter and Percy 1980, Mitchell and Olson 1981,

Mitchell 1983, Mitchell 1986). For example, when the text information of an advertisement was held constant, Mitchell (1986) found the valence of the emotional response to the visual image affects both A_{ad} and attitude-toward-the-brand.

Attitude Toward Homosexuality

A recent (1994) public opinion poll conducted by a reputable marketing research firm showed that 39% of the American public found the homosexual lifestyle unacceptable (*San Francisco Chronicle*, June 20, 1994). While this is down from 59% since 1976, a majority of Americans polled in 1994 believed that homosexuals are not good role models, gay relationships are morally wrong, and that gay couples should be barred from adopting children. Clearly, this poll demonstrates that a substantial portion of the American public holds a negative attitude toward homosexuals and homosexuality. The evidence of increased acceptance of homosexuality as an alternative lifestyle may simply indicate a growing tolerance of homosexuals in society; a qualified acceptance, given the expressed reservations on a number of specific questions on the roles of homosexuals in the society.

Attitudes toward homosexuality have been measured in a number of ways. Millham, San Miguel, and Kellogg (1976) measured attitude using 38 true-false items. The resulting data were factor analyzed and provided six dimensions of attitude toward homosexuality: repressive-dangerous, personal anxiety, preference for female over male homosexuals, cross-sexed mannerisms, moral reprobation, and preference for male over female homosexuals. Larsen, Reed, and Hoffman (1980) used 20 Likert-type scale items to create a Heterosexual Attitudes Toward Homosexuality (HATH) scale. Their study confirmed a pattern of anti-homosexual attitudes rooted in a conservative and punitive outlook where behavior is measured against religious ethics and morality.

An attempt to measure attitudes toward homosexuals in a social context was the Index of Homophobia developed by Hudson and Ricketts (1980). This index consisted of 25 Likert-type scale items, each dealing with an individual's reaction to homosexuality in a social setting. A modified version of the index demonstrated good reliability and content and factorial validity.

Herek (1984) gathered homosexuality attitude scales from a number of prior studies and extensively factor-analyzed data collected on those scales. Through repeated factor analysis with varying samples and rotational methods, Herek found a single factor emerged consistently that explained a large proportion of the variance in attitudes. Naming the factor "Condemnation-Tolerance (C-T)," Herek found it explained 35%-45% of the variance in attitudes, and correlated well with the Millham et al. (1976) scale. Furthermore, Herek found that additional factors discovered related to beliefs about homosexuals rather than attitudes, and explain relatively little of the variance encountered. Herek concluded that a unidimensional scale for measuring attitudes should consist of items related to condemnation and tolerance (the C-T scale), and such a scale provides a useful measure of attitude toward homosexuals. Herek provided 38 sample items for inclusion in the C-T scale.

Herek's C-T scale was chosen for the purpose of this study because unlike the restricted range of emotions and feelings covered in previous studies, the C-T scale includes items that characterize homosexuality as being "unnatural, disgusting, perverse, and sinful; as a danger to society and requiring negative social sanctions; and as a source of personal anxiety to the individual respondent, consequently leading to avoidance of gay men and lesbians" (Herek 1984). It thus captures the essence of definitions of the phenomenon described as homoerotophobia (Churchill 1967) and homophobia (Weinberg 1972, Morin and Garfinkle 1978).

RESEARCH HYPOTHESES

This research examines the use of homosexual visual imagery in advertising and its effects on A_{ad}. As noted earlier, visual imagery in advertising has been strongly linked to A_{ad}. Several studies have noted the negative attitude toward homosexuality in contemporary American society (cf. Weinberg 1972, Levitt and Klassen 1974). A recent Time/CNN poll revealed that 39% of those surveyed find the homosexual lifestyle unacceptable, 53% find homosexuality to be morally wrong, 57% said homosexuals are not good role models, 64% said homosexual marriages should not be recognized, and 65% said homosexual couples should not be allowed to adopt children (*San Francisco Chronicle*, June 20, 1994). The negative public attitudes toward homosexuality suggests that the depiction of homosexual images in an ad are likely to evoke strong negative reactions to the ad among individuals who do not approve of homosexuality.

At the same time, there is little research to suggest existence of any negative attitudes toward heterosexual lifestyles among homosexuals or bisexuals. Also, heterosexual imagery in advertising is so common that homosexuals' acceptance of and reactions to this form of imagery would most likely be muted. This suggests that heterosexual images in an ad are not likely to engender any strong differential responses to the ad. We therefore, posit the following hypotheses:

H_1: Attitude toward an ad with homosexual imagery will be more positive for individuals who hold tolerant attitudes toward homosexuality than for individuals who hold intolerant attitudes toward homosexuality.

H_2: Attitude toward an ad with heterosexual imagery will be no different between individuals who hold tolerant attitudes toward homosexuality and those who hold intolerant attitudes toward homosexuality respectively.

H_3: Among subjects who hold tolerant attitudes toward homosexuality, an advertisement with homosexual imagery will rate about the same attitude-toward-the-ad as an advertisement with heterosexual imagery.

H_4: Among subjects who hold intolerant attitudes toward homosexuality, an advertisement with homosexual imagery will rate less positive attitude-toward-the-ad than an advertisement with heterosexual imagery.

METHODOLOGY

Stimulus Design

An initial focus group was held to determine what types of images could be used in advertising to suggest homosexuality without the use of nudity or same-sex sexual contact. These limitations were placed to ensure realism of the advertising stimulus. Recommendations from the group included using fully-clothed male subjects shown in close physical proximity, with gestures implying a romantic involvement.

Two products were selected by the researchers for examination. One product was a pair of blue jeans with a brand name of a well-known American manufacturer, and the second product was a shampoo brand from a leading American manufacturer. Established brands were selected for examination to eliminate possible confusion in subjects from an unfamiliar brand name. A fashion item (jeans) was selected to approximate current experimentation by marketing practitioners with images of homosexuality in fashion advertising. A toiletry article (shampoo) was selected because no prior images suggesting homosexuality had been observed in the product category's advertising.

Black and white magazine-style advertisements were selected as a practical medium due to size, ease of reproduction, and low cost of design and preparation. Four advertisements were created: a male homosexual version and a heterosexual version for each of the two products. The advertisements were produced by a professional advertising designer who used professional models photographed by an experienced photographer. The heterosexual-couple models were posed identically to the homosexual-couple models. Advertising text copy was limited to the brand's logo and a single "catch phrase" from the brand's current campaign to enhance realism, and to limit a possible confound from text information.

In each advertisement, a couple is shown in close proximity with a gesture that intimates a romantic involvement. In the jeans ad, the couple is seated next to each other on a broad stairway overlooking a plaza. The person on the left has his/her arm around the subject on the right, and is engaged in animated conversation. In the shampoo ad, the couple are shown standing next to each other at a balcony, facing outward toward the viewer. The subject on the left has his/her hand running through the hair of the subject on the right.

When the advertising design was complete, the ads were pretested with both heterosexual and homosexual respondents to ensure that the couples depicted were perceived as romantically involved, and that the male/male couple was perceived as a homosexual couple. Results of the pretests indicated that the manipulations were successful for both versions and both products.

Measurement

A survey was prepared to measure a respondent's attitude-toward-the-ad, tolerance of homosexuality, age, and gender. Each respondent was asked to evaluate a single ad, which was presented following a brief set of instructions. The A_{ad} measures were seven point semantic differential scales suggested by MacKenzie and Lutz (1989). Reliability of the A_{ad} scales in the current research was excellent (Cronbach's alpha = 0.946). Tolerance of homosexuals was measured by nine selected items from Herek's (1984) C-T scale. The nine items used were selected based on their factor loadings in Herek's research (all in excess of 0.70) and in view of the research interest were oriented toward male homosexuality rather than female homosexuality. These include items characterizing male homosexuality as (1) wrong, (2) disgusting, (3) a sin, (4) a perversion, (5) a lifestyle that should not be condemned (reverse scaled), (6) an indicator of a decline in American morals, and the additional statements: (7) that a man should overcome any homosexual feelings, (8) that it is not a social problem (reverse scaled), and (9) that homosexual marriages are a ridiculous idea. Reliability of the selected C-T scales in the current research is excellent (Cronbach's alpha = 0.944).

To obtain a better understanding of the role that a subject's sexual orientation plays in evaluating the stimuli ads, measures of personal sexual behavior and erotic fantasy history and a self-categorization of sexual orientation were also collected. Personal sexual behavior and erotic fantasy histories were measured on seven-point scales suggested by Kinsey et al. (1948, 1953). Subjects were asked to categorize themselves by answering the following question: "If I had to categorize myself, I'd identify as" with three foils as choices (heterosexual, bisexual, homosexual).

Following administration of the survey, respondents were debriefed to ensure that they understood that the ads were research simulations and neither real ads nor potential advertising executions of the brand sponsors.

Subjects

A sample of 325 college student respondents was selected from a variety of graduate and undergraduate courses at two major universities. One of the universities is located in a major west-coast metropolitan area where there is a large and visible homosexual community. The other university is located in a college town in a southern state, with no appreciable homosexual community presence. Given the objective of this research, a stratified sample was deemed necessary to ensure representation in all the desired profiles. Two hundred fifty-six were from the first university and 69 from the second. Male subjects were 51.9% of the sample and female subjects made up 48.1%. The respondents ranged in age from 18 years to 61 years with 40.5% of them being in the 18-24 years age range, 36.1% in the 25-29 years age range, and 13.9% in the 30-34 age range. Out of 325 subjects, 317 reported their erotic fantasies: 189 (59.6%) had exclusively heterosexual fantasies, 20 (6.3%) had exclusively homosexual fantasies, and 108 (34.1%) reported a combination of homosexual and heterosexual fantasies. The majority of the 313 subjects who reported their adult sexual behavior mentioned exclusively heterosexual behavior (239, 76.4%), 24 (7.7%) reported exclusively homosexual behavior, whereas the remaining reported both heterosexual and homosexual behavior (50, 15.9%). Of the 317 subjects who responded to the self-categorization question, 245 (77.3%) individuals categorized themselves as heterosexual, 21 (6.6%) as bisexual, and 51 (16.1%) as homosexual. It is interesting to note that while the sexual behavioral reports closely match the self-categorization of sexual orientation, reports of sexual fantasy do not seem to be consistent with either the reported behavior or self-categorization. It seems that a large portion of those who have both heterosexual and homosexual fantasies report exclusively heterosexual behavior and categorize themselves as heterosexual. Scores on the averaged C-T scale ranged from 1 (extremely tolerant) to 7 (extremely intolerant) with 2.56 as the median. The mean score was 3.22 for males and 2.75 for females, suggesting more tolerance among females for male homosexuality.

RESULTS

Hypotheses

The first hypothesis predicts that attitude toward the homosexual ad would be more positive for individuals who have tolerant attitudes toward homosexuality than for individuals who have intolerant attitudes toward homosexuality. A median split of the averaged measure of the C-T scales was used to classify subjects as tolerant or intolerant. Thus, those with scores less than or equal to 2.56 on the C-T scale were placed in the tolerant group and the remainder were in the intolerant group. Mean differences in A_{ad} were then compared between the two groups to test the hypothesis. The tolerant group comprised 165 subjects with the following percentages reporting non-exclusively heterosexual (a) fantasies (63.8%), (b) behavior (54.5%), and (c) self-categorization (41.7%). The intolerant group comprised 160 subjects with an overwhelming majority reporting exclusively heterosexual fantasies (83.4%), behavior (96.8%), and self-categorization (96.8%).

Table 1 depicts the mean attitudes toward the homosexual and heterosexual ads for both the jeans and shampoo brands for the tolerant and intolerant groups. In addition, the table contains mean attitudes for groups classified in terms of their sexual fantasies, sexual behavior, and self-categorization of sexual orientation. These have been provided for the sole purpose of helping the reader better understand and interpret reactions to homosexual and heterosexual advertising. As expected, those with a tolerant attitude toward homosexuality displayed a better attitude toward the homosexual ad than did those with an intolerant attitude. For the jeans ad, the mean A_{ad} was 4.46 (n = 34) for the tolerant group but only 2.87 (n = 28) for the intolerant group, and this difference is statistically significant (F = 12.425, p = .001). With the shampoo ad, mean A_{ad} was 4.72 (n = 30) for the tolerant group versus 2.44 (n = 31) for the intolerant group, and again, the difference is statistically significant (F = 31.753, p < .001). Hypothesis 1 is therefore supported.

The second hypothesis suggests that there would be no differences in the reaction to ads portraying a heterosexual couple between those who have tolerant attitudes toward homosexuality and those who have intolerant attitudes.

Those with a more tolerant attitude toward homosexuality displayed a

TABLE 1. Attitude Toward the Ad: Mean Ratings (Sample Size) of Homosexual and Heterosexual Imagery Ads by Tolerance of Homosexuality and Sexual Orientation

| | Jeans | | Shampoo | |
| | Homosexual Imagery Ad | Heterosexual Imagery Ad | Homosexual Imagery Ad | Heterosexual Imagery Ad |
Category				
Intolerant of Homosexuality	2.87 [28]	3.39 [23]	2.44 [31]	3.70 [29]
Tolerant of Homosexuality	4.46 [34]	2.48 [30]	4.72 [30]	3.36 [30]
Exclusively Heterosexual Fantasies	3.07 [36]	3.33 [28]	2.78 [35]	3.70 [35]
Bisexual Fantasies	4.52 [18]	2.57 [21]	4.50 [18]	3.32 [20]
Exclusively Homosexual Fantasies	5.19 [7]	1.33 [3]	5.67 [4]	2.78 [3]
Exclusively Heterosexual Behavior	3.24 [45]	3.32 [37]	3.07 [41]	3.58 [47]
Bisexual Behavior	4.33 [9]	1.26 [9]	4.20 [10]	3.46 [8]
Homosexual Behavior	6.06 [6]	2.60 [5]	5.56 [6]	2.78 [3]
Self-Categorized Heterosexual	3.34 [44]	3.21 [37]	3.02 [45]	3.58 [48]
Self-Categorized Bisexual	2.67 [5]	2.83 [4]	5.58 [4]	3.67 [2]
Self-Categorized Homosexual	5.39 [12]	1.94 [11]	5.09 [11]	2.83 [6]

poorer attitude toward the heterosexual ad than did those with more intolerant attitudes. For the jeans ad, the mean attitudes were 2.48 (n = 30) for the tolerant group and 3.39 (n = 23) for the intolerant group, a difference which is statistically significant (F = 5.301, p = .025). With the shampoo ad, the mean attitude was 3.36 (n = 30) for the tolerant group and 3.70 (n = 29) for the intolerant group, a difference which is not statistically significant (F = 1.364, p = .248). Thus, Hypothesis 2 receives support with respect to the shampoo ad but not the jeans ad. The differences in the results for the two brands are discussed later.

The third hypothesis asserts that those who have a more tolerant attitude toward homosexuality would have similar attitudes toward ads portraying a homosexual couple as towards ads portraying a heterosexual couple.

Individuals with tolerant attitudes toward homosexuality had a poorer attitude toward the heterosexual jeans ad (2.48, n = 30) than toward the homosexual jeans ad (4.46, n = 34). This difference is statistically significant (F = 19.327, p < .001). Individuals with tolerant attitudes toward homosexuality had a poorer attitude toward the heterosexual shampoo ad (3.36, n = 30) than toward the homosexual shampoo ad (4.72, n = 30), with this difference being statistically significant (F = 11.570, p = .001). Overall, it seems that those with a more tolerant attitude toward homosexuality show a poorer attitude toward ads portraying heterosexuals than those portraying homosexuals which is contrary to our expectations in Hypothesis 3. This occurred possibly because the tolerant group includes homosexuals who would like to see homosexuals portrayed in ads and therefore, reacted more positively to the stimuli ads depicting a homosexual couple.

These results may also help us understand the reasons for the contradictory results in attitudes toward the heterosexual jeans and shampoo ads. Recall that attitude toward the heterosexual shampoo ad was similar for both the tolerant and intolerant groups, but was far lower for the heterosexual jeans ad with the tolerant group than the intolerant group. If we compare the mean ad attitude scores for the tolerant group (per Hypothesis 3), we observe that the difference in scores between the homosexual and heterosexual ad conditions is 1.98 (4.46-2.48) for the jeans brand, but is only 1.36 (4.72-3.36) for the shampoo brand. The tolerant group seems to prefer homosexual ads with a wider margin in the case of jeans. Perhaps, there is greater identification of the jeans brand's image with the homosexual lifestyle as compared to the shampoo brand's image. One reason for this is that advertisers of fashion items, including a number of jeans marketers such as Calvin Klein and Banana Republic (though neither brand was used in this study), have long targeted the homosexual community with ads depicting homosexual images in gay media outlets. The tolerant category includes those classifying themselves as homosexual who may not view the heterosexual jeans ad very favorably for this reason. This may account for the differential effects of the jeans and shampoo ads.

The fourth hypothesis (H4) proposes that those who hold intolerant attitudes toward homosexuality would have better attitudes toward ads portraying a heterosexual couple than ads portraying a homosexual couple.

Those with more intolerant attitudes toward homosexuality had a much better attitude toward the heterosexual jeans ad (3.39, n = 23) than toward the homosexual jeans ad (2.87, n = 28), but the difference in means is not statistically significant (F = 1.848, p = .180). These individuals had a better attitude toward the heterosexual shampoo ad (3.70, n = 29) than toward the homosexual shampoo ad (2.44, n = 31). As this difference is statistically significant (F = 17.124, p < .001), Hypothesis 4 receives mixed support for the two brands. As explained earlier, the depiction of homosexual lifestyles is prevalent in fashion advertising, including a few jeans brands, but not, to our knowledge, in advertising for shampoo brands. Negative reactions to the shampoo homosexual ad may have been stronger for this reason. This could explain the difference in findings for the jeans and shampoo brand ads.

Other Findings

As could be expected, attitude toward the homosexual ad for both brands was most favorable on the part of those reporting exclusively homosexual fantasies and behavior, and least favorable for those reporting exclusively heterosexual fantasies and behavior, with the attitudes of those reporting bisexual fantasies and behavior being somewhere in between. Also, those who categorized themselves as homosexual liked the homosexual ads better than did those who categorized themselves as heterosexual or bisexual. With the heterosexual ads, the pattern was generally reversed: those reporting exclusively homosexual fantasies and behavior had the least positive attitudes; those reporting exclusively heterosexual fantasies and behavior had the most positive attitudes; and those reporting bisexual fantasies and behavior had attitudes somewhere in between (except for the jeans ad). Individuals classifying themselves as heterosexuals also liked the heterosexual ads better than did those who classified themselves as homosexual.

Individuals with exclusively heterosexual fantasies, behaviors, and self-categorization seemed to find little difference between the heterosexual and the homosexual jeans ads but preferred the heterosexual shampoo ad to the homosexual shampoo ad, a product- or brand-related difference that we commented on earlier. Those who reported bisexual fantasies and behavior as well as those with exclusively homosexual fantasies, behavior and self-categorization found homosexual ads better than heterosexual ads. Individuals characterizing themselves as bisexual, however, gave similar ratings to the heterosexual and homosexual jeans ads but seemed to prefer the homosexual shampoo ad to the heterosexual shampoo ad. Caution must be exercised in interpreting these observations in view of the small cell sizes in some cases and, for that very reason, the non-use of statistical testing of differences.

CONCLUSIONS

In this study, an attempt was made to examine the effect of using homosexual imagery in advertising on individuals' attitude toward the ad.

Attitude toward the ad has been found to be a very important indicator of brand attitude and purchase.

In general, the findings suggest strong support for the hypothesis that attitude toward an ad with homosexual imagery was much more positive for those who had a tolerant attitude toward homosexuality than for those who were intolerant of homosexuality. At the same time, those more intolerant of homosexuality preferred the heterosexual ad to a similar homosexual ad.

These findings suggest that advertisers who wish to retain the loyalty of their traditional, mainly heterosexual market must be very careful about the likely "crossover" effect when they target homosexuals with advertising imagery that appeals to the homosexual audience. The saving grace is that a sizable segment of the heterosexual public seems to have a tolerant attitude toward homosexuality, and this group seems unaffected by the portrayal of homosexual lifestyles in advertising. However, the study does suggest that the unequivocal acceptance of images depicting the homosexual lifestyle in traditional media is as yet unlikely.

In general, those who were tolerant of homosexuality were likely to display less positive attitudes toward heterosexual imagery in advertising than those who were intolerant. Also, the tolerant group seemed to prefer the ad with homosexual images by a very wide margin over the ad with heterosexual images. While these findings are quite surprising given the abundance of heterosexual imagery in traditional advertising, discrepancies in findings between the two brands used in the study suggest that some brands that have possibly stronger associations with homosexual lifestyles are looked upon less favorably by those tolerant of homosexuality when they use heterosexual imagery. The "crossover" effect is apparent here, too.

Advertisers need to be aware that while using homosexual imagery in advertisements may alienate a segment of the population, it does create goodwill for the brand among homosexuals and those tolerant of homosexuality. However, appealing to these different segments through the use of homosexual imagery in advertisements in mainstream media is not a good idea. In light of the findings that the group intolerant of homosexuality reacted negatively to the homosexual imagery ad whereas the group tolerant of homosexuality responded negatively to the heterosexual imagery ad, ads depicting same-sex or opposite-sex couples probably ought to be "micro" targeted, i.e., targeted specifically to the tolerant and intolerant groups respectively.

The differential impact for the two brands in this study indicates the role that a brand's symbolism may have in the use of homosexual imagery in ads. It seems that some brands that are more strongly associated with homosexual lifestyles might elicit only a muted response from those who might otherwise react differently. This issue needs to be explored further.

A few limitations of this study suggest that generalization of its findings must be made with caution. First, the findings reported were observed in the circumstances of this study, i.e., stand-alone stimuli and survey not placed in any particular magazine or other context. The acceptance of homosexual images may be different in other contexts or situations. For example, acceptability may be higher in a fashion magazine vis-à-vis a newsmagazine. The sample size of homosexuals in this study, though higher than the reported proportion of homosexuals in the general population, was quite small. Subsequent research could use stratified sampling procedures to enhance the proportion of homosexual respondents. Also, the study examined only the immediate effects of exposure to an ad, and did not look at the long-term "crossover" effects.

To the best of our knowledge, this is the first study to investigate this issue. This field of inquiry is almost devoid of research, and several future research issues spring to mind. Certainly, the long-term effects of positioning with homosexual imagery need to be examined. Consistent with research suggesting that strongly held brand attitudes are somewhat resistant to change, it could be that in the long term, such imagery has little effect on brand attitudes and therefore brand purchase behavior. In addition, brand symbolism should be considered to determine if brands have different symbolic meanings for homosexual and heterosexual consumers. While this study examined reactions to male homosexual images in ads, future research might profitably look at responses to the use of female homosexual images in ads. The intriguing reactions of tolerant individuals (including homosexuals) to heterosexual images in ads suggests that there is an interesting and important area of research: what is the attitude of homosexuals toward heterosexuals and heterosexuality? We also recommend a more comprehensive examination of attitudes toward advertising in general and especially toward both homosexual and heterosexual imagery in ads among heterosexuals, homosexuals, and bisexuals to ascertain the differences, if any, in opinions of and the evaluation processes employed by these groups.

NOTE

1. Homosexual population estimates range from 2.8% (Laumann et al. 1994) to 10% (Kinsey et al. 1948, 1953). The variation may, in part, be attributed to widely differing definitions of homosexuality. Smaller numbers are generally reported when respondents are asked to categorize themselves. Higher numbers are reported when respondents are asked about their sexual behavior and fantasies.

REFERENCES

Batra, R. & Ray, M. L. (1985). How advertising works at contact. In Alwitt, L. F. & Mitchell, A. A. (Eds.), *Psychological Processes and Advertising Effects: Theory, Research, and Application*. Hillsdale, NJ: Lawrence Erlbaum Associates.

Churchill, W. (1967). *Homosexual Behavior Among Males*. New York: Hawthorn.

Edell, J. A. & Burke, M. C. (1986). The relative impact of prior brand attitude and attitude toward the ad on brand attitude after ad exposure. In, Olson, J. & Sentis, K. (Eds.), *Advertising and Consumer Psychology*, 3. New York, NY: Praeger Publishers.

Fishbein, M. & Ajzen, I. (1975). *Belief, Attitude, Intention, and Behavior: An Introduction to Theory and Research*. Reading, MA: Addison-Wesley Publishing Co.

Gardner, M. P. (1985). Does attitude toward the ad affect brand attitude under a brand evaluation set? *Journal of Marketing Research*, 22 (2), 192-8.

Herek, G. M. (1984). Attitudes toward lesbians and gay men: A factor-analytic study. *Journal of Homosexuality*, 10 (1), 39-51.

Hudson, W. W. & Ricketts, W. (1980). A Strategy for the Measurement of Homophobia. *Journal of Homosexuality*, 5 (4), 357-373.

Kinsey, A. C., Pomeroy, W. B., & Martin, C. E. (1948). *Sexual Behavior in the Human Male*. Philadelphia, PA: W. B. Saunders Company, 636-655.

Kinsey, A. C., Pomeroy, W. B., Martin, C. E., & Gebhard, P. H. (1953). *Sexual Behavior in the Human Female*. Philadelphia, PA: W. B. Saunders Company, 468-476.

Larsen, K. S., Reed, M., & Hoffman, S. (1980). Attitudes of heterosexuals toward homosexuality: A Likert-type scale and construct validity. *Journal of Sex Research*, 16 (3), 245-257.

Laumann, E. O., Gagnon, J. H., Michael, R. T., & Michaels, S. (1994). *The Social Organization of Sexuality: Sexual Practices in the United States*. Chicago, IL: University of Chicago Press, 292-297.

Levitt, E. E. & Klassen, A. D., Jr. (1974). Attitudes toward homosexuality. *Journal of Homosexuality*, 1 (1).

Lutz, R. J. (1985). Affective and cognitive antecedents of attitude toward the ad: A conceptual framework. In Alwitt, L. F. & Mitchell, A. A. (Eds.), *Psychological Processes and Advertising Effects: Theory, Research, and Application*. Hillsdale, NJ: Lawrence Erlbaum Associates.

MacKenzie, S. B. & Lutz, R. J. (1989). An empirical examination of the structural antecedents of attitude toward the ad in an advertising pretesting context. *Journal of Marketing*, 53 (1), 48-65.

Millham, J., San Miguel, C. L., & Kellogg R. (1976). A factor-analytic conceptualization of attitudes toward male and female homosexuals. *Journal of Homosexuality*, 2 (1), 3-10.

Mitchell, A. A. (1983). The Effects of Visual and Emotional Advertising. In Harris, R. (Ed.), *Information Processing Research in Advertising*. Hillsdale, NJ: Lawrence Erlbaum Associates.

_____. (1986). The effect of verbal and visual components of advertisements on brand attitudes and attitude toward the advertisement. *Journal of Consumer Research*, 13 (2), 12-24.

Mitchell, A. A. & Olson, J. C. (1981). Are product attribute beliefs the only mediators of advertising effects in brand attitudes? *Journal of Marketing Research*, 18 (3), 318-322.

Morin, S. F. & Garfinkle, E. M. (1978). Male homophobia. *Journal of Social Issues*, 34 (1), 29-47.

Muehling, D. D. & Laczniak, R. N. (1988). Advertising's immediate and delayed influence on brand attitudes: Considerations across message-involvement levels. *Journal of Advertising*, 17 (4), 23-34.

Rossiter, J. R. & Percy, L. (1980). Attitude change through visual imagery in advertising. *Journal of Advertising*, 9 (2), 10-16.

San Francisco Chronicle (1994). Some Progress Found in Poll on Gay Rights. (June 20), Reuters News Service.

Shimp, T. A. (1981). Attitude toward the ad as a mediator of consumer brand choice. *Journal of Advertising*, 10 (2), 9-15.

Weinberg, G. (1972). *Society and the Healthy Homosexual*. New York: St. Martin's.

The Social Marketing of Project ARIES: Overcoming Challenges in Recruiting Gay and Bisexual Males for HIV Prevention Counseling

Douglass S. Fisher, MA
Rosemary Ryan, PhD
Anne W. Esacove, MPH/MSW (cand.)
Steven Bishofsky, MA
J. Marc Wallis, MSW (cand.)
Roger A. Roffman, DSW

University of Washington

SUMMARY. This paper reports on the development, implementation, and evaluation of a social marketing campaign designed to

Douglass S. Fisher is Director of Marketing for Project ARIES. Rosemary Ryan is Research Assistant Professor in the School of Social Work at the University of Washington and Research Director for Project ARIES. Anne W. Esacove is an MPH/MSW candidate. Steven Bishofsky is a research consultant. J. Marc Wallis is a research consultant. Roger A. Roffman is Associate Professor in the School of Social Work at the University of Washington, and the principal investigator and Director/Project ARIES. This research was supported by grant number 5RO1MH46792 from the National Institute of Mental Health (NIMH), Bethesda, Maryland. The authors wish to thank Cher Gunby for her valuable technical assistance in the preparation of the manuscript. Correspondence should be addressed to Douglass S. Fisher, MA, Innovative Programs Research Group XD-39, University of Washington, Seattle, WA 98195. E-mail: *dsfisher@u. washington.edu*

[Haworth co-indexing entry note]: "The Social Marketing of Project ARIES: Overcoming Challenges in Recruiting Gay and Bisexual Males for HIV Prevention Counseling." Fisher, Douglass S. et al. Co-published simultaneously in *Journal of Homosexuality* (The Haworth Press, Inc.) Vol. 31, No. 1/2, 1996, pp. 177-202; and *Gays, Lesbians, and Consumer Behavior: Theory, Practice, and Research Issues in Marketing* (ed: Daniel L. Wardlow) The Haworth Press, Inc., 1996, pp. 177-202; and: *Gays, Lesbians, and Consumer Behavior: Theory, Practice, and Research Issues in Marketing* (ed: Daniel L. Wardlow) Harrington Park Press, an imprint of The Haworth Press, Inc., 1996, pp. 177-202. Single or multiple copies of this article are available from The Haworth Document Delivery Service [1-800-342-9678, 9:00 a.m. - 5:00 p.m. (EST)].

177

recruit clients for Project ARIES, an AIDS prevention study funded by the National Institute of Mental Health. Marketing channels employed for the campaign included advertising in the gay press, generating coverage in the mainstream press, distributing materials to HIV testing centers and other health and social service providers, and displaying posters in gay bars and baths.

While these approaches all succeeded in eliciting inquiries from individuals engaging in high risk sexual behaviors, they differed in several respects, including their ability to reach specific subgroups that are often underserved by more traditional programs, such as men of color, younger men, and men who self-report as being closeted. Promotional materials displayed in gay bars and baths resulted in the highest percentage of callers who, after inquiring about the program, decided to participate in the counseling. Coverage in the mainstream press was the most successful in reaching closeted men, men who were less active in the gay community, and individuals who did not self-identify as gay. Display and classified ads in the gay press produced the highest number of initial inquiries. Finally, recruitment of participants via materials distributed to HIV test sites and other service providers was the most effective in reaching men who were HIV-positive. *[Article copies available from The Haworth Document Delivery Service: 1-800-342-9678.]*

INTRODUCTION

By comparison to social change campaigns which have been around as long as people have tried to redress social ills or advance social causes, the formal application of traditional marketing principles to social change efforts is a more contemporary phenomenon (Kotler and Roberto, 1989). In 1971, the term "social marketing" was applied to the use of marketing strategies to advance social causes, ideas, or behavior (Kotler and Roberto, 1989). In 1985, the American Marketing Association officially revised their definition of marketing to include ideas as entities which can be promoted: "Marketing is the process of planning and executing the conception, pricing, promotion and distribution of ideas, goods and services to create exchanges that satisfy individual and organizational objectives" (Fine, 1991). Today, in order to effect societal changes, social institutions no longer question the need to market their ideas or products. Rather, the challenge is determining which strategy to use and how to implement it (Fine, 1991).

Since 1982, when AIDS began to emerge as a significant public health concern, there has been a proliferation of social change campaigns designed to influence public awareness of the problem. Kotler (1982) identifies four types of health-related changes that campaigns are designed to effect: (1) *cognitive change* (public information or public education campaigns), (2) *action change* (campaigns designed to elicit a particular response during a given period), (3) *behavioral change* (campaigns designed to help people change some aspect of their behavior for the sake of their health) and (4) *value change* (campaigns designed to alter beliefs or values). This paper reports on the development, implementation, and evaluation of an action change campaign that was designed to recruit clients for Project ARIES, an AIDS prevention study funded by the National Institute of Mental Health.[1] We will describe the marketing plan that resulted in employing the following: (1) advertising in the gay press, (2) generating coverage in the mainstream press, (3) distributing materials to HIV testing centers and other health and social service providers, and (4) displaying posters in gay bars and baths. We evaluate the costs and differential effectiveness of these major components of the marketing plan in seeking to reach and enroll individuals in need of support to be sexually safer.

The Challenges of AIDS-Related Social Marketing Campaigns

As knowledge has emerged concerning sexual behaviors that present high risk for HIV transmission, public health specialists and gay activists have vigorously promoted educational campaigns that appear to be effective in enhancing knowledge, changing attitudes, and modifying behaviors among many gay and bisexual men (Becker & Joseph, 1988; Coates et al., 1988; Ekstrand & Coates, 1990; Martin, Garcia, & Beatrice, 1989; McCusker, Stoddard, Zapka, Zorn, & Mayer, 1989; Stall, Coates, & Hoff, 1988). These outcomes notwithstanding, considerable evidence has consistently pointed to continuing high risk sexual behavior among a minority of gay and bisexual males, some of whom have failed to initiate behavior change while others have periodically slipped back to unsafe behaviors after adopting safer behavioral patterns for a period of time (Adib, Joseph, Ostrow, & James, 1991; Ekstrand & Coates, 1990; Kingsley et al., 1990).

Thus, in this second decade of AIDS, the field of public health is faced with two difficult tasks. First, new behavior change interventions must be developed that will facilitate both the initiation as well as the maintenance of change in those gay and bisexual individuals who have not as yet successfully adopted stable safer sex behavior patterns. Epidemiologists point to the need for particular emphases for these new interventions with men who have sex with men and: (a) do not self-identify as gay, (b) are younger, (c) have less formal education, or (d) are men of color (Peterson, Coates, Catania, Middleton, Hilliard, & Hearst, 1992; Hays, Kegeles, &

Coates, 1990; Stall et al., 1992). However, because unsafe behavior continues to be reported among many other strata within this diverse population, new prevention efforts are needed across the board for men who have sex with other men.

Yet, even if empirically supported and theoretically sound risk-reduction approaches are designed, the second important task faced is that of social marketing, i.e., the application of marketing methods in the planning for and implementation of efforts to motivate the target population(s) to adapt to new ideas or to make behavioral changes beneficial to themselves and society (Fine, 1990; Kotler and Roberto, 1989). Promotional messages must be constructed that will effectively motivate individuals to participate in prevention counseling. Methods that will succeed in delivering those messages to specific audiences must then be selected. Because even the most effective of tomorrow's interventions can fail through lack of awareness and motivation to participate, the challenge of marketing HIV-prevention programs is of key importance to public health.

Barriers to Social Marketing

At least two important barriers have the potential for obstructing social marketing concerning AIDS prevention interventions. The first has to do with the complexities of the relationship between public health and the mass media. The second pertains specifically to aspects of AIDS and societal attitudes towards homosexuality.

The regulatory environment of the mass media has made it difficult to communicate health information to the public. Decreased public service time for public health messages, greater message competition (especially on television), and media gatekeepers' (the individuals who influence what and how stories are covered in the media) sensitivity to the potential for offending segments of the audience can have the effect of preventing the dissemination of important public health guidance. Moreover, public health specialists and media gatekeepers may disagree concerning what is newsworthy. Finally, in recognizing that repetition of information is an important component of public education, public health specialists may be discouraged by media gatekeepers' unwillingness to devote ongoing attention to an issue (Atkin & Arkin, 1990).

Taylor and Henderson (1992) list four reasons why social marketing specific to AIDS is a particularly difficult challenge. First, it is probable that the lethal nature of AIDS induces denial behavior in some individuals. Risk reduction marketing themes must therefore overcome avoidance attitudes concerning personal vulnerability. Rather than relying on simple slogans urging people to be safe, messages designed to overcome denial will need to stimulate awareness and interest, and to present the issues in ways that strike target groups as relevant and understandable. Second, the taboo nature of public communication of sexual behavior may lead both the government and the mass media to restrict or obstruct candid and explicit educational messages. Content that may be acceptable for widespread dissemination may nonetheless be ineffectual in influencing treatment-seeking behavior. Third, some homophobic media gatekeepers may be unwilling to associate themselves with AIDS prevention groups due to perceived risks of stigmatization. Finally, the fact that AIDS and AIDS-risk behavioral changes are still relatively new and not well understood makes it inevitable that the content of social marketing will need to change as new knowledge emerges. Indeed, some messages that appear to be sound at one point may later be seen as ineffective or perhaps even harmful (Odets, 1994).

In assessing today's requisites for the social marketing of AIDS prevention interventions, one cannot help but be struck by the immensity of the task. To effectively motivate the gay or bisexual man who is acting unsafely, social marketing campaigns will need to incorporate information that acknowledges his losses, his feelings concerning how he has been affected by the epidemic, and his conflicting thoughts about personal choices in sexual behavior. Clearly, the complexity and sexually intimate content inherent in these themes reduces the likelihood of their being disseminated via the mass media. Yet in order to reach some in the gay and bisexual population who remain at high risk (e.g., those who do not self-identify as gay, men with less formal schooling, younger men, men of color, and those who are disadvantaged economically), the mass media may offer the strongest potential for effective message delivery. In brief, complex messages targeting specific hard-to-reach segments of the gay and bisexual populations are needed, and the most promising mechanisms of message delivery are often unavailable or very difficult to access.

Overcoming Barriers to Serving Individuals at High Risk

In developing this project's preventive intervention we recognized that homophobic societal attitudes lead many gay and bisexual males to be closeted and thus isolated from social supports for reducing HIV transmission risk. To overcome the barriers to reaching these individuals, we designed and are evaluating a 14-session group intervention delivered entirely by telephone while permitting anonymous participation. We named the program Project ARIES.

Prior research had demonstrated the effectiveness of cognitive-behavioral group counseling in reducing unprotected sexual behavior in gay and bisexual males (Kelly, St. Lawrence, Hood, & Brasfield, 1989; Roffman, Beadnell, Downey, & Ryan, 1992). By using teleconference technology, permitting anonymous enrollment, and providing a toll-free line, we hoped to overcome geographic and psychological obstacles to working with individuals who remained at high risk and were unlikely to be able or willing to seek risk-reduction supports from agencies that required in-person contact.

This four-year study had the primary objective of determining the extent to which exposure to the intervention led to reduced risk behavior. An additional objective was to evaluate the effectiveness of service delivery by telephone in enrolling men at high risk who otherwise might not have come forward for help. Finally, we hoped to examine the relative strengths of alternative marketing strategies in reaching various subgroups such as those who did not self-identify as gay, men of color, and those who were younger.

METHOD

Goals of Client Recruitment

Our timeline permitted a seven-month planning phase prior to the initiation of recruitment efforts. In developing general goals that would guide our marketing decisions, we determined that all components of the strategy would be required to further the following purposes: (1) to motivate individuals who were concerned about their ongoing unsafe sexual behavior to phone our office to learn about the program firsthand; (2) to reach individuals who were isolated from gay social networks and support; (3) to enroll an ethnically and socioeconomically diverse group of men at high risk of HIV transmission; and (4) to generate a sufficiently rapid flow of applicants so that there would be little or no delay in starting new groups.

The study design called for eligible individuals to be randomly assigned to treatment or wait-list control conditions. Eligibility was based on an individual's having had a minimum of three incidents of unprotected oral or anal sex with another man within the preceding three months. To facilitate statistical analyses concerning the effectiveness of the intervention, the project required that at least 320 individuals be enrolled, complete baseline assessment interviews, be randomized to join a counseling group or remain untreated, and then be reassessed. Control-condition participants were treated following their reassessment.

Our pilot studies with telephone counseling indicated that a substantial rate of attrition would be likely to occur during the enrollment period. We had found in our earlier work that many callers, on learning that the service involved participating in an intervention that was several months long as well as being interviewed several times, decided against participating. Based on our attrition projections, we calculated the need to generate a minimum of 1,882 calls of inquiry over an 18-month recruitment period. With this target in mind and using estimates concerning the percentage of adult males in the population who were sexually active with same-sex partners and engaging in high-risk sexual activities, we projected the size of the geographic region in which recruitment would need to take place. A region that included Vancouver, British Columbia, the states of Washington and Oregon, and northern California met this criterion. As will be noted below, we later expanded our marketing efforts to five additional states. Eventually, widely published news coverage of our program and the placement of display ads in gay publications that have regional distribution led to calls coming in from every state in the country.

Review of Previous Recruitment Efforts

With these recruitment goals in mind, we reviewed the lessons learned in our previous efforts to enroll participants for HIV risk-reduction counseling. Four marketing approaches had been effective: (1) advertising in local gay publications, (2) building a referral network of professional health care providers in HIV and sexually transmitted disease (STD) sites as well as AIDS service agencies, (3) displaying posters in gay bars and baths, and (4) generating feature stories in local daily newspapers. Attempts to publicize our program via radio and television public service announcements (PSAs) had been considerably less effective. Although radio station personnel accepted our PSA scripts, we could never get a firm commitment to have them read on the air. We also worked with an advertising agency to develop a television PSA. During this process we consulted with station managers and public affairs personnel regarding the content and the format of the PSAs. While all of these individuals were optimistic about running the finished product, to our knowledge it was aired only a few times.

Advisory Group, Focus Group, and Graphic Designers

Concurrent with the review of our previous recruitment efforts, we organized an advisory group for the purpose of generating ideas for our upcoming recruitment campaign. Group members were drawn from the local AIDS prevention field, an advertising agency, and academic specialties such as communications.

To enhance the campaign's effectiveness in recruiting men of color, we organized a focus group comprised of staff from a local AIDS agency that works specifically with racial minorities. The focus group members initially identified an array of potentially effective strategies for this purpose. Later they reviewed draft marketing products that had been developed based on their earlier input.

While setting up the focus and advisory groups, we sent letters to seven graphic designers, asking each to consider donating their professional services. Three were interested, and we determined that two of them had experience that would likely make for a good fit with the project's needs. Both agreed to take on some portion of the marketing design requirements.

With these idea-generating units in place, the marketing staff assumed the responsibility of providing feedback to each unit, communicating ideas, eliciting comments and suggestions, making needed revisions, and gradually working toward consensus.

Marketing Tools

Seven marketing tools were developed for use in three out of the four marketing channels we ultimately relied upon to promote the study: a series of five posters, newspaper display advertisements that were smaller versions of the posters, a brochure, one by three inch pads of tear-off business cards designed to be attached to the posters, various versions of a press release, a flyer called "A Brief History of Project ARIES," and an ARIES Fact Sheet.

The decision to create a series of posters, our flagship items in the campaign, was driven by several concerns. Focus group members believed that materials intended to reach and motivate men of color to participate needed to be targeted specifically to each racial and ethnic group. They argued that mixed ethnic images within any one brochure or poster would be less effective. As will be noted below, each poster in the series we subsequently produced conveyed a unique "face" of the project and its clientele. We hoped that men would see themselves in these publicity materials. We also hoped that offering a variety of posters would effectively keep our message "fresh" over time.

Since the posters were to be displayed in venues ranging from gay bars to public health clinics, we wanted designs that were not so overtly sexual as to limit their acceptability. Also, we strove for images appropriate for a professional counseling service program that provided an in-depth look at some of the psychological factors that are often barriers to safer intimate encounters. The five poster images and themes we developed were: (1) "Make the Connection"–a watercolor portraying hands and arms of persons representing racial diversity reaching towards a telephone, (2) "I Want It"–a European-American male image, with a simple statement of desire left intentionally vague, (3) "You Choose Who Knows"–an African-American male image with a statement that suggests the viewer is in control of self-disclosure, (4) "I Know What I Do Is Risky"–a Latino image accompanied by a statement that acknowledges that behavior change often requires more than knowledge about AIDS risk, and (5) "Afterward, I Worry About What I've Done"–a European-American male image with a statement that recognizes the commonly experienced after-effects of being unsafe, e.g., anxiety, worry, and stress.

While we intended to have all five posters printed prior to implementation of the recruitment phase, only two were available at the start. This delay worked to our advantage because a staggered production schedule made it possible to make minor copy revisions and to create a more effective campaign.

Approximately three months were required to usher the poster creation process through two advisory group meetings, two focus group meetings, numerous draft drawings from the designers, and several ARIES staff meetings to the point where we were ready to make final decisions.

Channels of Communication

With our review of previous efforts having been completed, and with the feedback mechanism in place, we developed a general strategy. Public service announcements on the radio and television were rejected because neither afforded us adequate control over placement. Moreover, the cost for TV-PSA production was prohibitive. Ultimately, the main components of the recruitment effort included generating feature stories in mainstream newspapers, placing display advertisements in the gay press, mailing informational material on a quarterly basis to a professional referral network (e.g., community based gay and AIDS service organizations and state level HIV/STD test sites), and quarterly mailings to gay bars and baths.

Advertising in Gay Publications

Advertising in gay publications proved to be the most reliable method of recruiting participants. Given the cost of buying ad space, it was also the single most expensive component of the overall campaign. However, we consistently saw a direct and immediate relationship between the appearance of these advertisements and incoming calls where men cited the ads as their source of information about the project.

In order to increase image and name recognition and in an effort to stretch our design budget, we decided to use slightly reworked versions of our five posters for these display advertisements. We also examined several gay publications to determine the ideal ad size and layout. A quarter page appeared to be the smallest size that would have the potential of being noticed. To maximize their eye-catching quality, we strove to keep copy to a minimum. The ads were designed to pique a reader's curiosity, not to tell the whole story. For a full explanation of the project, they had to contact us on the toll-free number. (See Figures 1 and 2.)

This initial ad campaign was six months long. Display ads were placed in seven gay publications on the West Coast, alternating issue run dates, except for monthlies in which we ran ads each month for six months. In an effort to avoid losing interest from readers, three different ads were rotated.

Every publication offered a discount for non-profit organizations and additional rate cuts for placing higher numbers of ads. For the first third of the campaign we took advantage of both discounts. However, when we expanded our recruitment area, we forfeited the frequency discounts in order to place ads in more publications. In the last two thirds of the campaign, we bought ad space in twenty new gay publications, including two with national distribution, and ran them half as often as those placed at the beginning of the campaign.

When there was a lull in the display ad campaign, there was a noticeable decrease in the number of incoming calls. It became evident that display advertising created a consistent flow of callers inquiring about the project. This predictability of response was not available through other means. Since maintaining a steady flow of inquiries was necessary for the timely assignment of men into counseling groups, having funding available for display advertising was highly important to the project.

Classified Ads and Press Releases in the Gay Press

Two additional marketing efforts were utilized with the gay press. We wrote what we hoped would be seen as interesting and provocative classified ads and sought to have them placed in the "looking for relationships/ sex" sections of the papers. In publications that would not permit placement of non-contact ads in those sections, we ran them under "Counseling." The latter seemed to be less effective. Nonetheless, given the very low cost of producing and placing classified ads, this seemed like a good alternative, especially if used in conjunction with display advertising.

Another strategy involved the writing and distribution to gay newspapers of a press release concerning the project. We purchased a media list

FIGURE 1

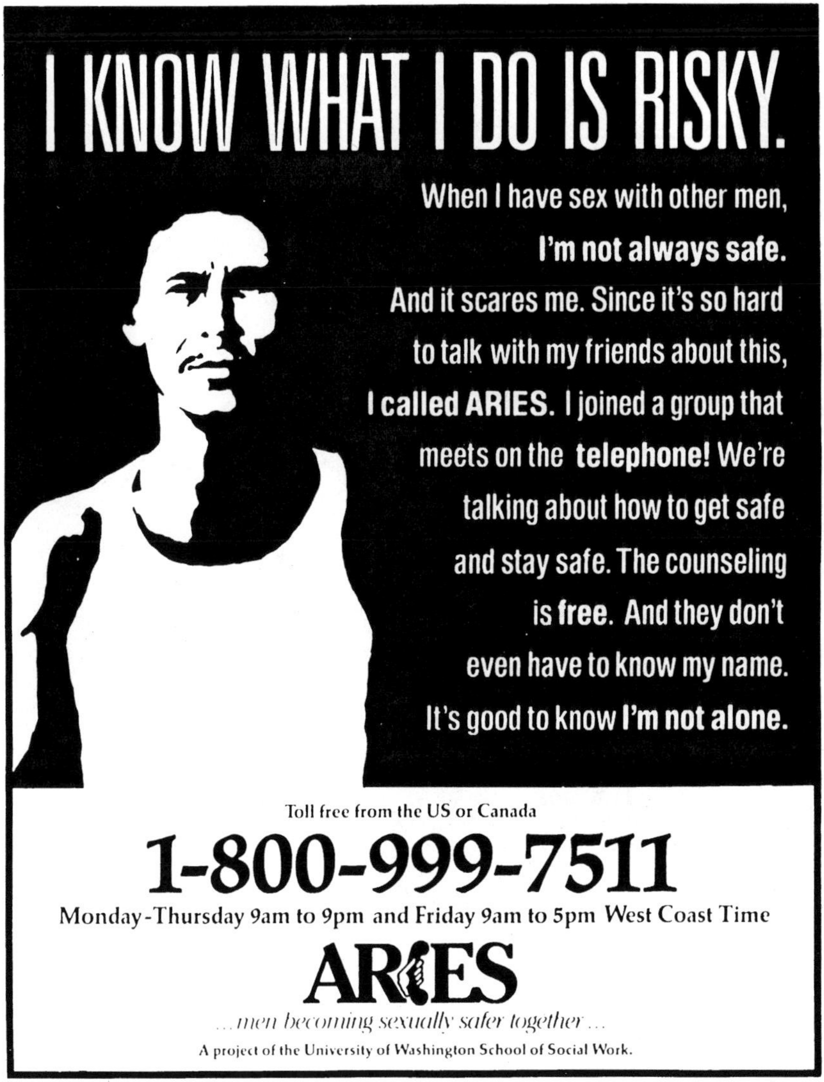

I KNOW WHAT I DO IS RISKY.
When I have sex with other men,
I'm not always safe.
And it scares me. Since it's so hard
to talk with my friends about this,
I called ARIES. I joined a group that
meets on the telephone! We're
talking about how to get safe
and stay safe. The counseling
is free. And they don't
even have to know my name.
It's good to know I'm not alone.
Toll free from the US or Canada
1-800-999-7511
Monday-Thursday 9am to 9pm and Friday 9am to 5pm West Coast Time
ARIES
...men becoming sexually safer together...
A project of the University of Washington School of Social Work.

FIGURE 2

from Renaissance House, the company that publishes the GAY YELLOW PAGES. Recognizing that some gay newspapers had limited personnel, releases were written so they could be printed directly as a news item.

Feature Stories in the Mainstream Press

Generating news coverage and feature stories in the mainstream press was a major recruitment component because we believed that this medium would be effective in reaching men who were closeted. Prior to seeking press coverage, we contacted two of the men who had participated in our telephone counseling pilot project and asked if they would consent to being contacted for press interviews. Both agreed, and we assured them that they would be able to maintain their anonymity. News coverage with a personal angle turned out to be an effective and low cost marketing mechanism.

We then generated a list of all metropolitan daily newspapers in our multi-state recruitment region and telephoned each paper to find out which reporter might handle a story about our program. For certain newspapers, the medical reporter was identified as most appropriate. More commonly, however, reporters who wrote about general lifestyle issues turned out to be the most interested.

The ARIES Project director, a University of Washington faculty member, initiated our contacts with the newspapers because we hoped that being contacted by a professor would catch the reporter's attention. We created a press packet that included a cover letter, a press release, and a brief history of Project ARIES. The director sent this packet to reporters with a note that he would be calling them to follow up on the letter.

Eliciting reporters' interest was more difficult than we had imagined. We had thought that an innovative program of this nature would be perceived as newsworthy by reporters eager for new angles on the AIDS epidemic. Often this was not the case. Quite commonly, when the project director made his follow-up calls, the reporter would ask him to mail the materials again because the first packet had been lost or discarded. It became evident that when they had initially glanced at our materials, many reporters failed to see local relevance for a program that was physically located outside of their communities. When we emphasized that the toll-free telephone number essentially located the intervention in their community, many then saw the relevance and ran the story.

After a feature story about ARIES was published in the *Los Angeles Times* in June of 1992, we received numerous calls from men in southern California. That story also was distributed via a national wire service and carried by newspapers in many U.S. communities. As a consequence, men interested in ARIES called from all around the country. A subsequent article written by a reporter with the Associated Press and distributed nationwide resulted in a similar boost in our incoming calls.

Largely as a result of this coverage, we decided to expand recruitment from a regional to a national focus. We made decisions about where to expand our efforts by consulting 1991-1992 data from the Centers for Disease Control pertaining to each state's number of AIDS cases. As a consequence, we added New York, New Jersey, Florida, Texas, and Illinois. The project benefited in several ways. Working with men across multiple time zones meant that the scheduling of data collection interviews and group sessions could be more evenly distributed over our work day. It also increased the rate of new client inquiries to the project. Finally, this news coverage aided us in approaching other newspapers for publicity. Being able to say ARIES had been covered by the *Los Angeles Times* helped us to get a foot in the door.

While we clearly benefited from this coverage, there were also some negative consequences to gaining national attention via the mainstream press. We became highly visible to the general public, including individuals who reacted negatively to what we were doing. Since our toll-free number was mentioned in all news coverage, it became easy for those who wanted to voice their disapproval to call us at our expense. Several "right wing" groups encouraged their members to call and object to our use of tax dollars to help gay and bisexual men in the fight against AIDS.

Advertising in Racial/Ethnic Minority Newspapers

As part of our effort to actively recruit men of color, we bought display ad space in ethnic/racial minority newspapers in Los Angeles, the San Francisco Bay Area, Portland and Seattle. Using ads with the African-American and Latino images, we ran a minimum of four placements in each paper. This was a costly campaign and did not appear to be effective in generating inquiries to the project.

The Professional Referral Network

Prior to mailing promotional materials to local AIDS service organizations and HIV/STD testing agencies, we approached the lead AIDS organization and the appropriate public health department officials in each state and asked for their assistance. If they agreed to support the marketing of our services, we asked them to provide us with a list of the relevant service agencies in their state and permission to use their name in a cover letter as having endorsed ARIES. With one exception, our requests were granted.

Materials were mailed to local service providers on a quarterly basis. Each mailing updated them on the progress of the program. The packets included a cover letter, a new poster, a set of brochures, one or two pads of tear-off business cards, and an ARIES Fact Sheet. If an article about the project had recently been published in a newspaper in their region, we included a copy in the packet. We hoped that these stories in the press would add to our credibility, thus enhancing the likelihood that the local service provider would display and distribute our materials.

Materials in Gay Bars and Baths

Using listings in the Damron Address Book, we initiated quarterly mailings of ARIES posters, brochures, and tear-off business cards to gay bars and baths in each of the eight states. Both bars and baths are venues where large numbers of men congregate socially, often in search of sexual partners, thereby making them important places to display project materials. Methods other than mailings, such as calling the bars and hiring a "runner" to post materials, all proved to be too costly to pursue.

RESULTS

In this section, we begin by examining the efficacy of each of our four major marketing strategies in generating inquiries. We then examine the percentage of callers within each recruitment source who were interested in counseling, were both interested and eligible, and who actually began the program.

Because ARIES was a research project, its participants had to complete as many as seven individual telephone interviews over at least a five-week period before they could join a counseling group. Thus, in an attempt to make these data useful for the staff of a nonprofit agency that might offer a similar prevention program in the future (but without the considerable research component), we have designated completion of the first baseline assessment interview as comparable to the status of beginning treatment in a conventional agency context.

We also report in this section the differential capacity of each marketing strategy to elicit inquiries from members of specific subgroups (e.g., younger men, those who do not self-identify as gay, etc.) which tend to be underserved by AIDS prevention programs. Finally, we present data concerning the costs associated with each of our marketing efforts, emphasiz-

ing the costs within each marketing category per caller who began participation in the program.

Responses from the Target Population

We were able to determine how 4,481 out of 4,649 callers (96 percent)
had heard about the program. The 2,500 men who were interested in safer
sex counseling accounted for 55.8 percent of these calls (see Table 1).
Other calls came from health care professionals wanting information
about the project, from persons seeking some other form of counseling
assistance, and from individuals who wanted to voice their objections to
the program.

The gay press generated the highest number of calls from men interested in counseling (n = 849). The numbers of callers interested in counseling who identified the mainstream press (n = 582) or the professional
referral network (n = 538) as the means through which they had learned
about the project were quite similar to each other. It must be noted, however, that the volume of calls from each source is at least in part a reflec-

TABLE 1. Client Flow from Initial Call to First Interview by Recruitment
Source[1]

	Total	Gay Press	Mainstream Press	Professional Referrals	Bars & Baths	Other
All Callers	4,481[2]	1,450	1,180	887	278	686
# Interested in Counseling	2,500	849	582	538	187	344
% of all callers	*55.8*	*58.6*	*49.3*	*60.7*	*67.3*	*50.1*
# Interested & Eligible	1,720	607	358	396	143	216
% of all callers	*38.4*	*41.9*	*30.3*	*44.6*	*51.4*	*31.5*
# Completing First Baseline	614	230	119	138	58	69
% of all callers	*13.7*	*15.9*	*10.1*	*15.6*	*20.9*	*10.1*
% of interested & eligible callers	*35.7*	*37.9*	*33.2*	*34.8*	*40.6*	*31.9*

[1] In addition to one of our four main recruitment sources, 64 callers named a second venue
through which they had heard about ARIES. These callers were assigned to the main
recruitment source they named. Another 22 callers named two out of four main recruitment
sources. To assign them to a single recruitment source, we grouped them by the pairs of
sources they had cited, e.g., gay bar and mainstream press, gay press and professional
referral. Each sub-group contained an even number of men. Using a random start within
each subgroup, we alternated assignment to one recruitment source or the other.

[2] We were able to gather recruitment source data on 4,481 out of 4,649 calls.

tion of how we chose to differentially allocate our marketing funds. Thus it is more informative to examine the proportion of callers from each recruitment source who were interested in counseling, met our eligibility criteria, and actually began the program by completing the first baseline interview.

Materials displayed in bars and baths produced the highest proportion of callers interested in counseling (67.3 percent). The mainstream press produced the lowest proportion, with just under half of those callers expressing interest in our services. Approximately 60 percent of those who heard about ARIES through the gay press or via professional referrals were seeking counseling. The "other" category included individuals who either identified word-of-mouth or other sources of information as the means through which they had learned about the program.

Eligibility by Referral Source

To be eligible for the program, callers had to be male, 18 years of age or older, and report three or more instances of unprotected oral or anal intercourse with another man in the previous three months. Of the 2,500 callers who were interested in counseling, 1,720 (69%) met these eligibility criteria. Highest interest and eligibility rates occurred among men recruited via the bars and baths (51.4%), followed by professional referrals (44.6%), and gay press (41.9%). Only 30.3% of those recruited through the mainstream press were both interested and eligible.

Initial Participation by Referral Source

Of the 1,720 men who were eligible, 614 chose to enroll and completed the first step in the pretreatment interviewing process (i.e., first baseline assessment). Completion rates for this interview were highest among those recruited from bars and baths (20.9 %), followed by the gay press (15.9 %), professional referral (15.6 %), and mainstream press (10.1 %). The reader will note that overall, just over a third (35.7 %) of the individuals who had called and were both interested and eligible subsequently moved ahead to completing the first baseline interview, thus being classified as having "begun the program."

Profile of Participants by Referral Source

The data presented in Table 2 pertain to 545 men who completed the first baseline assessment and identified either the gay or mainstream press, professional referral, or bar and bath as their route of recruitment. With

TABLE 2. Selected Respondent Characteristics

	Gay Press $n = 230$	Mainstream Press $n = 119$	Professional Referrals $n = 138$	Bars & Baths $n = 58$
Mean Age (years) [1]	34.6	37.6 [a]	33.5 [b]	36.7
Mean # Gay-Oriented Activities [1,2]	2.6 [b]	1.9 [a]	2.7 [b]	2.6
Mean # of HIV Services Available [3]	1.4	1.4	1.4	1.6
% Closeted [1,4]	44.8 [b]	63.6 [a]	38.4 [b]	36.2 [b]
% Anonymous Enrollment [1]	26.1 [b]	42.9 [a]	18.9 [b]	24.1 [b]
% Sex with a Woman [5]	19.8	27.4	25.6	19.6
% Other than Gay [1,6]	18.8 [b]	34.2 [a]	16.7 [b]	24.6 [b]
% Men of Color [1,7]	21.1 [b]	8.4 [a]	17.2 [b]	17.2 [b]
% Unprotected Anal Sex [8]	53.0	49.6	59.4	43.1
% Tested for HIV [1]	85.2 [b]	82.4 [b]	93.5 [a]	82.8 [b]
% of Tests That Were Positive [1,9]	13.0 [a]	8.3 [a]	22.4 [b]	18.8 [b]
Level of Education				
% HS or less	16.7	12.0	13.8	14.3
% Some College	36.0	42.7	36.2	37.5
% College degree or more	47.3	45.3	50.0	48.2

[1] $p < .05$. Means and proportions with different superscripts ("a" or "b") are significantly different from each other. Means and proportions without superscripts do not differ significantly from the others.
[2] This variable is a count of participation in up to five different types of activities over the past five years. Included are: volunteering time to gay causes, participating in gay marches or wearing a gay button, participating in gay social activities, attending gay counseling or support groups, and attending gay cultural events. Scores range from 0 to 5.
[3] Perceived availability in respondent's community of 3 types of HIV prevention services: professional counseling for safer sex issues, self-help groups in which safer sex issues are discussed, and workshops or classes on safer sex. Scores range from 0 to 3.
[4] Self-rated as: definitely in the closet; mostly in the closet; or half in, half out. Those classified as not closeted rated themselves as mostly out of the closet or completely out of the closet.
[5] Within previous 12 months.
[6] Self-identified as bisexual, heterosexual or straight.
[7] Self-identified race/ethnicity as other than White/European descent.
[8] Within previous 12 weeks.
[9] Includes only those men who had tested and knew their results. Total n = 461: 192 for gay press, 96 for mainstream press, 125 for professional referrals, and 48 for bars and baths.

interval level data, we used one-way analysis of variance and Scheffe's multiple comparisons tests to detect statistically significant differences between the group means of the four major recruitment sources. For dichotomous variables, we conducted contingency table analyses and partitioned resulting chi-square values to identify which specific inter-group differences were statistically significant. Because the partitioning was suggested by the data and not planned a priori, only chi-square values exceeding significance levels of p < .05 for a 4 × 2 table were considered statistically significant (see Fleiss, 1981).

As noted above, Project ARIES was offered by telephone in an attempt to overcome a number of factors that were identified as potential barriers for men seeking HIV prevention services. These barriers include being younger, having less education, being closeted, not identifying as gay, being a man of color, and participating in fewer gay social activities. In several respects, the mainstream press proved to be the most effective route to enrolling these hard to-reach men.

Compared to other publicity sources, men recruited through the mainstream press were significantly more likely to be closeted, to enroll anonymously, and to self-identify as other than gay. These men also engaged in fewer gay-oriented activities than men citing gay press or professional referrals. However, it is important to note that all recruitment sources produced substantial numbers of men with these characteristics. The mainstream press was significantly less effective than the other methods in attracting men of color. On average, mainstream press recruits were older, though the difference reached statistical significance only in comparison to men referred by other service providers.

Men referred by professional sources were significantly more likely than others to have been tested for HIV. Along with patrons of bars and baths, they were also more likely to have tested positive than men who learned of ARIES through the gay or mainstream press.

No significant differences were found between recruitment sources in perceived availability of HIV prevention services in participants' communities, reported sexual activity with women during the previous year, level of education, or the proportion who had engaged in unprotected anal sex within the previous twelve weeks.

Marketing Costs Per Caller by Referral Source

One of the ways to evaluate the efficiency of a marketing plan is to measure output (in this case, number of ads placed, posters distributed, etc.) in relation to input (in this case, the dollar cost of implementing the plan) (Fine, 1990). We have chosen a variation on this method of evaluation. Table 3 provides input data concerning the costs associated with labor with the production of marketing tools, and with implementing the marketing plan for each of the four major channels of communication. We relate these input costs to the numbers of callers who cited each of the four major channels of communication to come up with the costs within each channel for three categories of callers: all individuals who called, all

TABLE 3. Marketing Costs

	Gay Press	Mainstream Press	Professional Referral	Bars & Bath	TOTALS
LABOR COSTS[1]					
EXECUTIVE DIRECTOR[2]					
labor hours	4	30	3	3	40
labor cost	$94	$702	$70	$70	$936
DEPARTMENT HEAD[3]					
labor hours	569	342	1071	294	2276
labor cost	$8,535	$5,130	$16,065	$4,410	$34,140
PROFESSIONAL STAFF[4]					
labor hours	447	455	1142	495	2539
labor cost	$4,783	$4,869	$12,219	$5,297	$27,168
CLERICAL SUPPORT[5]					
labor hours			66	52	118
labor cost			$383	$302	$685
TOTAL LABOR HOURS	1020	827	2282	844	4973
SUB TOTAL LABOR	$13,412	$10,701	$28,737	$10,079	$62,929
COSTS FOR PRODUCT					
graphic design	$399	$119	$1,038	$519	$2,075
printing	770	230	17,887	8,942	27,829
phone costs	233	273	624		1,130
advertising	40,274	12,011			52,285
postage			2,359	1,180	3,539
runners				1,192	1,192
TOTAL COSTS	$41,676	$12,633	$21,908	$11,833	$88,050
GRAND TOTAL FOR LABOR, PRODUCTION AND IMPLEMENTATION	$55,088	$23,334	$50,645	$21,912	$150,979
COST/CALL – ALL CALLS	$38	$20	$57	$79	
COST/CALL – INTERESTED AND ELIGIBLE CALLERS	91	65	128	153	
COST/CALL – COMPLETED BASELINE ONE	$240	$196	$367	$378	

1 All salary rates are taken from the 1992 Wage & Benefit Survey of King County Nonprofit Organizations conducted by United Way of King County. Rates are based on the average monthly salary by responsibility level for an agency with an annual budget of between $500,001 - $1,000,000. The hourly breakdowns in the following notes do not include benefits. In the United Way survey, benefits averaged 20% of payroll costs.
2 Executive Director – "Top paid manager. Responsible to Board of Directors for overall direction and supervision of agency affairs, employees, programs and activities." ($23.40/hour)
3 Department Head – "Primary responsibility is for management of a component or DEPARTMENT of agency services or administration. Involves supervision of three or more employees or volunteers. The supervisor does not perform the same work as do those under his/her supervision except in cases of emergency." ($15.00/hour)
4 Professional Staff – "Under general supervision, is responsible for complex tasks within a work plan or project. Applies professional skills and knowledge of a specialized field to perform work without specific directions. Uses considerable judgment. May have regular contact with clients and/or community in area of employee's job specialty." ($10.70/hour)
5 Clerical Support – "Under close supervision, receives on-the-job training in basic skills required for entry-level, routine repetitive jobs." ($5.80/hour)

callers who were interested and eligible, and all callers who proceeded to complete the first baseline assessment interview.

Because we hope to make these data useful for nonprofit HIV prevention agencies, in this table we report the estimated labor costs that would have been incurred if this program had been offered in that organizational context rather than by a university research staff. The 4,973 labor hours devoted to marketing by members of our staff were equivalent to the workload of 2.4 full-time employees over a one year period.

Labor costs were highest in relation to the professional referral network, with much of this effort being devoted to developing the poster themes and designs, generating the lists of referral agencies in eight states, and communicating with these agencies via the telephone and mail. In terms of overall marketing costs, however, we spent more of our funds in the gay press category than elsewhere. The bulk of those dollars went to paying for display advertising in gay newspapers and magazines.

Just over half ($12,011) of the cost for mainstream press marketing was for the placement of display advertisements in racial/ethnic minority newspapers. Unfortunately, we found that this publicity method was largely ineffective in recruiting men of color.

When seeking to determine the differential effectiveness of our expenditures for each marketing channel, we found that recruitment via the mainstream press was least expensive on a per-call basis ($196 per caller who began the program) and publicity in the gay bars and baths was most expensive ($378 per such caller).

DISCUSSION

In developing a marketing plan for Project ARIES, we sought to accomplish two key objectives. First, we projected the need to elicit at least 1,882 calls of inquiry over an 18-month recruitment period in order to enroll a sufficient number of participants to permit statistical analyses of the intervention's effectiveness. Second, we wished to assess the relative utility of alternative marketing strategies in recruiting clients. In particular, we were concerned with reaching individuals underserved by traditional services whose sexual behaviors placed them at high risk of HIV transmission.

The first objective was met, with the marketing efforts succeeding in generating 2,500 inquiries from men who were interested in the program. As anticipated, attrition of applicants during the project's extensive enrollment process was considerable.

In evaluating outcomes of the marketing efforts, several conclusions were drawn that would appear relevant for future service providers. First, in making it possible for individuals to inquire via a toll-free telephone call in which anonymity is permitted, a project such as this is likely to receive many contacts from people who will choose not to become clients. Some will be individuals who seek counseling for gay identity issues and have nowhere else to turn. Others, individuals who are contemplating but not yet committed to obtaining help in modifying their behavior, will be tentatively shopping around. Still others will be venting their anger at the program's support for the gay community. Consequently, agencies offering this type of service will need to train their intake staff with current gay social service referral knowledge, with skill in assisting ambivalent individuals in overcoming their tentativeness so they can learn about the program, and with the patience and fortitude to cope with angry or homophobic members of the public.

Reaching men who have sex with men and who are still struggling to adopt stable patterns of safer sexual behavior appears to require multiple marketing approaches. Our data indicate that each such approach has its own strengths and contributions in reaching diverse elements within this target population. Each approach also has unique liabilities. For example, project staff cannot control the content or timing of news coverage, nor can they insure that project materials will be displayed and distributed by clinics, bars, etc. Paid advertisements afford greater certainty of exposure, but newspapers retain control over section and page placement. Lastly, there were considerable differences between the costs per eligible caller when looked at by recruitment source. This alone would be an inadequate way of deciding how to appropriate marketing funds as it could lead to decisions which are cost-efficient but which inhibit the achievement of the broader recruitment objectives.

Gay Bars and Baths

Our marketing efforts via the gay bars and baths were the most expensive in terms of cost per caller who began the program. Because we had invested the fewest marketing dollars in this category, we were not surprised that the smallest number of callers cited this method of hearing about our program. We also realized that we had very little control over whether materials were actually posted. In general, we could only hope that bar personnel would recognize the value of the program and make the materials available to their patrons. We do want to note, however, that a higher percentage of callers citing the publicity in bars and baths turned out to be interested in the program, eligible to participate, and motivated to begin as participants than was true for the other major sources of information about the study.

In this category, our marketing cost per caller who began the program was $378. While this approach led to a higher percentage who became clients, it was not more effective than the other strategies in reaching members of the underserved target subgroups.

Mainstream Press

Our experiences with mainstream press and gay bars/baths marketing contrasted sharply in two important respects. First, while the gay bar/bath route was the most expensive in terms of the cost per caller who began the program by completing the first baseline interview, the mainstream press approach was the least costly in this regard. Second, while the gay bar/bath approach generated the highest percentages of callers who were interested, eligible, and who completed the first research interview, the mainstream press approach had generated the lowest percentages of each of these types of caller. However, the advantages of marketing the program via the mainstream press were most evident when considering its superiority in reaching individuals who were closeted, chose to enroll in the program anonymously (presumably indicating that they would have been unlikely to seek in-person risk-reduction counseling services), engaged in fewer gay-oriented activities (possibly indicating that they had fewer social supports for safer sex), and were less likely to self-identify as gay.

Gay Press

We chose to invest more of our marketing funds in the gay press than in any other category. It is not surprising, therefore, that the highest number of callers (n = 1,450) cited this source when making their initial call to our project. When compared with gay bars/baths and the mainstream press, the per-caller costs of this publicity approach fell in the middle of the range. Also, intermediate percentages of callers went on to begin the program. The advantage of this method was that it provided us with maximum control over the content of the message and the frequency with which it appeared. In a project where creating a consistent client flow was essential, this avenue created a welcome predictability in terms of inquiries about the study.

Professional Referral Network

Once again, both the per-caller costs and the percentages of clients beginning the program who cited this marketing mechanism fell into an intermediate position. Yet, as has been observed with each of the strategies discussed thus far, the outcomes from utilizing this approach demonstrated some unique advantages. A higher percentage of individuals citing profes-

sional referrals reported that they were HIV positive. While the dissemination of materials via this network was dependent upon health-care professionals' believing in the project, posting materials, and remembering to
use us as a referral, this method proved to be quite consistent in providing
a steady flow of callers.

CONCLUSION

While many gay and bisexual individuals have successfully reduced
their risk of HIV transmission, a substantial minority have not done so. As
public health specialists continue in their efforts to design and assess new
AIDS-prevention approaches, the challenges in marketing these programs
remain formidable. Moreover, when conducting research where the strength
and applicability of conclusions about an intervention are dependent upon
the volume and diversity of those who are enrolled (Ashery and McAuliffe,
1992), a well-planned marketing strategy plays a key role in achieving those
ends (Fine, 1990; Kotler and Roberto, 1989). The social marketing plan
executed by ARIES staff resulted in exceeding our goals in terms of numbers of men we needed to enroll for the project. We were also successful in
recruiting a diverse client population who remain at high risk for HIV
transmission. The approaches utilized in marketing Project ARIES were
equally effective in reaching individuals engaging in unprotected anal intercourse, but differed in their capacities to reach those who were younger,
men of color, non-self-identified as gay, engaged in a minimum of gay
social supports, closeted, and HIV positive. The approaches also offered the
staff varying levels of control over content and placement of information
about the project.

NOTE

1. ARIES is an acronym for AIDS Risk Intervention and Education Series. We
are indebted to Dr. Jeffrey Kelly and his colleagues for permitting us to adopt the
Project ARIES name which they had created for their pioneering AIDS-prevention intervention.

REFERENCES

Adib, S. M., Joseph, J. G., Ostrow, D. G., & James, S. A. (1991). Predictors of
relapse in sexual practices among homosexual men. *AIDS Education & Prevention*, 3, 293-304.
Ashery, R. S., McAuliffe, W. E. (1992). Implementation issues and techniques in

randomized trials of outpatient psychosocial treatments for drug abusers: Recruitment of subjects. *American Journal of Drug Alcohol Abuse*, 18 (3), 305-329.

Atkin, C., & Arkin, E. B. (1990). Issues and initiatives in communicating health information. In C. Atkin & L. Wallack (Eds.), *Mass Communication and Public Health*. Newbury Park, CA: Sage.

Becker, M. H., & Joseph, J. G. (1988). AIDS and behavioral change to reduce risk: A review. *American Journal of Public Health*, 78, 394-410.

Coates, T. J., Stall, R. D., Catania, J. A., & Kegeles, S. M. (1988). Behavioral factors in the spread of HIV infection. *AIDS*, 2 (suppl. 1), 239-246.

Ekstrand, M. L. & Coates, T. J. (1990). Maintenance of safer sex behaviors and predictors of risky sex: The San Francisco Men's Health Study. *American Journal of Public Health*, 80, 973-977.

Fine, S. E., (Ed.) (1990). *Social Marketing*. Needham Heights, MA: Simon & Schuster, Inc.

Fleiss, J. L. (1981). *Statistical Methods for Rates and Proportions*. Second Edition. New York: Wiley.

Hays, R. B., Kegeles, S. M., & Coates, T. J. (1990). High HIV risk taking among young gay men. *AIDS*, 4, 901-907.

Kelly, J. A., St. Lawrence, J. S., Hood, H. V., & Brasfield, T. L. (1989). Behavioral intervention to reduce AIDS risk activities. *Journal of Consulting and Clinical Psychology*, 57, 60-67.

Kingsley, L. A., Bacella, H., Zhou, S. Y. J., Rinaldo, C., Chmiel, J., Detels, R., Saah, A., Van Raden, M., Ho, M., Armstrong, J., & Mernoz, A. (1990). *Temporal trends in HIV seroconversion: A report from the Multicenter AIDS Cohort Study (MACS)*. Paper presented at the 6th International Conference on AIDS, San Francisco.

Kotler, P. (1982). *Marketing for Nonprofit Organizations*, 2nd ed. Englewood Cliffs, NJ: Prentice-Hall, Inc.

Kotler, P. & Roberto, E. L. (1989). *Social Marketing*. New York, NY: Macmillan, Inc.

Martin, J. L., Garcia, M. A., & Beatrice, S. T. (1989). Sexual behavior changes and HIV antibody in a cohort of New York City gay men. *American Journal of Public Health*, 79, 501-503.

McCusker, J., Stoddard, A. M., Zapka, J. G., Zorn, M., & Mayer, K. H. (1989). Predictors of AIDS-preventive behavior among homosexually active men: A longitudinal study. *AIDS*, 3, 443-448.

Odets, W. (1994). AIDS education and harm reduction for gay men: Psychological approaches for the 21st century. *AIDS & Public Policy Journal*, 9, 1-18.

Peterson, J. L., Coates, T. J., Catania, J. A., Middleton, L., Hilliard, B., & Hearst, N. (1992). High-risk sexual behavior and condom use among gay and bisexual African American men. *American Journal of Public Health*, 82, 1490-1494.

Roffman, R. A., Beadnell, B., Downey, L., & Ryan, R. (1992). *Preventing relapse to unsafe sex in gay and bisexual males*. Poster presented at the annual meeting of the American Public Health Association, Washington, D.C.

Stall, R., Barrett, D., Bye, L., Catania, J., Frutchey, C., Henne, J., Lemp, G., & Paul, J. (1992). A comparison of younger and older gay men's HIV risk-taking behaviors: The Communication Technologies 1989 Cross-Sectional Survey. *Journal of Acquired Immune Deficiency Syndromes*, 5, 682-687.

Stall, R. D., Coates, T. J., & Hoff, C. C. (1988). Behavioral risk reduction for HIV infection among gay and bisexual men: A comparison of published results from the United States. *American Psychologist*, 43, 859-864.

Stoner, M. R. (1986). Marketing of social services gains prominence in practice. *Administration in Social Work*, 10, 41-52.

Taylor, D. W., & Henderson, K. (1992). AIDS and Ontario's public education campaign: A social marketing calamity. *Canadian Journal of Administrative Sciences*, 9, 58-65.

Marketing
to the Homosexual (Gay) Market:
A Profile and Strategy Implications

M. Wayne DeLozier, PhD
Jason Rodrigue, MBA

Nicholls State University

SUMMARY. This article describes a significant market to which marketers must devote greater attention. The gay market is well-educated, has high discretionary income, is informed socially and politically, is dedicated to career and home ownership, and places greater importance on friendship networks than do most Americans. Although a potentially lucrative market segment, gays represent a difficult segment to reach since alienation by other segments could be an explosive factor for many businesses. *[Article copies available from The Haworth Document Delivery Service: 1-800-342-9678.]*

Since the homosexual community is comprised mainly of white males, the composite profile of the homosexual market segment is that of gay men. The homosexual market can be further broken down into subseg-

M. Wayne DeLozier is Distinguished Professor of Marketing at Nicholls State University. Jason Rodrigue is a licensed property and insurance agent for a large regional insurance agency. Correspondence should be addressed to Dr. M. Wayne DeLozier, College of Business Administration, Nicholls State University, Thibodaux, LA 70310. E-mail: *delozierw@cenac.nich.edu*

[Haworth co-indexing entry note]: "Marketing to the Homosexual (Gay) Market: A Profile and Strategy Implications." DeLozier, M. Wayne, and Jason Rodrigue. Co-published simultaneously in *Journal of Homosexuality* (The Haworth Press, Inc.) Vol. 31, No. 1/2, 1996, pp. 203-212; and: *Gays, Lesbians, and Consumer Behavior: Theory, Practice, and Research Issues in Marketing* (ed: Daniel L. Wardlow) The Haworth Press, Inc., 1996, pp. 203-212; and: *Gays, Lesbians, and Consumer Behavior: Theory, Practice, and Research Issues in Marketing* (ed: Daniel L. Wardlow) Harrington Park Press, an imprint of The Haworth Press, Inc., 1996, pp. 203-212. Single or multiple copies of this article are available from The Haworth Document Delivery Service [1-800-342-9678, 9:00 a.m. - 5:00 p.m. (EST)].

ments of black homosexuals, older homosexuals, and lesbians. However, the focus of many marketers should be on white gay men since this is the largest and most profitable subsegment of the homosexual market.

To date, there is no reliable information as to the number of homosexual individuals in the United States. The two most widely cited studies are somewhat contradictory. The Kinsey Institute in 1948 estimated the homosexual population of the United States from six percent to sixteen percent (6%-16%) of the total adult population (Weekes, 1989). However, a more recent study conducted by the Alan Guttmacher Institute revealed that only 1.1 percent of adult males were found to be exclusively homosexual (Ybarra, 1993). While the Kinsey range is not a very useful estimate of the gay population, The Guttmacher study also has its limitations. "Gay leaders question the study's accuracy, saying homosexuals are reluctant to identify themselves" (The Wall Street Journal, 1993, A1).

Although both studies have limitations, they indicate that a market comprised of homosexuals does exist. This homosexual market segment is often ignored in the marketing strategies of businesses in the United States, leaving virtually untouched a market segment that may comprise as much as sixteen percent (16%) of the total market. Why do businesses continue to neglect such a sizable market segment? What strategies can marketers use to reach the gay market without alienating present market segments?

THE HOMOSEXUAL MARKET (THE GAY COMMUNITY)

Demographics

What are the demographics of the homosexual market? To begin, homosexuals are predominately white and male, with the black lesbian being perhaps one of the smallest subsegments of the homosexual population (Hetherington and Orzek, 1989; Loiacano, 1979). Gays as a group are relatively well-educated, with over fifty-nine percent (59%) having a college degree. The average homosexual in America reports an annual income in excess of $55,000–much of this disposable income (Rigdon, 1991). The occupations of homosexuals cover the full spectrum of occupations, but seem to be concentrated among middle-to-lower level, white-collar or service-sector occupations (Lynch, 1987).

Psychographics

What are the psychographics (i.e., activities, interests, and opinions) of the homosexual market? Weekes (1989) noted that, as a group, homosexuals tend to travel extensively, that they spend considerable money on clothing, and that they are dedicated to the arts. However, the authors acknowledge that the exact figures used by Weekes were taken from Overlooked Opinions panel research data. These data have been criticized by *The Wall Street Journal* and *The Advocate* as being overstated. Homosexuals also tend to be very aware of the current social issues and are often politically active regarding them (Loiacano, 1979). Among homosexuals living in suburban areas, a strong orientation towards career-building and home ownership is common (Lynch, 1987). Also common is a high priority on a long-term love relationship and a deep appreciation for the importance of friendships (Lynch, 1987). Dennis Altman observes that, "Over the years, numbers of people have said to me that they place more importance on their friends than their lovers . . . " (Altman, 1982, p. 190).

Personality Traits

There is a pronounced personality difference between homosexuals and heterosexuals of the same gender. Male homosexuals overwhelmingly tend to be less masculine, more tender-minded, and less dominant than heterosexual males. At the same time, however, homosexual males are more unconventional and less submissive to authority than heterosexual males (Duckitt and duToit, 1989). On the other hand, Hassell and Smith (1975) found that female homosexuals are more dominant, independent, and tough-minded than heterosexual females. While not entirely unexpected, these results do fit the common stereotypes of gay males as being feminine and gay females as being tough and masculine.

Composite Profile

The demographic and psychographic characteristics presented allow for a type of composite profile for use in developing marketing tactics for a product or service to homosexuals. The following characteristics define the composite homosexual:

1. Well-educated
2. Has high discretionary income
3. Informed socially and politically
4. Dedicated to career and home ownership
5. Usually a white male
6. Places great importance in friendship networks

Of course, these characteristics represent only the predominant, average characteristics of the homosexual population as a whole, but within that population are significant subsegments such as black homosexuals and lesbians. Another significant segmentation is by age. John Lee (1989) reports that among liberated homosexual communities, significant cultural differences and segregation appear between the younger and older members of the community. The older homosexuals tend toward a more settled lifestyle than the younger homosexuals.

The six profile characteristics listed above indicate a market that has considerable purchasing power. However, some marketers are still reluctant to pursue this gay market. One reason marketers avoid the homosexual market is fear of driving heterosexual customers away (Weekes, 1989). This fear is a legitimate concern since heterosexuals comprise the lion's share of the market. Another factor in the avoidance of the homosexual market is the AIDS crisis. There is a tremendous backlash against gays because of this disease, and even though AIDS is now predominantly spread through heterosexual contact (Nevett and Schleede, 1989), marketers do not wish to get caught in this backlash.

Still, given the fact that the homosexual market is potentially significant, some businesses are starting to risk being associated with it. What can a marketer do to tap into the gay market, and at the same time, not lose any of his present heterosexual market? Well-known companies like Fox Network, The Gap, and Absolut Vodka took steps toward this end. Fox Network's television show, "Melrose Place," introduced one of its characters as gay hoping to quietly gain a bigger gay audience. Similarly, The Gap, in its attempt to impress the show's gay viewers, modeled all of the *Melrose Place* stars in its "Individuals of Style" campaign (Miller, 1992). Absolut Vodka, along with other liquor companies, has advertised in *The Advocate*, a gay magazine, for the past eleven years (Miller, 1992). Now, according to the census, over forty-nine percent (49%) of gay households drink vodka (Rigdon, 1991). Lately, Absolut, in its ads for the magazine, has targeted cities with large gay populations, such as San Francisco, Miami, and Los Angeles (Miller, 1992). All three of the above-mentioned companies have taken deliberate steps at parallel segmentation by trying to capture the gay consumer without upsetting heterosexuals. Other companies involved in low-profile advertising strategies aimed at homosexuals include Banana Republic, Levi Strauss, Calvin Klein, and Remy-Martin Cognac.

MARKETING STRATEGIES

Before actively undertaking a marketing effort aimed at the homosexual market, a marketer must determine if a separate marketing effort is necessary. For instance, market segmentation based on sexual orientation would probably be appropriate if marketing financial services geared toward unmarried domestic partners, fiction novels containing gay or lesbian overtones, or flags with rainbow-colored stripes (Summer, 1992; Jefferson, 1993). However, when marketing products such as motor oil, segmentation along homosexual lines may not be effective. Still, advertising in a gay magazine or publication could have positive effects regardless of the company's product.

If a separate marketing effort is warranted, a breakdown of the present market will disclose the percentage of homosexuals currently using the product or service. Management must then decide whether to attempt increasing the number of homosexuals using the product or service. In addition, management must decide if it wishes to further segment the homosexual market into niches such as black homosexuals, lesbians, and younger or older homosexuals and which of these niches, if any, deserve attention.

In marketing to homosexuals, the marketer is entering the world of niche marketing. Niche marketing is drastically different from the old world of mass marketing, especially in that even smaller market segments are segregated from the total market, and a marketing strategy is implemented for each segment. The goal is to produce many small payoffs which, when added together, generate a substantial return on investment (Schiller, 1989). In this sense, marketers can look at the homosexual market as a group of niches segmented by gender, race, and age. Marketers can then develop strategies aimed at capturing these markets if they are deemed large and profitable enough.

Packaging and Brand Names

Product packaging is a very important and visible part of the overall marketing of a product. The task here is to effectively market a product to both the homosexual and the heterosexual markets at the same time without offending either market. Although not proven empirically, heterosexuals may avoid a particular brand if accepted by homosexuals. If marketers believe that heterosexuals will shun the product if accepted by gays, then a three-pronged approach can be utilized. Americans tend to identify more with brand names than producer names (Schiller, 1989), but due to the lure of cheaper brands, popular brand names worldwide are no longer commanding a premium price from consumers (Schiller, 1993). Regardless, the answer to the packaging problem remains the same–separate brand names for the same product. In this way, one brand can be marketed to homosexuals and the other brand can be marketed to heterosexuals. Both brands can be produced with the same production equipment with the only differences being the product package and the brand names. The payoff is that the homosexual market is satisfied and the heterosexual market is not identified with the homosexual brand; therefore, the heterosexual market is not alienated.

PROMOTION

Public Events

Perhaps one of the most visible means of attracting a particular market segment is to offer sponsorship in activities considered important by that particular market segment. In this case, marketers could offer product sponsorship to gay-oriented and gay-organized events such as the annual parade in the predominately gay Montrose section of Houston, Texas. A business can also sponsor AIDS research and make public such sponsorship. Another area that often requires corporate sponsorship is that of the arts. Because gays are more likely than the average American to attend operas, ballets, classical concerts, and museums, a marketer can generate considerable awareness among the gay community through sponsorship of such events. The drawback here is the visibility generated by these events. Although not proven empirically, the marketer will run a greater risk of alienating present heterosexual markets with the high-profile advertisements of public sponsorships, but the marketer will also reach a larger gay market with these high-profile sponsorships.

Media Advertising

The use of highly targeted media is effective in reaching niche audiences and thus appropriate for marketing to the homosexual segment. In advertising products to the gay market, a three-pronged approach can be utilized. The first part of this approach is the use of direct mail advertisements. In this case, direct mail marketing offers an excellent solution to the alienation problems of marketing to the homosexual market. By sending the advertisements directly to the gay market segment, the marketer does not indicate to the heterosexual market that the same product is being marketed to gays. The biggest problem with direct mail is identifying the gay population towards which the advertisements are directed. Perhaps the best way to alleviate this problem is to use mail-order catalogs targeting gays. Gay catalogs such as *Lambda Rising* and *A Different Light* have extensive gay customer lists (Summer, 1992). When the direct mail advertisements are correctly routed to the intended gay market, the target market is reached without upsetting present market segments.

A similar approach is advertising in gay-oriented magazines and publications. In the Houston-area market, two such gay-oriented publications are the *Montrose Voice* and *This Week in Texas*. National publications also exist to reach the gay market. *The Advocate* and *Genre* are gaining a sizable following by businesses willing to risk marketing to gays (Rigdon, 1991). Since the heterosexual market supposedly does not read such publications, there is little chance of "upsetting the boat" by advertising in these gay publications. One advertiser in such a publication was quoted as saying, "Only gays read the ads, so who's to know?" (Weekes, 1989, p. 48). One gay-oriented publication feels that the homosexual market is very loyal and that businesses that choose to advertise in gay publications will be seen by the gay market as deserving patronage (Weekes, 1989).

Another possible media advertising approach is the utilization of cable TV, syndicated TV, and advertising spots on video cassette tapes. Four of the largest ten television market areas have large gay populations (TV/Radio Age, 1989) (Appendix A). These four areas are New York, Los Angeles, the San Francisco Bay Area, and Houston. As can be seen, these four markets are very large and offer great potential for exploitation by marketers–especially in the cable and syndicated television markets (Appendix A). However, network television is rapidly losing its advertising market to alternative forms of advertising such as direct mail, magazines, and cable and syndicated television (Direct Marketing, 1989). Besides, when targeting a segment that may be as small as 1.1 percent of the population, television audiences are far too large. Perhaps further evolution of a "gay/lesbian" cable network will warrant more television ads.

While television advertising is high-profile and may cause some loss of heterosexual customers when marketing a product to both gay and heterosexual markets, advertising on video cassette tapes is more along the lines of gay publication advertising. Movies that are aimed at the homosexual market and movies that are consistently rented or purchased by homosexuals are good targets for co-sponsorship advertisements. Again, the goal of VCR advertising is low-profile advertising that reaches the homosexual market without alienating the heterosexual one.

CONCLUSION

As noted, the gay market is potentially significant to marketers both in terms of size and purchasing power. As much as sixteen percent (16%) of the U.S. population is thought to be gay. The average homosexual reports an average income of $55,000 annually–much of this money is disposable income because of fewer fixed commitments such as raising children. These factors combine with others to indicate that the gay market can no longer be neglected by marketers.

However, in marketing a product or service to homosexuals, marketers run the risk of alienating their present heterosexual markets. This alienation can happen partly as a result of AIDS and its connection with homosexuals. Some heterosexual people do not wish to be connected in any way, shape, or form to the homosexual community. Examples of homophobia can be seen by religious leaders, Republican leaders, and entertainment and news media. George Bush called gays "anti-family" people who are not normal and who have made the wrong choice, and Pat Robertson believes that gays are unfit parents (Marcus, 1992). Also, "the entertainment and news media continue to promote negative stereotypes of lesbians and gay men" (Davidson, 1991, p. 73). Howard Stern and Rush Limbaugh often use the terms "dyke" and "fag"; meanwhile, television shows like *Quantum Leap* and *Mr. Belvedere* portray gays as murderers and sex molesters (Davidson, 1991). This homophobia presents a unique challenge to marketers–marketing a product effectively to both the homosexual and heterosexual markets at the same time. This challenge can be partially met through the use of direct mail marketing to homosexuals, and advertising in gay-oriented magazines and publications. Marketers can also introduce separate brands of the same product and market one brand to the gay market and one brand to the heterosexual market. Another approach is for marketers to sponsor socially responsible events such as the arts, or perhaps sponsor AIDS research. A sponsorship ties the product to something the entire society accepts as positive and avoids the alienation trap. The key to successfully marketing products to both the homosexual and the heterosexual markets is sensitivity. The marketer must be aware of the available marketing channels and must monitor results closely as well as assure that all target markets are being reached and that the desired effects are achieved.

The major problem is the conflict that marketers have between selling products to heterosexuals and homosexuals that are the same or are identified as the same from the same company. The homosexual market is there. How do we handle it? The very difficult problem is that we have *very* little research on gays and their purchasing behavior. We need more consumer research on this minority. Although not proven empirically, the relatively large incomes of gay people indicate that they control a sizable amount of purchasing power even if they do represent as little as 1.1% of the population. Hence, this market segment is profitable and needs more attention.

REFERENCES

Altman, D. (1982). *The Homosexualization of America, The Americanization of the Homosexual.* New York: St. Martin's Press.

Davidson, C. (1991). Can We End Media Bias Against Gays. *USA Today* (magazine) (November), 72-74.

Direct Mail Revenues, Expenditures Rising. *Direct Marketing* (July 1989), p. 7.

Duckitt, J. H. & duToit, L. (1989). Personality Profiles of Homosexual Men and Women. *Journal of Psychology*, 123 (Sept.), 497-505.

Gay-Rights Activists Worry Their Power Will Be Hurt by New Survey. *The Wall Street Journal*, April 16, 1993, p. A1.

Hassel, J. and Smith, W. L. (1975). Female Homosexuals' Concepts of Self, Men, and Women. *Journal of Personality Assessment*, 39, 154-159.

Hetherington, C. & Orzek, A. (1989). Career Counseling and Life Planning with Lesbian Women. *Journal of Counseling and Development*, 68 (Sept./Oct.), 52-56.

Jefferson, D. J. (1993). Businesses Offering Products for Gays Are Thriving. *The Wall Street Journal*, April 22, p. B2.

Lee, J. A. (1989). Invisible Men: Canada's Aging Homosexuals: Can They Be Assimilated into Canada's 'Liberated' Gay Communities? *Canadian Journal on Aging*, 8(1), 79-97.

Loiacano, D. K. (1979). Gay Identity Issues Among Black Americans: Racism, Homophobia, and the Need for Validation. *Journal of Counseling and Development*, 68 (Sept./Oct.), 21-25.

Lynch, F. R., (1987). Non-Ghetto Gays: A Sociological Study of Suburban Homosexuals. *Journal of Homosexuality*, 13(4), 13-42.

Marcus, E. (1992). 'They're Not Telling the Truth.' *Newsweek*, Sept. 14, p. 41.

Miller, C. (1992). Mainstream Marketers Decide Time Is Right to Target Gays. *Marketing News*, 26(15), pp. 8, 15.

Nevett, T. & Schleede, J. M. Jr. (1989). Marketing in the AIDS Era. *Business Horizons* (Nov.-Dec.), pp. 90+.

Rigdon, J. E. (1991). Overcoming a Deep-Rooted Reluctance, More Firms Advertise to Gay Community. *The Wall Street Journal*, July 18, B1-B2.

Schiller, Z. (1989). Stalking the New Consumer. *Business Week* (August), pp. 54+.

_____ . (1993). Procter & Gamble Hits Back. *Business Week* (July 19), 20-22.

Summer, B. (1992). A Niche Market Comes of Age. *Publishers Weekly* (June 29), 36-40.

TV Market Rankings–1989-90. *Television/Radio Age* (Sept.1989), pp. 60+.

Weekes, R.V. (1989). Gay Dollars. *American Demographics* (October), pp. 45+.

Ybarra, M. J. (1993). Christian Groups Press Gay People to Take a Heterosexual Path. *The Wall Street Journal* (April 21), pp. A1, A6.

APPENDIX A

TV Market Rankings 1989-1990

RANK	AREA	TV HOUSEHOLDS
1	NEW YORK	7,043,900
2	LOS ANGELES	4,939,400
3	CHICAGO	3,124,800
4	PHILADELPHIA	2,704,400
5	SAN FRANCISCO BAY AREA	2,200,700
6	BOSTON	2,105,800
7	DALLAS/FORT WORTH	1,728,900
8	DETROIT	1,723,500
9	WASHINGTON	1,701,700
10	HOUSTON	1,453,200

Source: 1989-1990 Arbitron estimates

Some Comments on "Marketing to the Homosexual (Gay) Market: A Profile and Strategy Implications"

Subodh Bhat, PhD

San Francisco State University

SUMMARY. This article addresses some of the issues raised in the article "Marketing to the Homosexual (Gay) Market: A Profile and Strategy Implications." Strategic segmentation theory and practice suggest that segments should be based on consumers' responses or behaviors in relation to the marketer's product, thus calling into question the existence of a supposedly homogenous homosexual segment and the resultant profile of the average person in that segment. *[Article copies available from The Haworth Document Delivery Service: 1-800-342-9678.]*

In their article, DeLozier and Rodrigue present a profile of the "homosexual" market segment and suggest marketing strategies to reach this target segment. While there may be a need for what I think is their overall objective, i.e., to present a perspective on positioning products to the homosexual community, their article has many assumptions, descriptions,

Subodh Bhat is Associate Professor of Marketing at San Francisco State University. Correspondence should be addressed to: Department of Marketing, San Francisco State University, 1600 Holloway Avenue, San Francisco, CA 94132. E-mail: *sbhat@sfsu.edu*

[Haworth co-indexing entry note]: "Some Comments on 'Marketing to the Homosexual (Gay) Market: A Profile and Strategy Implications'." Bhat, Subodh. Co-published simultaneously in *Journal of Homosexuality* (The Haworth Press, Inc.) Vol. 31, No. 1/2, 1996, pp. 213-217; and: *Gays, Lesbians, and Consumer Behavior: Theory, Practice, and Research Issues in Marketing* (ed: Daniel L. Wardlow) The Haworth Press, Inc., 1996, pp. 213-217; and: *Gays, Lesbians, and Consumer Behavior: Theory, Practice, and Research Issues in Marketing* (ed: Daniel L. Wardlow) Harrington Park Press, an imprint of The Haworth Press, Inc., 1996, pp. 213-217. Single or multiple copies of this article are available from The Haworth Document Delivery Service [1-800-342-9678, 9:00 a.m. - 5:00 p.m. (EST)].

and prescriptions on market segmentation that deserve clarification and amplification for the lay reader. The intent of this paper is to clarify the role of segmentation. This paper will first deal with the general issues in segmentation and then go on to examine specific points raised in the DeLozier and Rodrigue paper.

Let me first clarify what a "market segment" is and how and why segmentation as a strategy works. As understood by theorists and savvy practitioners, a market segment is a set of consumers who are different from consumers in other sub-markets, but similar to each other, in terms of their responses to a firm's marketing mix. Since a marketing mix comprises strategies for the 4 P's, i.e., product, price, promotion, and place (distribution), consumers' responses for segmentation purposes are usually construed in terms of responses to the 4 P's. Differences in consumers' responses across segments suggest that a segment can be profitably targeted with unique marketing strategies different from strategies employed in targeting other segments.

The underlying economic rationale comes from the price discrimination literature in economics (Wind 1978). In a market characterized by heterogeneous demand, "optimal profits can be achieved if the firm uses consumers' marginal responses to price, i.e., price elasticities, to define mutually exclusive segments and sets price (or output) so that marginal profits in each segment are equal" (Claycamp and Massy 1968, p. 388). Similarly, in a broader marketing context, a firm can use consumers' marginal responses to the 4 P's to identify segments and decide product, price, promotion, and distribution strategies for the different segments to equalize marginal profits in each segment and thus maximize total profits (Claycamp and Massy 1968, Wind 1978).

This conceptually sound and strategically meaningful perspective stands in contrast to approaches sometimes used in segmentation. Some practitioners and academics tend to view segments in terms of differences in demographic, socioeconomic and generic psychographic variables. For example, they talk of segments in terms of the "Generation X" segment, the "senior citizen" segment, or in this context, the "homosexual" segment. There are several problems that arise with such an approach. Claycamp and Massy (1968) and Wind (1978) present a comprehensive review of the problems that arise from taking such a perspective; some of these problems are summarized in the following discussion.

One useful way to understand segmentation is to distinguish between "bases of segmentation" and "descriptors of segments." Bases of segmentation are the underlying characteristics that differentiate segments, such as consumers' price elasticity, needs or benefits sought, media usage, deal proneness, and shopping patterns. Once segments are identified on these bases, they can then be described in terms of their demographic, socioeconomic, or psychographic profile. These latter characteristics are called "descriptors of segments" (Wind 1978). Wind (1978) proposes a general segmentation model where the bases are dependent variables and the descriptors are independent variables.

In a general sense, using a descriptor as a basis for segmentation is "stereotyping," i.e., assuming that every one who fits the descriptor would behave in the exact same way. For example, every member of so-called "Generation X" would be imbued with a set of common preferences and behaviors. This "stereotyping" may not be meaningful from the marketing point of view.

More importantly, descriptors do not provide any insight that can be used directly for guiding marketing strategies. That a person is a member of Generation X tells marketers little about how to effectively target this person, since not all Generation X members have exactly similar product, promotion, distribution, and pricing needs. When one differentiates between bases and descriptors, markets can be profitably segmented for *different reasons*. For example, a person can be classified in one segment based on the benefits sought from the product, in another segment based on frequency of purchase, and yet another based on price elasticity. If we used a stereotypic descriptor to decide segments, such flexibility in marketing strategy would be lost. And in doing so, we would not be using the very foundation of segmentation: the division of markets into segments at the margin to reap maximum profits.

The use of descriptors as bases for market segments also does not allow for differences in how individuals in a "segment" might view different firms and brands. Not everyone in a demographic or psychographic "segment" would have exactly similar views about the marketing activities of different firms and brands.

That the strategic and nonstereotypic perspective of segments and segmentation is now well accepted is seen in both the conceptual and the "practical" models in recent literature (Dickson 1982, Doyle and Saunders 1985, Bucklin and Gupta 1992, Grover and Srinivasan 1992).

In the context of the article by DeLozier and Rodrigue, it seems that the authors have not incorporated some of these additional perspectives of segmentation theory and practice. More strategic insights can be gained by applying these current perspectives to the segmentation strategies reported by DeLozier and Rodrigue, and to those reported in the popular press. The overall result is a simplistic view of segmentation that offers little strategic insight for marketers.

I now wish to comment on some specific aspects of the article. The opening sentence, "Since the homosexual community is comprised mainly of white males, the composite profile of the homosexual market segment is that of gay men," is one example of a limitation of that approach. Even if one accepts the premise that all homosexuals behave exactly the same way so that marketers can target them as one segment, it is a tactical stretch to use white gay males to exemplify the entire homosexual community.

The authors cite several studies that claim that between 1-16% of the U.S. population is homosexual, and say that the size indicates the presence of a segment. Size doesn't necessarily indicate a segment. The size of a segment is the result of segmentation, not a basis.

The authors' breakdown of sub-segments by gender, race, and psychographics in the homosexual community could be problematic in implementation. A person's gender, race, and sexual orientation cannot guide marketing strategy; it is only the manner in which an individual reacts to a specific component of a specific firm's marketing mix that can be used to group individuals based on their common reactions. Thus, marketers may not benefit from the profile of the average "homosexual," i.e., someone who is white, male, dedicated to the arts, less masculine, travels extensively, and so on. A composite profile is an example of stereotyping and the use of such a composite profile as a guiding post of a marketing strategy geared toward homosexuals may result in a less than optimum strategy.

The authors refer to marketing to homosexuals as an example of "niche marketing." A niche, as generally used in marketing, is a group of consumers who have a special product, promotion, distribution, or pricing need. Since all homosexuals likely do not have the same needs, the homosexual community cannot be regarded as a "niche." It would be a very rare product, promotion, distribution, or pricing need where all homosexuals have exactly similar needs and these needs are different from the needs of other segments; only in that event would there be a "homosexual niche." One may be able to envisage such a niche in estate and retirement planning, and benefits package design; of course, the niche would also include unmarried heterosexual couples. No such niches would probably exist in such commonly used products and services as beer or hairstyling.

One of the article's strategic prescriptions, the idea of separate brand names for the same product (one targeted to homosexuals and another to heterosexuals to avoid "crossover" associations) bears some questioning. First, the idea of branding is to differentiate a firm's product from that of competitors, not to differentiate it from one segment to another. Secondly, as an accompanying article (Bhat, Leigh and Wardlow 1995) finds, there are a considerable number of heterosexual consumers who do not respond negatively to a brand's associations with homosexuality. Additionally, because most heterosexuals do not read or view media specifically targeted to homosexuals, it would not be a bad idea to promote the same brand but position it differently in different media. That, rather than the establishment of separate brands, seems to be a logical and cost-effective answer. DeLozier and Rodrigue approve of and several marketers already use such an approach (e.g., Levi Strauss, Calvin Klein, Banana Republic).

While understanding the needs of the homosexual community, including any special needs, is and should be of great importance to marketers, DeLozier and Rodrigue's view of the homosexual community or niche gives marketers a starting point for strategic targeting. Additional strategic insights can be had through a rigorous review of current segmentation theory and its application in the context of the homosexual community.

REFERENCES

Bhat, S., Leigh T. W., & Wardlow, D. L., (1995). The Effect of Homosexual Imagery in Advertising on Attitude Toward the Ad. *Journal of Homosexuality*, 31(1/2).

Bucklin, R. E. & Gupta, S. (1992). Brand Choice, Purchase Incidence, and Segmentation: An Integrated Approach. *Journal of Marketing Research*, 29 (May), 201-215.

Claycamp, H. J. & Massy, W. F. (1968). A Theory of Market Segmentation. *Journal of Marketing Research*, 5 (November), 388-394.

Dickson, P. R. (1982). Person-Situation: Segmentation's Missing Link. *Journal of Marketing*, 46 (Fall), 56-64.

Doyle, P. & Sanders, J. (1985). Market Segmentation and Positioning in Specialized Industrial Markets. *Journal of Marketing*, 49 (Spring), 24-32.

Grover, R. & Srinivasan, V. (1992). Evaluating the Multiple Effects of Retail Promotions on Brand Loyal and Brand Switching Segments. *Journal of Marketing Research*, 29 (February), 76-89.

Wind, Y. (1978). Issues and Advances in Segmentation Research. *Journal of Marketing Research*, 15 (August), 317-337.

Out of the Closet
and into the Marketplace:
Meeting Basic Needs
in the Gay Community

John E. Bowes, PhD

University of Washington

SUMMARY: This study suggests that an emerging, popular market profile legitimizing gays as a lucrative niche may need qualification. Those targeting the gay community encounter subtlety and contradiction that traces to a history of exclusion and discrimination. Using data from a major Seattle (WA) survey, the study examines barriers to securing goods and services. While basic demographics such as gender have a strong influence on perceived barriers, other issues such as a need to conceal one's orientation, abuse encountered, and means to complain are examined. In short, to those seeking characteristics of a potentially powerful market segment, this study seeks to identify and discuss market areas most likely to drive gays and lesbians back into the closet. *[Article copies available from The Haworth Document Delivery Service: 1-800-342-9678.]*

John E. Bowes is Associate Professor of Communications at the School of Communications at the University of Washington. Correspondence should be addressed to: School of Communications, DS-40, University of Washington, Seattle, WA 98195. E-mail: *jbowes@u.washington.edu*

[Haworth co-indexing entry note]: "Out of the Closet and into the Marketplace: Meeting Basic Needs in the Gay Community." Bowes, John E. Co-published simultaneously in *Journal of Homosexuality* (The Haworth Press, Inc.) Vol. 31, No. 1/2, 1996, pp. 219-244; and: *Gays, Lesbians, and Consumer Behavior: Theory, Practice, and Research Issues in Marketing* (ed: Daniel L. Wardlow) The Haworth Press, Inc., 1996, pp. 219-244; and: *Gays, Lesbians, and Consumer Behavior: Theory, Practice, and Research Issues in Marketing* (ed: Daniel L. Wardlow) Harrington Park Press, an imprint of The Haworth Press, Inc., 1996, pp. 219-244. Single or multiple copies of this article are available from The Haworth Document Delivery Service [1-800-342-9678, 9:00 a.m. - 5:00 p.m. (EST)].

INTRODUCTION

Likened by some advertisers to a market that is "upscale and cutting edge," gay and lesbian consumers have achieved a visibility unthinkable a few years ago ("Overcoming," 1991). Indeed, anecdotal accounts suggest a vibrancy to this marketing niche that spells profits for advertisers and positive recognition for the gay/lesbian community. In the past several years, major national advertisers–Phillip Morris, Shearson-Lehman, Nestlé, Columbia House, Gap Stores, Miller Brewing, and Hiram-Walker–have come to advertise in the gay/lesbian press. IKEA, a national furniture chain, recently featured in national TV ads a "loving" gay male couple buying a dining table (Gay and Lesbian Alliance, 1994a, p. 1). Increasingly, mainstream advertisers have contributed as sponsors to major gay community events such as the 1993 March on Washington and the 25th Stonewall Anniversary in 1994 (Goldman, 1994; Horovitz, 1993).

The marketing attention has encouraged a rash of new gay/lesbian publications in the last 5 years, mostly "lifestyle" magazines (Gay and Lesbian Alliance, 1994b). The gay press (weekly or monthly tabloid publications) claims circulation figures which top 30,000 in several markets with 65 newspapers collectively making claim to over 3 million readers (Wilke, 1994; "Lesbigay press," 1992).

Increasingly, marketing specialists have found the demographics of gays and lesbians attractive. In a study sponsored by major gay newspapers, Simmons reported (for 1988) gay incomes well above national averages generated by high proportions of managers and other professionals (Overlooked Opinions, 1993). More recent data suggest income differences may be exaggerated (Boulard, 1994), but that many attractive consumer characteristics remain (Elliott, 1994). A readiness by gays and lesbians to travel, use charge cards, and drink wines has not only attracted the trendy travel industry and vintners, but the old guard of banking and telecommunications services as well. More basic characteristics–high levels of self-employment, concentration in top markets, heightened concern with physical well-being and stress–suggest a consumer group that is open to new technologies, health care, and self-improvement.

The importance of group identity to marketing has long been recognized. Models of life goals, values, and demographics have long been built to distinguish important consumer profiles as a key to motivation (Kahle et al., 1986). Appealing to these profiles has had presumed success in promoting products as diverse as American Express cards and imported beer to the gay community. While these are important signals, they may not span the concerns of the gay community. Indeed there are allegations that the popular marketing profile of the gay community is inaccurate, ignoring the closeted, the poor, and possibly lesbians (Fejes and Petrich, 1993, p. 411).

Jansen (1994) argues, for example, that gays as a new, better-than-average consumer niche have been overestimated; they merely mirror the straight world's income, ethnic, and occupational strata. Common sampling methods used to assure representation are foiled by concealment and the reactiveness of asking if a respondent *is* gay or lesbian. Economically secure gays, it is argued, are more likely to be openly so, and accessible to market research measures. But perhaps more important than demographic inaccuracies are differences in a *psychosocial* profile for gays that "create[s] a lot of different tensions; higher levels of stress . . . feelings of victimization and cynicism towards dominant-culture institutions like government or business" (Jansen cit. Briggs, p. 47).

We suggest in this paper that a simple market profile offered in the enthusiasm of legitimizing gays as a market force may need qualification. Those targeting the gay community encounter a terrain of subtlety and contradiction that is only beginning to come to light. Much of this complexity traces to a history of exclusion and discrimination that is encountered in reaching out to the gay community. Using data from a city government-commissioned survey of gays and lesbians in Seattle, Washington, we sought to augment the basic market profile in several key respects:

- Is the marketplace uniformly seen as open by the gay community? What were market areas that were seen as less accessible? There is ample evidence of marketing directed at the gay community; there is rather less on whether lesbians and gays can get needed goods and services and still be openly gay.
- What were market sectors that required greater levels of concealment of being gay or lesbian in order to do business? And did such action improve success in meeting needs?
- Were there significant differences across key market areas by gender? Did lesbians encounter different barriers than those encountered by gay men?
- Were there means to communicate discrimination problems? What was done, if anything?
- Are gays and lesbians optimistic about their future and/or feeling supported in both the gay and majority community?

In short, positive marketing to the gay community involves conveying both respect for its differences and affirmation of its claims to rights in the society. Clearly, this status can't be determined from surface demographics, but from questions specific to these conditions. More precisely, to those seeking the characteristics of a potentially powerful market segment, it is useful to know market areas most likely to drive gays and lesbians back into the closet.

CONCEPTUAL BASIS

A constant in advertising research over the past three decades has been a concern with audience problems and needs. Codified as a "uses and gratifications approach" to explaining media influence, it has become enshrined both as conceptually fertile for understanding what audiences gain from the media and as a practical focus for editors and advertisers interested in providing "useful" and congenial content to satisfy their audiences (Katz & Blumler, 1974; Frank & Greenberg, 1980). For decades, marketing professionals have been urged to respond "more intelligently to *people*, and their wants and needs, rather than to *products*" (Mortimer, 1959).

Analysis of uses and gratifications experienced by general population samples conventionally rests on two dimensions (Rubin, 1981, 1983). *Instrumental* uses speak to specific consumer needs addressed by the media while *ritualistic* gratifications suggest content that may reinforce a social environment, provide passive entertainment, and sustain a comforting culture. On both grounds, marketing information aimed at gays can win or fail. Messages touting instrumentally needed services may fail recognition by the gay community because the social environment suggested may be alien. Clearly the reverse obtains: much may be risked by mainstream marketing in catering to the gay community, a potentially alien landscape to the straight community.[1]

While ambivalence of mainstream media is reasonably clear towards gay-positive content, that of gay media is more subtle. Levin (1993) notes that as gay and lesbian publications achieve advertising success, the "economic logic of national advertising begins to drive publications aimed at the lesbian and gay community." Fejes (1993) comments that the "heterosexism permeating the national media and advertising now affects the media of the gay and lesbian community" (p. 411).

The publishers of *Urban Fitness*, a successful publication with arguably the highest circulation of any magazine targeting the gay community, maintains that as a matter of policy it is unconcerned with what its readers do in their bedrooms. As the publisher, Jim Herman, commented, "Mr. Corporate American can't comprehend a homosexual." Like other growing gay and lesbian publications, it sees profits in temporizing the militant or sexually suggestive content that once was characteristic of the medium

(O'Donnell, 1994). In short, reaction that might exclude publications from majority favor bring about content shifts to a cleaned-up gay image, "heterosexualized" for mainstream advertisers. The gay community, then, finds itself controversial not only in general circulation media, but also increasingly tested in its own. Specific implications of discrimination, political isolation, and sexuality itself seem muted in marketing to the gay community.

By its very definition, *mass* media has to balance the need of majority interests against those of specialized minorities. As Kessler put it, media are the reflection of the homogenous middle. The tyranny of audience ratings and readership studies forces a consistency on content that is designed to attract the most and offend the fewest possible (Kessler, 1984). In a system where circulation is money in the bank, it is foolish for media professionals to stray far from this formula.

For minorities, getting content relevant to their particular needs can be frustrating. A generation of occasional research highlights the needs met (and unmet) by the African American press and the ethnic press linked to immigrant arrivals from Asia, Europe and elsewhere (Greenberg et al., 1970).[2] Sexual minorities, however, have had even less attention to their everyday needs. Larry Gross (1991) comments, "they [the media] mostly show us as weak and silly, or evil and corrupt, but they exclude and deny the existence of normal, unexceptional, as well as exceptional lesbians and gay men."

Arguably, a poor record of understanding the gay/lesbian community contradicts a generation of audience and marketing research that attempts to better target audiences by addressing their needs. From the '70s makeover of newspapers to increasingly reflect the daily needs of suburban readers to "soft news" television directed to consumer product evaluation, home fix-up and travel, the news business has found potential in everyday problem-solving (Stamm, 1985). Academic research sporadically has investigated audience needs for everyday living and problem solving (Dervin, 1976). Advertising and marketing have pulled away from simple considerations of audience size to more complex motivational formulations, based in needs, aspirations, and lifestyles of specialized segments (Stamm & Bowes, 1991).

Such data are rudimentary for the gay community. The simple demographics of high disposable incomes and affinity for luxury goods are enticing for marketing, but may ignore psychosocial complexities of suspicion, concealment, and alienation of gay consumers, just as they ignore possible reactions from the straight community. There have been many studies in recent years of discrimination encountered by gays and lesbians in their respective communities (Herek & Berrill, 1990; Comstock, 1991). But few have examined barriers on a service-by-service basis, or the means used to cope with such problems.

We were particularly interested in those areas having anecdotal evidence of problems: child day care, housing, financial services, and accommodation by hotels and restaurants. Marketing plans might usefully consider past discrimination or, perhaps more importantly, the *expectation* of problems by gays and lesbians based on such a history. By considering these fears and negative anticipation, we believe many institutions will more humanely and effectively market to the gay and lesbian community than solely demographic profiles would suggest.

Conceptually, we hope to show the difficulty gays and lesbians endure in resolving the dilemma of gaining attention and respect from majority institutions. One cannot advance against discrimination in the marketplace without taking action, yet action may bring on unwanted attention and abuse. Alienation from the majority community is understandable, but not a practical option for gay consumers. Though the general community can (and has) ignored gays and lesbians, the reverse really isn't possible. Those who recognize the special pressures of being gay or lesbian may enjoy market success well beyond accounting for simpler characteristics of high disposable incomes and an affinity for luxury goods. As mainstream commerce targets gay consumers, it should learn the subtleties embodied in a history of discrimination. While our data do not consider marketing messages directly or test their invigoration through accounting for gay social attitudes, they strongly suggest that this link may be valuable to consider in a climate of individual caution and distrust of institutions.

Finally, marketing professionals may realize a higher social purpose in their advertising by recognizing problems gay consumers have in openly approaching mainstream institutions. Editorially, the media has been a vehicle of assimilation and cohesion for minorities, bridging isolation, and providing a sense of community (Greenberg et al., 1970). Marketing has been the commercial parallel of this attention, substantiating that a minority is recognized for its purchasing power and valued materially for its needs.

METHOD

This study is based on an opportunity survey of gays and lesbians in the Seattle metropolitan area which focused on discrimination and hate crime victimization. While it does not have the desirable controls on representation present in strict quota or random sample studies, it employed basic quota controls (gender, neighborhood, and minority status) keyed to the Standard Metropolitan Statistical Area (SMSA) for Seattle-Everett, Washington, as defined by the US Bureau of the Census (Friedli, 1990). The survey secured gender balance and representation from people of color.[3] Questionnaires were distributed in numerous venues including gay/lesbian support groups, book stores catering to the gay/lesbian community, and gay/lesbian community and social centers. In addition, many surveys were distributed at Seattle's Gay/Lesbian Pride Week festival in June 1990. The bulk of the surveys were distributed between May 1990 and January 1991. Few if any of the questions were time-sensitive in the short term. The questionnaire was designed for self-administration. It could be picked-up and returned anonymously from several distribution points, or be openly requested by mail or telephone. Completion time for the questionnaire was about 20 minutes.

The questionnaire was developed over a period of a year and a half, beginning in early 1989. Many individuals in the community representing a variety of interests and perspectives contributed, with a prototype based on a survey constructed by Dr. Walter Tunstall and distributed in Richmond, Virginia.[4] Approximately 2,500 surveys were used of which 1,291 were completed and coded in machine-readable form, tested for coding errors, and processed with SPSS. This 52% response rate could be considered good, given the organization of volunteers that distributed and managed the survey. Since there are no census data sets or random samples that further define this population, it is not possible to determine "representativeness" beyond this rough evaluation. Of the 1,291 respondents, some 52 identified themselves as bisexual and 27 failed to answer this classification item. All were included in the analyses.

Questions about daily difficulties focused on 9 areas: children (day care, adoption), health care (emergency care, visitation), government services (welfare, schools), general services (restaurants, hotels), religious organizations (churches, religious counselors), financial institutions (mortgages, banks), housing (rentals, purchase), employment (promotions, harassment) and AIDS (housing, insurance).[5]

"Difficulties" in each instance referred to problems encountered because one was lesbian or a gay male. For example, the question concerning problems with renting or buying housing was phrased, "Have you ever been prohibited or discouraged from renting or buying an apartment or house with a non-related same-sex roommate or partner." With service industries, respondents were asked, "Have you experienced difficulties with any of the following services because you are gay or lesbian." Each item under a general topic, such as housing or financial services, was the basis of an index of difficulties endured because the respondent was gay/lesbian. These subsidiary scales making-up indices are summarized in Appendix A. The kind of difficulty experienced was disaggregated for physical and verbal violence.

Originally, questions about frequency of changing behavior, frequency of violence, and being openly gay socially and at work were continuous scales or indexes. When used as independent variables, these were dichotomized to assist graphic presentation. Simple statistical testing was done of group differences using t-tests for separate variance estimates. Significance is indicated where appropriate.

FINDINGS

Paradoxically, given the attention to gays as a market niche, less than 0.2% of the interviewees mentioned mainstream media or advertising as a source of help or information with meeting personal needs. Seattle's gay press went unmentioned as a source of problem-solving assistance.[6] The media–gay and straight–were largely irrelevant.[7] In part, this may be traced to the open-ended nature of questions designed to pick-up sources' help beyond individual action or government and civic action groups, but they are significant by their absence, nevertheless. Our focus, however, is open to a range of actions taken by the gay community to meet its needs.

The principal results of this study form a progression; from difficulty meeting everyday needs because one is gay or lesbian, through changing behavior to avoid detection, to problem-solving actions and their consequences.

Difficulty in Resolving Problems Because Gay/Lesbian

Difficulty was scaled on a five step basis from "never" to "always." Results in Figure 1 show generally a low problem incidence for our respondents. Children, religious organizations, housing, and employment proved to be the most troublesome, but in mean only approached a "rarely" difficulty level. Seattle is a venue with an established tradition of tolerance, and more to the point, statutory protection for gays and lesbians in housing and accommodation. City and state government, and the region's largest employers, the Boeing Corporation, Microsoft, and the University of Washington, provide job discrimination protection as well. The region has been an international leader in policy about and treatment of AIDS. As such, the region may show a "best case" situation with difficulty levels that are perhaps modest in contrast to other, presumably less tolerant, places.

For marketing considerations, despite the low *level* of difficulty, some areas were mentioned by more respondents: health care, financial services, and "general" service industries. Open-ended responses indicated the poor legal standing of gay and lesbian couples, and feared embarrassment caused problems with mortgages, making joint health care decisions, taking loans and applying for credit, and sharing hotel accommodation.

Education and minority status had little effect on difficulties experienced, but gender did (Figure 2). Across a broad range of circumstances, gay men reported fewer difficulties than lesbians with the sole exceptions of religion and AIDS. Ironically, as shown later (Figure 10), gay men were more likely to be openly gay, while lesbians were more likely to conceal or change behavior to avoid difficulties. Throughout our findings, lesbians encountered more problems and suffered more negative consequences. Religious involvement was *not* appreciably different for gay men and lesbians (gay men were very slightly more active) leaving this difference in want of satisfactory explanation. AIDS, with its concentration among gay men, explains this remaining difference.

Changing Behavior to Avoid Problems

Likely the most punishing self-imposed restriction for gays and lesbians is the need to change behavior from normal to avoid abuse from the straight population and its institutions. This can be highly situational: gays and lesbians are "out" in varying degrees depending on their circumstances. Family settings differ from the workplace and from church. Sadly, in this study, the family required the most concealment, followed by the workplace, religion, and appearing in public. Taken together, these places typically comprise the bulk of one's waking hours. Figure 3 shows such reactions affected the preponderance of the sample, with some diminution for religion and the courts. Happily for areas most sensitive to marketing: retail, recreation, health, and financial services, the least amount of concealment was necessary. Levels of change are mostly intermediate on a five step scale, approximating "sometimes necessary."

A central question is if those changing behavior experienced less difficulty in solving everyday problems. Concealment of being gay or lesbian can make practical sense if it reduces difficulty. Ironically, for our respondents, it didn't. Those who changed behavior the most (high changers) experienced the most difficulties. Figure 4 shows all problem areas as more difficult for these individuals, particularly in critical areas such as housing and employment.

AIDS problems and general services showed the greatest differences. The logic of concealment leading to more problems makes better sense if

FIGURES 1 and 2

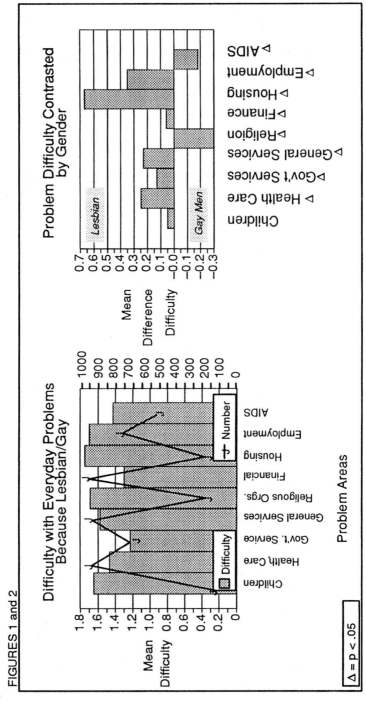

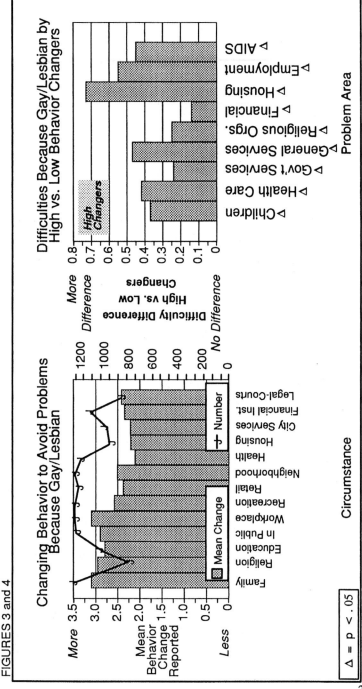

FIGURES 3 and 4

Changing Behavior to Avoid Problems
Because Gay/Lesbian

Difficulties Because Gay/Lesbian by
High vs. Low Behavior Changers

229

the causation is reversed: experiencing difficulties may force concealment. Determining causation from a single wave field study is risky at best. The causal patterns here may not be simple, unidirectional ones.

Barriers to Problem Solving

Violence experienced by gays and lesbians is of central interest in a time of rapid increase in hate crimes (Turque et al., 1992). More particularly, the threat of violence abrogates personal freedom and access to the full resources of society. In this study, violence is conceptualized as both verbal and physical. Threat, intimidation, and name-calling are examples of the former, while beating, slapping, and pushing around characterize the latter. In our data, violence levels are substantial. Fully 65% of respondents suffered verbal abuse from strangers, while some 12% had been physically assaulted.

Despite seemingly pervasive violence, the levels reported in this study are generally lower than those found in other U.S. cities. Berrill (1990) summarizes ten studies, nine of which show verbal abuse ranging from 80% to 87%. Physical abuse ranged from 6% to 35%. The variation, aside from actual differences, may trace to how violence is defined. Robbery, for example, is included in some studies as anti-gay violence, but may not have been perpetrated because the victim is gay or lesbian.

Not surprisingly, those most abused tend to perceive more difficulties with everyday situations because they are gay/lesbian (Figure 5). Again, simple causation is difficult to assume. Having encountered violence, we may be more sensitive to difficulties. Conversely, difficulties themselves may be part of or lead to violent confrontation.

A third (34%) of our respondents reported taking no action in response to abuse from "general problems," a combined category of health, children-related and government agencies and businesses. When asked why no action was taken (Figure 6), respondents were consistent across three major problem areas (for this analysis, "general problems" was contrasted with employment difficulties and outright attacks). In a plurality of cases, respondents believed reporting would "make the situation worse," especially for violent abuse. Other reasons, such as fearing exposure, belief than no one was interested, and not knowing how to complain, composed the balance of responses.

Gender is important to the equation of being open and suffering the consequences. In this sample, lesbians fared poorly compared to gay men in a number of ways (Figure 7). Women reported more verbal attacks, more behavior change, and concealment of being gay, but were slightly more inclined to take action on problems. Gay men were more likely to be

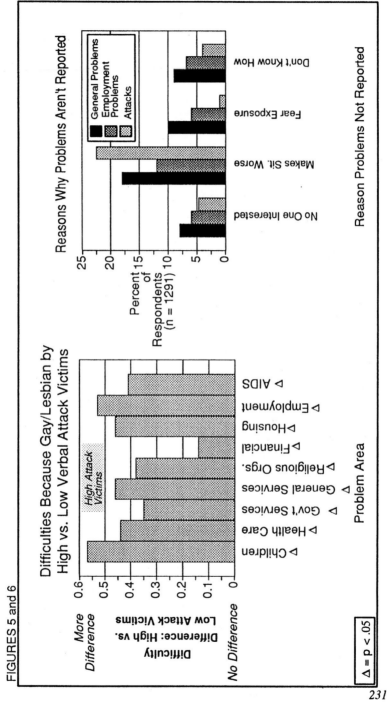

FIGURES 5 and 6

Difficulties Because Gay/Lesbian by
High vs. Low Verbal Attack Victims

Reasons Why Problems Aren't Reported

openly gay. In other studies, women have been less prone to physical violence but more likely to encounter verbal violence in family or home settings (Comstock, 1992). A problem in these contrasts is a higher level of violence against women in American society than men, regardless of gender preference. Victims may not know whether an attack is born of anti-woman or anti-lesbian sentiment, or both. In other surveys, lesbians also reported greater discrimination, fear of violence, and victimization in nongay venues. This may help explain greater concealment of being gay and feelings of difficulty in dealing with straight society (Gross, et al., 1988).

We also made comparisons by education and minority status. Less educated respondents were more prone to physical attack but otherwise were not distinguishable from those with more than high school educations. Minority status showed one strong finding: a greater tendency to be closeted both socially and at work. The increased victimization of gay and lesbian minorities noted in other studies (e.g., Comstock, 1991) was not a significant effect here.

Alienation and Problem Solving

The rite of passage a gay man or lesbian makes in being openly gay often coincides with a commitment to a community of like individuals who supply needed social (and often) material support. In part, too, this can be a negative process of movement away from a majority straight community that may have little positive to offer the openly gay man or lesbian (Herdt & Boxer, 1992). Classically, causal themes in alienation grow from institutions or governments that resist transfer of power to their clients, and, secondly, from incapacity of the victimized to assert their rights. The consequences are feelings of worthlessness, futility, and distrust (Pool, 1973). Our interest was in seeing the influence of affiliation with both the gay/lesbian and straight community upon problem solving and being openly gay. More tangentially, we wanted to explore the likelihood that mainstream media and marketing efforts could be distinguished as instruments of straight society and thus discounted as of little credence to gays and lesbians.

Some alienation from the general community prevails (43%) over those claiming no alienation (30%, Figure 8). Nearly 60% of respondents felt no alienation from the gay/lesbian community. Community identity thus seems clearly differentiated: a hesitant tie to the mainstream and a stronger affiliation with the minority.

Finally, we address disaffection not in absolute terms, but in contrast to what respondents feel they enjoy as life quality compared to their heterosexual counterparts (Figures 9 and 10). While the modal response is same-

FIGURES 7 and 8

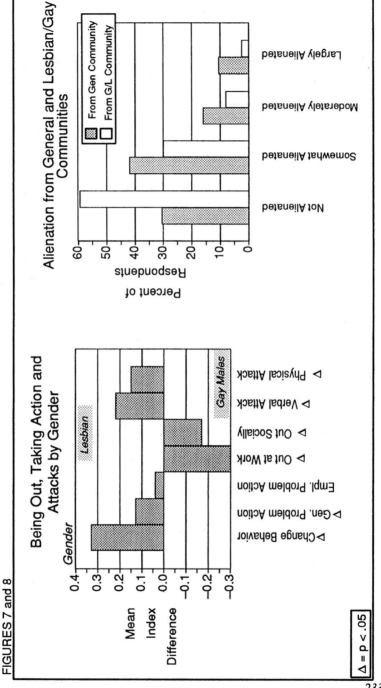

Being Out, Taking Action and Attacks by Gender

Alienation from General and Lesbian/Gay Communities

FIGURES 9 and 10

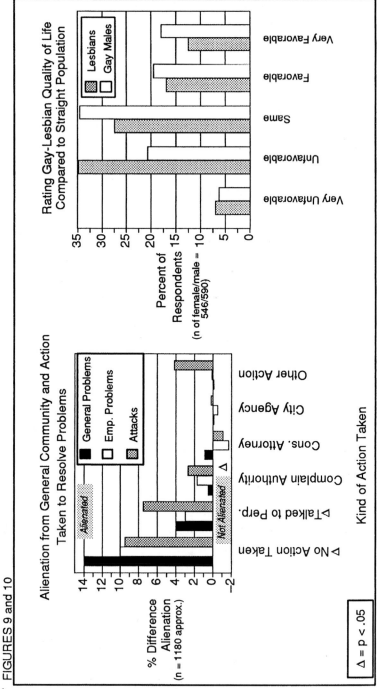

Alienation from General Community and Action Taken to Resolve Problems

% Difference Alienation (n = 1180 approx.)

General Problems
Emp. Problems
Attacks

Alienated

Not Alienated

No Action Taken ◁
◁Talked to Perp.
Complain Authority   △
Cons. Attorney
City Agency
Other Action

Kind of Action Taken

△ = p < .05

Rating Gay-Lesbian Quality of Life Compared to Straight Population

Lesbians
Gay Males

Very Favorable
Favorable
Same
Unfavorable
Very Unfavorable

Percent of Respondents

(n of female/male = 546/590)

ness with the straight population, gay men collectively view their situation as notably better than lesbians. In earlier comparisons (see Figures 2 and 7), lesbians suffer the effects of discrimination more intensely, so it should come as no surprise that they collectively view themselves as generally worse off than their straight counterparts.

CONCLUSIONS

There are both descriptive and conceptual issues of importance from this and similar studies. We did not find exceptionally high levels of perceived difficulty across a broad range of circumstances and institutions because one is gay or lesbian. Even on detailed breakdown of our general problem categories (general services consisted of 6 subcategories, for example),[9] the problems remained uniformly moderate. The greatest perceived difficulty across all 64 sub-categories was the securing of employee benefits for a same-gender spouse. Yet, differences among them in terms of numbers affected and level can suggest to media and others what proves most troublesome for most. Religious organizations, for example, were among those who provided the most problems for our respondents, but affected comparatively few of them (Figure 1). Employment issues, in contrast, affected nearly everyone.

Abuse, both verbal and physical, is at astonishing levels–if slightly less so in this study venue than in other communities. Problems of children, employment, housing, and general services link most visibly with high verbal abuse victims.[10] For media, particularly gay owned, these topical breakdowns suggest coverage possibilities, not based on precipitating events, but on day-to-day needs. For marketing specialists, they represent not only perceptions to be overcome in proffering services to the gay/lesbian community, but rewards both psychic and monetary in successfully doing so.

Does the gay community cope with its problems with straight society and do so openly? Concealment ("changing behavior") to avoid problems because one is gay/lesbian was relevant to almost all respondents, yielding with uniformity a "sometimes" response. The tendency was pronounced for lesbians and didn't seem to lessen their difficulties. The implication for the mainstream media is an old one; it is easy to underestimate the distinctiveness and breadth of gay community feeling since much can be hidden from view. For the marketing community, concealment masks the potential of this segment as well as its problems.

The prevailing response to problems was to take no action, particularly with abuse (Figure 7). This apparent stasis must be examined in light of rapid increases in gay/lesbian visibility and activism over the past two decades. From near total invisibility and marginalization, gay issues now command significant attention from the mainstream media. Well-organized groups take up a variety of gay causes with both the government and the media. Twenty years ago, this would have been largely unthinkable. We are perhaps seeing the bare beginnings of similar attention by mainstream marketing professionals. Organizations such as the Gay and Lesbian Alliance Against Defamation (GLAAD) are in place to monitor both media coverage and marketing campaigns for their inclusiveness and prejudices.

The data do suggest much work still remains to be done with the coverage of gay and lesbian issues as opposed to that of, perhaps, major political issues. The media have given the gay/lesbian community increased attention, but much of it remains colored by stereotypes or focused on divisive political agendas and the threat of AIDS. Marketing and its most visible manifestation, advertising, have walked a narrow path between alienation of a powerful and possibly homophobic majority, and catering to a lucrative new consumer group. But, for nearly all of the respondents in this study, the mainstream community, the majority media, and marketing are remote from the personal problems of being gay.

Some of the reasons for this inaction are based on a lack of knowledge; but more stem from a fear of retribution ("making the situation worse") and the belief that no one would be interested. The media's forte is in providing information and reporting major events, but they are less willing to provide clear support in defending gay rights, giving emotional support, and in exposing subtle discrimination and daily abuse. Advertising's advantage is in targeting products, and appeals to a minority community, but very little of this effort shows gays and lesbians thematically. For the most part, mainstream ads grace gay publications, unaltered. The media and advertisers have moved mainstream content to gay publications, but they have barely included the gay community, positively, in their content mix for consumption by the majority community. That our respondents believed their needs were ignored is hardly remarkable.

About 70% of our respondents felt at least somewhat alienated from the majority community and more than 40% from the gay/lesbian community. The media's influence on nurturing community attachment is murky at best and is locked in difficult causal reasoning that is not especially clear on whether press use leads or follows community involvement (Stamm & Weis, 1984). The influence of advertising "inclusion" is even less apparent. The strongest focus of gay community activism, AIDS, likely owes its organizational momentum not so much to media leadership, but to the techniques of public relations, lobbying, activist confrontation, and fund-raising. The silence of all but a few media outlets to the growing AIDS crisis in the early 1980s has been well documented (Shilts, 1988).

Methodological problems abound with descriptive studies of this kind. Beyond the simple variability people hold for the questions asked (e.g., what does "alienation" mean?) come the implications of the answers given. Concealment or changing behavior in the straight world, for exam-ple, cloaks as a uniform percentage poignant comments like "Most of us [gay/lesbians] act the way we do to make straights comfortable." Or, "As a lesbian, I continually monitor my behavior and appearance to ward off verbal attacks."

Causation and logic also can be easily confused or reversed. Do les-bians encounter more difficulty and suffer greater violence and alienation because they are lesbian, or women, or both? Parallel studies with con-trasting populations rarely exist to provide the contrasts necessary to con-trol such artifacts. Do the media follow or lead the agenda on gay issues? Does marketing to gays have a positive net effect on sales? Careful panel or matched group studies essential to clear causal delineation are costly and difficult. They are virtually absent in consideration of gays and the media.

Sampling is a consistent threat to external validity. It is almost impossi-ble to field a probability sample of a large, geographically diverse gay and lesbian sample–at least with acceptable costs and safety for interviewers (Harry, 1986). Accidental samples tap the willing and articulate (book stores constituted major distribution points for the present study; hardly the place for marginally literate or TV-addicted respondents to secure a questionnaire). Further, when a misplaced questionnaire itself may reveal a closeted respondent, few may be willing to take a chance despite precau-tions and assurance of anonymity. In short, the population represented could easily be skewed to the those "out," articulate, and living in heavily gay-populated neighborhoods near questionnaire distribution points.

RECOMMENDATIONS

While much has been written on minority needs, the mass media, and marketing, little discussion has been directed to the gay community. Hope-ful signs are present in the study of gays and lesbians in media institu-tions–as reporters, primarily[11]–and in histories of gays in the entertain-ment industries.[12] But these are more organized and accessible populations.

The breadth of the gay/lesbian community is more difficult to reach and describe. Simple demographics provide a useful beginning, but ignore the unique and troubled history of this emerging market segment. Seeing advertisements for gay-owned businesses may help the gay audience feel legitimized and connected to their community, yet may serve no immediate problem-solving need. News of an openly gay state representative defending a school's budget has little to do with particular gay community needs, but it does serve as a powerful symbol of political legitimacy for the community. Both situations, while quite different superficially, may provide a validation of the gay community as legitimate and its citizens as substantial.

Going beyond demographics to understand consumer motivation and values holds promise for gains in the gay community as with other target groups. In a recent advertisement, five Pacific Northwest hotels built their joint advertisement on the idea that "people stay with us without any [personal] reservations." The copy went on to promise that "comfortable means more than a well-appointed guest room. It means you feel great about who you are and where you're staying."[13] Accompanying the copy was a picture of a gay male couple having a convivial discussion in the hotel bar. The acceptance and welcome are clear and the advertisement confronts an issue of ease in choosing lodging with a same-gender mate. The hotels' locales have significant gay populations, so the advantages of such targeting may be obvious in a sophisticated hospitality market that specializes in groups from Japanese tourists to backpackers. But extension of the advertisement's placement beyond major, culturally diverse cities may be questionable.

Our present analysis suggests the utility of psychosocial characteristics in addition to traditional demographic indicators. Marketing appeals that reassure, validate, and offer open access to products and institutions for the gay community may encounter consumer wariness and resistance. Promotions that simply patronize the gay media and remain unchanged from their mainstream character may avoid offending the heterosexual world, but it is questionable whether they realize their potential by engaging needs particular to the gay community.

How much should the majority media generally, and marketing in particular, pay attention to specific minorities? Our working premise here is that there may be a gain for marketing programs in doing so, but that the advantages may be qualified. Marketing that mixes gays and lesbians in with the majority community evokes the same notoriety witnessed a generation ago when African-Americans were, for the first time in the mainstream media, allowed to hold a bowl of Jello, or brush with Crest toothpaste. Mainstream ads reprinted in the gay press afford little more than an extension of traditional marketing reach. But marketing depicting gays and gay lifestyles in the majority community carries a very different set of assumptions. All of these campaigns may at first glance attract the loyalty of a community starved for recognition and legitimacy. But do the closeted or fearful respond favorably? And what of a possible backlash by an offended heterosexual community?

Moreover, the problems of alienation, concealment, and inaction in the face of discrimination beg the question of whether the media really provide a means of breaking this cycle. As described earlier, empirical studies of press and community are few and causality is suspect. While progressivist views of media from the early years of the century suggest media leadership fosters social justice, there is little hard data that sustains this comforting view (Baldasty, 1993). A research need definitely exists as gays and lesbians seek to strongly effect social change.

Aside from conceptual problems, there is a host of methodological needs. Time-based studies to check causation alleviate the difficult logic that tries to tease causal progressions from single-shot studies. Contrasts in coverage and slant of gay-directed and mainstream media could better describe the unique role each may have in the gay community. Sampling and cooperation are recurrent problems in a community, where significant numbers remain closeted and fearful of the confidentiality of their answers. Lesbians and gays of color were especially difficult to contact. The use of social clubs, organizations, and other intact groups was essential to this study. These techniques need to be refined. Finally, the needs of lesbians are significantly different from those of gay men and need to be considered separately. Combining them in the aggregate obscures many important, distinct relationships that are based in gender.

Capitalizing on existing data remains a problem. Organizations such as GLAAD provide a valuable monitoring and archiving resource of the media's treatment of gays and lesbians. Yet, no widely known parallel structure exists for archiving scholarly studies of gays and lesbians in the media. Groups such as the ICPSR (Intercollegiate Consortium for Political and Social Research) provide a distribution mechanism for social-science data on a broad range of issues. A cooperative or parallel structure is needed to archive mass-media data for the gay/lesbian community. Electronic networks, such as the Internet, provide low-cost, efficient means of information retrieval and distribution.[14]

These recommendations simply suggest improved collection and sharing techniques of what have been mostly exploratory and descriptive data. They are, perhaps, essential first steps toward conceptualization and can act as models that better *explain* how the majority media, marketing, and marginalized communities interact.

NOTES

1. This last problem is clear from studies of those viewing high levels of "Christian broadcasting," such as Pat Robertson's *700 Club.* These groups show yet another gratification served: *reaction* (Abelman, 1987). In addition to instrumental and ritualistic needs, Christian content provides an alternative; a rejection of conventional media fare and its transgressions on fundamentalist culture. Groups like the Traditional Values Coalition regularly promote advertiser boycotts and protest write-in campaigns to networks offering "positive views of homosexuality." Research suggests a fertile ground for these appeals: high television users are more critical of gays regardless of the respondent's political leaning (Gross, 1984), and there is evidence of a widespread wish among parents that children not watch programs with gay or lesbian characters (Schmalz, 1984).

2. For example: Kim, Young T. "A communication approach to the acculturation process: A study of Korean immigrants in Chicago." *International Journal of Intercultural Relation* 2, no. 2 (Summer, 1978). pp. 197-224. For contrast: Serena E. Wade. "Media and the disadvantaged: A review of the literature." ERIC. (Stanford, CA, 1969) 24 p.

3. In this sample, some 48.5% were female, 51.5% were male; minority representation was at 10.6%. Some 67.8% had some college education, 12.5% completed high school and 19.7% had even less formal education. Median and modal income was in the $20,000 to $25,000/yr. range category with 3.6% unemployed, 1.9% retired and 12.9% self-employed. Mean age of the sample was 35 years. Some 54% were in a "committed same sex relationship" having lasted an average of 5.0 years while 12.2% of the respondents were parents or co-parents (4.5%). Dominant political affiliation (62%) was Democrat, with 17% indicating Republican and the balance other affiliations or independent. A majority of 52.9% were "not active" with religion while the balance indicated they were active. More complete data are available in Elkin & Johanson (1991).

4. There are a number of sources for advice on surveys of the gay/lesbian community. Notable are: Herek & Berrill (1990) and Comstock (1991) pp. 31-55 and appendices.

5. Data specific to each component are available from the author. The raw data set is archived at the University of Washington's Center for Social Science Research and Computation and is available on request to: Archivist, CSSCR, DK-45, University of Washington, Seattle, WA 98195, or by anonymous ftp to *augustus.csscr.washington.edu/pub/hatedata.txt*

6. Seattle has one exclusively gay newspaper, *The Seattle Gay News*, published weekly since the mid-1970s. Another, more recent publication, *The Stranger*, appeals to a mix of straight and gay youth.

7. Sources of assistance in discrimination cases were determined from structured items listing coworkers, work supervisors, city officials/agencies and lawyers. Open-ended (respondent-specified) items were available for "other" sources. The incidence of gay and straight media assistance was taken from these items.

8. In Figures 2,4,5,7 and 9, chart bars represent average *differences* between groups of respondents, such as gay men contrasted to lesbians. The direction of the bar (above or below the zero line) shows which of the two groups compared was stronger or greater on a characteristic or problem area. The length of the bar, whether negative or positive-going, shows the extent of difference. Longer bars mean bigger group differences. All such differences were tested statistically. The delta [Δ] symbol shows differences that would be apparent in 19 of 20 similar samples drawn, or an alpha error of 5%. A delta placed *beneath* a label means that all contrasts grouped for the label were significant. In a few cases where only some differences in a group attained significance, the delta was moved adjacent to the applicable bar.

9. This listing is found in Appendix A.

10. Similar associations could not be computed for physical abuse victims due to small subsample sizes.

11. See, for example, Bernt & Greenwald, 1992.

12. For example: Richard Dyer. *Gays and Films*. New York, NY: Zoetrop, 1984.

13. Advertisement was sponsored by a consortium of 5 Seattle (WA) and Portland (OR) hotels. It appeared in October, 1994, issues of *The Advocate*, a national circulation current affairs magazine targeting the gay community.

14. There are several Internet resources of relevance to scholars of gay/lesbian media issues. The *Queer Resources Directory* is possibly the most productive and may be accessed by an Internet web (WWW) browser, URL *http://www.cs. cmu.edu:8001/Web/People/mjw/Queer/MainPage.html*

REFERENCES

Baldasty, G. (1993). *The Commercialization of News in the Nineteenth Century.* Madison, WI: U. of Wisconsin Press, 1993.

Berrill, K. T. (1990). Anti-gay violence and victimization in the United States: An overview. *Journal of Interpersonal Violence* 5, (3) (September): 274-294.

Boulard, G. (1994). Numbers: No matter what you say about gay income levels, there's now a study to back you up. *The Advocate.* No. 665 (October 4), 30-31.

Comstock, G. D. (1991). Empirical data on victims. In *Violence Against Lesbians and Gay Men.* New York: Columbia U. Press.

_____. (1992). Victims of anti-gay and lesbian violence. *Journal of Interpersonal Violence* 4, 101-106.

Dervin, B. (1976). Information: An answer for every question? A solution for every problem? *Journal of Broadcasting* 20, 323-344.

Elkin, S. & Johanson G. (1991). *A Survey of the Seattle Area Gay and Lesbian Community: Identity and Issues.* Seattle Commission for Lesbians and Gays, co-sponsored by The Seattle Office for Women's Rights and the Lesbian Resource Center, Seattle, WA.

Elliott, S. (1994). A sharper view of gay consumers. *NY Times* (June 9), C1, 17.

Fejes, F. & Petrich K. (1993). Invisibility, homophobia and heterosexism: Lesbians and gays in the media. *Critical Studies in Mass Communication* (December), 396-422.

Frank, R. E. & Greenberg M. G. (1980). *The Public's Use of Television: Who Watches What and Why?* Beverly Hills: Sage.

Friedli, E. (1990). Population and human needs: Background report. *Report of the Office for Long-Range Planning.* Seattle, WA: City of Seattle [draft].

Gay and Lesbian Alliance Against Defamation. (1994a). Down the Drano. *GLAAD Media Watch.* January 14, p. 1.

———. (1994b). IKEA furnishes breakthrough. *GLAAD/NY Bulletin,* May/June, p. 1.

Goldman, K. 1994. Major firms are approached on sponsoring major gay event. *Dow Jones News* (March 15).

Greenberg, B., Dervin B. with Bowes, J., & Dominick, J. (1970). *Use of Mass Media by the Urban Poor.* New York: Praeger.

Gross, L., Aurand, S. & Adessa, R. (1988). *Violence and Discrimination Against Lesbian and Gay People in Philadelphia and the Commonwealth of Pennsylvania.* Philadelphia Lesbian and Gay Task Force, Philadelphia, PA.

———. (1991). Out of the mainstream: Sexual minorities and the mass media. *Journal of Homosexuality* 21 (1-2), 19-46.

Harry, J. (1986). Sampling gay men. *Journal of Sex Research* 22 (1) (February), 21-34.

Hartinger, B. (1994). New kid on the block: New health and fitness magazine is expected to be largest periodical aimed at the gay, lesbian community. *Dallas Voice* (November 16).

Herdt, G. & Boxer, A. (1992). "Introduction: Culture, history, and life course of gay men." In Gilbert Herdt (Ed.) *Gay Culture in America: Essays from the Field.* Boston, MA: Beacon Press.

Herek, G. M. & Berrill, K. T. (1990). Documenting the victimization of lesbians and gay men: Methodological issues. *Journal of Interpersonal Violence* 5 (3) (September) 301-315.

Horovitz, B. (1993). Finding new ways to appeal to gays and lesbians. *LA Times,* (February 23), p. 12.

Jansen, E. P. (1994). The incredible shrinking gay dollar. *Genre.* 23 (November), 42-47.

Kahle, L. R., Beatty S. E., & Homer P. M. (1986). Alternative measurement approaches to consumer values: The list of values (LOV) and values and life style (VALS). *Journal of Consumer Research* 13(3) (December), 405-409.

Katz, E. & Blumler, J. (1974). Uses and gratifications research. *Public Opinion Quarterly* 37 (4) (Winter), 509-523.

Kessler, L. (1984). *The Dissident Press.* Beverly Hills, CA: Sage.

Lesbigay press (1992). *NY Times,* March 2, p. 1.

Levin, G. (1993). Mainstream's domino effect. *Advertising Age* (January 18), pp. 30, 32.

"Mainstream radio for gays, lesbians." (1992). *Boston Globe* (November 30), p. 43.

Mortimer, C. G. (1959). "The Creative Factor in Marketing," 15th Annual Parlin

Lecture, Philadelphia Chapter, American Marketing Assn., May, 1959 as cited in Philip Kotler. *Management Marketing: Analysis, Planning and Control.* Englewood Cliffs (NJ): Prentice.

"Overcoming deep-rooted reluctance, more firms advertise to gay community." 1991. *Wall Street Journal* (July 18), p. B 1.

Overlooked Opinions. 1993. Gays at a glance. *The Northern Star.* Northern Illinois Univ. (April 27th).

Pool I. D. (1973). "Public opinion." In Pool, I. & Schramm, W. (Eds.) *Handbook of Communication.* Chicago: Rand McNally.

Rubin, A. M. (1981). A multivariate analysis of '60 minutes' viewing motivations. *Journalism Quarterly,* 58, 529-534.

_____ . (1983). Television uses and gratifications: The interactions of viewing patterns and motivations. *Journal of Broadcasting,* 27, 37-51.

Schmalz, J. (1993) "Polls find even split on homosexuality's cause." *New York Times* (March 5), p. A14.

Shilts, R. (1988). How the media mishandled the AIDS story. *ASNE Bulletin* 701 (January).

Stamm, K. (1985). *Newspaper Use and Community Ties: Toward a Dynamic Theory.* Norwood, NJ: Ablex.

Stamm, K. & Weis, R. (1984). Toward a dynamic theory of newspaper subscribing. *Journalism Quarterly,* 59, 382-389.

Stamm, K. & Bowes, J. E. (1991). *The Mass Communication Process.* Dubuque (IA): Kendall-Hunt.

Turque, B. et al. (1992). Gays under fire. *Newsweek* (September. 14), p. 39.

Wilke, M. (1994). Gay newspapers try new paths to growth. *NY Times* (May 30), p. 21.

Appendix A

Indexing of problem items involved averaging specific difficulties into composite measures. The list below shows the component scales, rated on a 1 (Never difficulty because lesbian/gay) to 5 (Always a Problem) basis. These were combined and averaged for each respondent, adjusting for unused items.

Index	*Problem Items*
Children	problems with courts, welfare, schools, day care, health care (specifically for children), foster parent licensing, adoption
Health Care	routine health care, emergency health, mental health, hospital visits, rape counseling
Government Services	welfare, food stamps, youth services
General Services	memberships, restaurant service, hotel accommodation, transportation, employment services, funeral arrangements
Religious Organizations	church membership, religious counseling
Financial Problems	banks, and savings and loan associations, credit unions, mortgage companies, store charge accounts
Housing	public housing, rental housing, housing purchase
Employment	job transfers, job security, barred from practice, lost clients, unequal treatment, fear of safety, under employed, not promoted, harassed by coworkers, harassed by supervisors, harassed sexually, fired or forced to resign, poor evaluations, poor job references, no benefits for same-gender partner
AIDS	employment, housing, insurance, hospitals, foster parents, adoption, routine health care, emergency health care, dental care, alcohol/drug treatment, public assistance, funeral/burial, religious organizations, banks/credit unions, courts, police

About the Contributors

Subodh Bhat, PhD, is Associate Professor of Marketing at San Francisco State University. His research interests include brand management, brand extension strategies, store choice, advertising effects, and services marketing. His work has appeared in *Journal of Marketing Research, Journal of Professional Services Marketing,* and has been presented at numerous conferences.

Steven Bishofsky has an MA in Communications Research and specializes in the public use of commercial media. He is currently researching the media's willingness to accept anti-smoking messages.

John E. Bowes, PhD, is Associate Professor of Communication in the School of Communications of the University of Washington. His research interests have centered on new telecommunications technologies and policy development, particularly changes in traditional media industries and industrial cultures. As well, Bowes has interests in public opinion, minorities, and the mass media. He is the co-author of several books and numerous articles on these and other interests.

Janeen Arnold Costa, PhD, is Assistant Professor of Marketing, David Eccles School of Business, and Adjunct Assistant Professor of Anthropology, University of Utah. Her research focuses on social and cultural dimensions of consumer behavior and marketing, including assessment of the role and influence of culture, gender, class, ethnicity, and cross-cultural marketing, particularly in the context of tourism. She organized and chaired two conferences on gender and consumer behavior in Salt Lake City in 1991 and 1993. Her research has been published in *Journal of Marketing, Advances in Consumer Research, Research in Consumer Behavior, Advances in Non-Profit Marketing,* and *Anthropological Quarterly.* In addition to numerous books and conference proceedings, she is the editor of the recent volume *Gender Issues and Consumer Behavior* (Sage, 1994).

Maria-Cristina Curran, BA, is a recent graduate of the University of Georgia where she received dual degrees in psychology and philosophy. She plans to attend a counseling psychology graduate program with an emphasis on drug addiction therapy.

M. Wayne DeLozier, PhD, is Distinguished Professor of Marketing at

Nicholls State University. He has authored and co-authored twelve college textbooks and has published numerous articles and papers. He serves on the editorial review boards of *Journal of the Academy of Marketing Science* and *Journal of Business Research*. He is past editor of *Journal of Experiential Learning and Simulation*.

Anne W. Esacove, MPH/MSW (cand.), is completing her graduate work at the University of Washington and has over eight years of experience working to promote sexual health.

Douglass S. Fisher, MA, directed Seattle's sexual minority crisis and I&R hotline and worked with clients in private practice for several years before joining the Innovative Programs Research Group at the University of Washington. As Director of Marketing for Project ARIES, Doug is responsible for the creation and implementation of all IPRG social marketing campaigns.

Anthony Freitas, MS, is a doctoral student in communication at the University of California, San Diego. His research focuses on formations of the queer, diseased, and foreign body and self within popular and scientific communities.

Tania Hammidi, BA, is a research associate in Textiles and Clothing at the University of California, Davis. Her research within visual culture focuses on lesbian and transgender representations and the negotiation of multiple identities.

Oscar Huidor, BS, graduated from the University of California at Davis with a major in Sociology and a minor in Textiles and Clothing. He is currently a Junior Sales Manager for Lisa Jenks Jewelry in New York City. His research interests include the role of clothing in person perception, and the connections between gift exchanges and social relationships.

David A. Jones, MS, is a doctoral student in Counseling Psychology at The Ohio State University. His research interests include sexual orientation self-disclosure and AIDS-related multiple loss.

Susan Kaiser, PhD, is Professor of Textiles and Clothing and Associate Dean for Human Health and Development in the College of Agricultural and Environmental Sciences at the University of California, Davis. Her current research explores how subjectivities become mobile and material through intersecting identities expressed through appearance styles. She is the author of *The Social Psychology of Clothing: Symbolic Appearances in Context*, and has published in such journals as *Clothing and Textiles Research Journal* and *Symbolic Interaction*.

Thomas W. Leigh, PhD, is Associate Professor and Terry Research Fellow in the Marketing Department at the University of Georgia. His current research interests include a wide range of sales force issues. He has published in *Journal of Marketing Research, Journal of Marketing, Journal of*

Consumer Research, Journal of Advertising Research, Journal of Purchasing and Materials Management, Journal of Personal Selling and Sales Management, and *Journal of the Academy of Marketing Science,* among others. Dr. Leigh is active in the American Marketing Association and has participated extensively in executive education programs and corporate consulting.

sidney matrix is a graduate student working in the fields of lesbian life-writing and personalist lesbian cultural theory and criticism. Currently she is editing a collection of lesbian personalist essays, and readying for publication selections of her thesis "(Un)Authorized Disclosures: Performing in Lesbian: Writing and Lesbian: Theory."

Michelle R. Nelson, PhD (cand.), holds an MA in Journalism and Mass Communication from the University of Wisconsin-Madison. Her master's thesis explored the use of synesthesia and metaphor in print advertising headlines. Currently, Michelle is a doctoral student in the Institute for Communication Research at the Advertising Department of the University of Illinois at Urbana-Champaign. Her research interests include the psychological and social processes that affect consumer culture, exploring differences found in members of minority groups and subcultures who deviate from the dominant society.

Peter J. Newman, Jr., holds an MA in Advertising from the University of Illinois at Urbana-Champaign. He is planning to begin his doctoral studies at the University of Illinois in fall 1995, with research interests in the role of advertising and mass media on gay socialization and the acceptance of homosexuality in the United States.

Lisa Peñaloza, PhD, is Assistant Professor of Advertising at the University of Illinois. Her research interests focus on the ways in which social difference is expressed in consumer behavior and in marketing practice. Along those lines, she has investigated the effects of nationality, race/ethnicity, gender, and sexuality on marketers' and consumers' behavior. In addition, she is interested in the effects of market practice on culture in the global economy, and in the contributions of post-positivistic philosophy of science to marketing research.

Jason Rodrigue, MBA, is a licensed property and insurance agent for a large regional insurance agency based in Louisiana. He earned both BS (economics) and MBA from Nicholls State University.

Roger A. Roffman, DSW, is Associate Professor of Social Work at the University of Washington where he also directs the school's Innovative Programs Research Group. Roger's recent research has focused on designing and evaluating clinical and community interventions in addictive disorders, AIDS prevention, and domestic violence.

Margaret Rucker, PhD, has been conducting research on gift-giving norms, perceptions and practices for the last decade. She is particularly interested in the effects of culture, ethnic identity, and sex as well as the sexual orientation of giver and recipient on perceptions of value and equity. Papers based on her work have been presented at a variety of professional meetings including those of the Academy of Marketing Science, American Psychological Association, Pacific Sociological Association, International Textile and Apparel Association, Popular Culture Association, American Marketing Association, and the Association for Consumer Research.

Nancy A. Rudd, PhD, is Assistant Professor of Consumer and Textile Sciences at The Ohio State University in Columbus. She teaches undergraduate and graduate courses in the areas of aesthetics and dress and human behavior. Her research examines the use of clothing and appearance management strategies for special-needs consumers and other consumer cultures that may be stigmatized by society, including post-mastectomy women, the elderly, people with body image disorders, and homosexual men. The focus of her research is on the assessment of functional, aesthetic, and psychosocial needs that should be considered in product development, marketing, and use, with a goal of enhancing feelings of self-esteem and perceived quality of life among these consumers.

Rosemary Ryan, PhD, is currently Research Director for Project ARIES in the Innovation Programs Research Group at the University of Washington. She is also a member of the Seattle-King County HIV/AIDS Planning Council which sets service priorities and makes funding decisions for HIV/AIDS prevention and care services in the Seattle metropolitan area.

J. Marc Wallis, MSW (cand.), has worked in HIV/AIDS prevention and education with adults and adolescents. He is currently working as a student therapist while pursuing his MSW in clinical social work at Columbia University.

Andrew S. Walters, PhD, is Research Fellow at the University of California, San Francisco. His professional interests include pediatric health, applied health psychology, and human sexuality. He has published articles in pediatric adjustment to chronic illness/disease, adolescent sexual behavior, and educational strategies for therapists and sexuality educators to reduce homophobia/homonegativism.

Daniel L. Wardlow, PhD, is Associate Professor of Marketing at San Francisco State University. His research interests are in advertising effects, logistics strategy, and public policy. He is the co-author of the recent book *International Logistics*; he has published in *Journal of Macromarketing*, and has presented work at many conferences.

Index

Notes: Reference sources and authors are not indexed unless: title of publication is cited in full, or; author is directly quoted and named in full.

Page numbers followed by "n" indicate end-of-chapter Notes.

Page numbers preceded by *mentioned* indicate intermittent discussion of topic.

IKEA 69,91,93,162,220
Iconography, gay/lesbian
  in advertising 30-31,37
  in apparel/accessories 96,97
  Nazi assignment of 36
Intercollegiate Consortium for
    Political and Social
    Research (ICPSR) 239
Internet 239,241n14
Interview 128

*Janus Report of Sexual Behavior,
    The* 24
Jeffy, Eamon 72,73

Kinsey Institute 24,204
Kmart Corporation 162

Lambda Rising 208
lang, k.d. 92
Latinos; Latino market. *See also*
    Persons of color
  consumption patterns 23
  development of gay/lesbian market
    and, compared 19-20
  marketing representations of 14
  self-identification by 21
  social movement 14,19-20,22
Legal status of homosexuals
  daily life problems related to 227.
    See also under
    Discrimination
  legal sanctions against rights 136
    by Colorado 35,37,38n7
  protective legislation for
    homosexuals' rights
    and domestic partnership
    ordinances 136
  and oppositions to
    proposed/listing 14,15,19,
    35,136,150

in Seattle 226
states' statutes 136
Legitimation. *See* Social legitimation
Lesbian Avengers 37
Lesbians
  and celebrity lesbians, visibility
    of 92
  of color 204
  discrimination/difficulties, and
    coping strategies 227,230,
    235,237,239
  erotic representations of
    lesbianism and 72-80
    homophobic/lesbophobic
      elements of 74-75,76,77,
      79,80
    lesbian-consumer
      appropriations and
      translations of 74,75-80
    as male-authored for male
      audiences 74,75,77-78,
      79,80
    pulp fiction novels and
      industry 72-74,79
  market participation and
    consumption patterns
    26-27,86
  market targeting of 76,91-92,101
  personality traits 204
  style and appearance
    political-correctness and shifts
      from 92,99,100-101
    subcultural expressions
      mentioned 95-101
  as subaltern to males 101
  violence toward 230,232
Lesbopholia of erotic representations of
    lesbianism 74-75,76,77,79,80,80
Levi Strauss 30,206
Limbaugh, Rush 210

March on Washington (1993) 220
Market research; consumer research:
    gay and lesbian *See also*
    Consumer profile

Haworth
DOCUMENT DELIVERY
SERVICE

This valuable service provides a single-article order form for any article from a Haworth journal.

- *Time Saving:* No running around from library to library to find a specific article.
- *Cost Effective:* All costs are kept down to a minimum.
- *Fast Delivery:* Choose from several options, including same-day FAX.
- *No Copyright Hassles:* You will be supplied by the original publisher.
- *Easy Payment:* Choose from several easy payment methods.

Open Accounts Welcome for . . .
- Library Interlibrary Loan Departments
- Library Network/Consortia Wishing to Provide Single-Article Services
- Indexing/Abstracting Services with Single Article Provision Services
- Document Provision Brokers and Freelance Information Service Providers

---

MAIL or *FAX* THIS ENTIRE ORDER FORM TO:

Haworth Document Delivery Service
The Haworth Press, Inc.
10 Alice Street
Binghamton, NY 13904-1580

or FAX: 1-800-895-0582
or CALL: 1-800-342-9678
9am-5pm EST

PLEASE SEND ME PHOTOCOPIES OF THE FOLLOWING SINGLE ARTICLES:

1) Journal Title: _____
   Vol/Issue/Year: _____ Starting & Ending Pages: _____
   Article Title: _____

2) Journal Title: _____
   Vol/Issue/Year: _____ Starting & Ending Pages: _____
   Article Title: _____

3) Journal Title: _____
   Vol/Issue/Year: _____ Starting & Ending Pages: _____
   Article Title: _____

4) Journal Title: _____
   Vol/Issue/Year: _____ Starting & Ending Pages: _____
   Article Title: _____

(See other side for Costs and Payment Information)

COSTS: Please figure your cost to order quality copies of an article.

1. Set-up charge per article: $8.00

               ($8.00 × number of separate articles) _____

2. Photocopying charge for each article:

               1-10 pages: $1.00 _____

               11-19 pages: $3.00 _____

               20-29 pages: $5.00 _____

               30+ pages: $2.00/10 pages _____

3. Flexicover (optional): $2.00/article _____

4. Postage & Handling: US: $1.00 for the first article/

               $.50 each additional article _____

        Federal Express: $25.00 _____

        Outside US: $2.00 for first article/

               $.50 each additional article _____

5. Same-day FAX service: $.35 per page _____

GRAND TOTAL: _____

METHOD OF PAYMENT: (please check one)

❏ Check enclosed ❏ Please ship and bill. PO # _____

               (sorry we can ship and bill to bookstores only! All others must pre-pay)

❏ Charge to my credit card: ❏ Visa; ❏ MasterCard; ❏ Discover;

               ❏ American Express;

Account Number: _____ Expiration date: _____

Signature: **X** _____

Name: _____ Institution: _____

Address: _____

_____

City: _____ State: _____ Zip: _____

Phone Number: _____ FAX Number: _____

MAIL or *FAX* THIS ENTIRE ORDER FORM TO:

Haworth Document Delivery Service	or **FAX:** 1-800-895-0582
The Haworth Press, Inc.	or **CALL:** 1-800-342-9678
10 Alice Street	9am-5pm EST)
Binghamton, NY 13904-1580	